Elizabethan Sonnets

Edited by

Maurice Evans

Professor of English,
University of Exeter

Dent, London, Melbourne and Toronto
Rowan and Littlefield, Totowa, N.J.

All rights reserved
Printed in Great Britain by
Biddles Ltd., Guildford, Surrey
and bound at the
Aldine Press, Letchworth, Herts.
for
J. M. Dent & Sons Ltd
Aldine House, Albemarle Street, London
First published in the U.K. (Everyman's University Library), in 1977
First published in the U.S.A. (Rowman and Littlefield University Library)
by Rowman and Littlefield, Totowa, N.J., in 1977

This book is set in Journal Roman Medium 10 on 11 point

Dent edition   LC 78-395110
Hardback ISBN 0 460 10554 X
Paperback ISBN 0 460 11554 5

Rowman and Littlefield edition

British Library Cataloguing in Publication Data

The Elizabethan sonnet.
    1. Sonnets, English
    I. Evans, Maurice
    821'.04   PR1195.S5

    ISBN 0—460—10554—X
    ISBN 0—460—11554—5 Pbk

Contents

Elizabethan Sonnets

Introduction

The fulfilment and the frustration of passion have been the two great subjects of love poetry since time began, and whether, in Yeats's words, the imagination dwells most upon a woman won or a woman lost is a question not easily answered. The Petrarchan sonneteer, however, would have no doubts about the matter: the love sonnet is the most committed form of that poetry of frustration which, taking its origin from Ovid, came down the centuries picking up refinements and elaborations on its way. From the Provençal love song and medieval Amour Courtois it gained romantic colouring and something approaching religious fervour on the one hand, and formal structure and a set of conventions on the other. From Petrarch, after Ovid the most influential love poet of the western world, it absorbed a new personal and lyrical intensity and became especially associated with the sonnet form. Petrarch is the bridge between medieval and Renaissance, converting what had been predominantly narrative into lyric, but handing on, nevertheless, essentially traditional attitudes in a form which remained relatively unchanged for the next two hundred years. There were minor accretions with the High Renaissance — a touch of Neo-Platonism from fifteenth-century Italy; and more important, a new image of Cupid to temper that of the fierce and merciless deity of the Middle Ages. This is the sportive child, blind Cupid with his little bow and arrows, who derives from Anacreon and the *Greek Anthology*, among the classical Greek texts rediscovered by the Renaissance humanists. The mixture, handed on by the post-Petrarchan Italian sonneteers to the French Pléiade in the middle of the sixteenth century, reached England effectively only by the 1580s. The Elizabethan love sonnet is at the end of an unbroken tradition of love poetry which reaches back through the *Roman de la Rose* to classical antiquity.

The Elizabethan sonneteer inherited, therefore, not only the basic Petrarchan situation of the adoring lover and the unresponsive mistress but also a large number of traditional *topoi* inseparable from it, which offer elaborations upon the central theme and time-honoured modes for their expression. The sonnet lady, for example, the longed-for but unreachable Stella or Idea or Diana, is likely at some point in her story to fall ill, or be misled by 'venomous tongues', or tear up her lover's poems or treat him less kindly than her lap dog or pet sparrow. The lover in his turn will suffer the tempestuous and warring passions of love: he will lie awake all night, or if he sleeps, have erotic dreams of his mistress: he will hear her singing or watch her as she plies her needle or steal a kiss while she sleeps: he will itemize all her beauties and he will protest the power of his verse to keep that beauty alive in spite of the ravages of time. These and similar stereotypes make up the body of most sonnet sequences and are expressed through conventional images as essential to the sonnet tradition as the situations themselves: the unsuccessful siege of the fortress of love and the innumerable variations on the metaphor of love's war, for example: the lover as the ship in the storm; the hot ice and freezing fire which afflict him; the lady's eyes like the sun to burn, her eyelashes like nets to catch him; her eyebrows the bows for Cupid's arrows; her face the cherry tree on which her lips are cherries. One has only to read a few of the cycles to recognize the underlying framework of event and style which they have in common, and to see that these form the poetic medium of the genre. The Petrarchan sonnet is the most 'conventional' of forms, and a large part of its appeal to the Renaissance writer lay in the challenge it offered to emulate what others had done before.

For all but the greatest of Renaissance sonneteers, the sonnet is less concerned with the exploration of love itself than with the processes by which a moment of passion is transformed into a polished artefact. In discussing the sonnet in his *Defence of Ryme*,[1] Daniel praises its capacity to shape the 'unformed Chaos without fashion' of our imagination into 'an Orbe of order and forme' (p. 138); and this is something encouraged by the very shape of the sonnet, with its elaborate organization of rhymes and its fourteen lines giving just enough scope to erect a verbal structure which is complete and easily perceived. The term most commonly associated with the sonnet is the 'conceit', which is the basic conception of the organization within the poem, the rhetorical figure upon which the framework of an individual sonnet depends: and a good sonnet in Renaissance terms is one in which the conceit is worked out perfectly in fourteen lines so that form and content fit each other like hand and glove. To quote Daniel again,

Besides, is it not most delightfull to see much excellently ordred in a small roome, or little gallantly disposed and made to fill up a space of like capacitie, in such sort, that the one would not appeare so beautifull in a larger circuite, nor the other do well in a lesse. (p. 138)

The conceit takes innumerable forms. Among the commonest are the single metaphor extended through the whole sonnet and reaching its natural climax in the last line (*Amoretti*, 14: *A and S*, 49: *Zepheria*, 37, for example); the classical myth applied as an allegory of the lover's state (*Delia*, 5: *Amoretti*, 23); the debate (*Idea*, 38: *A and S*, 34); the paradox (*A and S*, 61, 62); the pattern of anaphora worked out with perfect symmetry through the three quatrains and the couplet (*Amoretti*, 1: *Diana*, 9), to name only a few obvious types. None of these are mutually exclusive, and any of them can be worked out in conjunction with any other or with a central argument, often in the form of a dilemma which is resolved in the final couplet. Spenser is particularly fond of this kind of conceit, as in *Amoretti*, 30, for example, which, beginning with the traditional comparison that 'My love is lyke to yse, and I to fyre', asks how two such opposites can co-exist, and answers that it is love's unique power to perform miracles. Giles Fletcher plays some

[1] *Poems and A Defence of Ryme* ed. A. C. Sprague, 1950.

amusing variations upon the same theme in *Licia*, 41 and 42. Again, in *Amoretti*, 43, Spenser asks, 'Shall I then silent be or shall I speake?', for if he speaks he is overwhelmed by his mistress's wrath, and if he stays silent his heart will break. The answer is to teach his heart and eyes the language of silent communication which her wit will soon learn to construe. The final couplet, which is a feature of so many English sonnets even when in other respects they are Petrarchan in form, lends itself to the summing up or the solution of paradox or dilemma and gives to the sonnet, in consequence, the quality of epigram.

The conceit is probably the most important dimension of the sonnet, and something which the Elizabethan poet and his reader, trained alike in rhetoric, were more aware of than we are. If this were not so, I do not think that Spenser would have left his *Amoretti*, 64 in the form in which we have it. It is a conventional icon of the mistress's parts but framed in terms of the scents of garden flowers:

> Comming to kisse her lyps, (such grace I found)
> Me seemd I smelt a gardin of sweet flowres:

Thus her lips smell like gillyflowers, her bosom like a strawberry bed, her breast like lilies and so on very pleasantly, as long as the reader keeps his mind fixed upon the idea of scent, to the exclusion of all other considerations. But if one forgets the terms of the conceit and allows the attention to stray into the world of vision and colour, for example, the consequences are unfortunate: 'her ruddy cheekes lyke unto Roses red' is passable in terms both of scent and of colour, but 'her lovely eyes Lyke Pincks but newly spred' (i.e. opened) is certainly not. Either the Elizabethans had the capacity to exclude from their consciousness everything which is outside the terms of the central conceit, or else Spenser has fallen down through using images too strongly loaded with traditional visual associations.

That poets composed their sonnets with these elaborate schemes consciously in mind is demonstrated most explicitly in the works of one of the earliest and dullest of the tribe, Thomas Watson, whose

Passionate Centurie of Love[1] came out in 1582. His poems are not strict sonnets, being all of eighteen lines, and he calls them 'passions', although he clearly makes no distinction between them and the strict quatorzain. Watson prefaces each Passion with a little précis in prose which outlines the conceit and sometimes analyses the specific method. Thus, number 41 is based on 'that figure in Rhetorique . . . called . . . of the Latines *Reduplicatio*'; number 3 'is all framed in manner of a dialogue, wherein the Author talketh with his owne heart . . .'; in number 4, 'The chiefe grounde and matter of this Sonnet standeth uppon the rehearsall of such thinges as by reporte of the Poets, are dedicated unto Venus.' Watson is one of the most minor and academic of Elizabethan sonneteers but he nevertheless defines, however crudely, the general practice. We shall see that even Astrophel sets about writing his sonnets in the same deliberate way, and that Sidney's objection is not to the method itself but to the material it uses.

Because of its preoccupation with the conceit, the Elizabethan sonnet cycle is not primarily a narrative form but rather the by-product of narrative. Occasionally, as in the songs which Sidney weaves throughout *Astrophel and Stella*, the story is told explicitly; but normally it is too traditional to need telling, and the various episodes can be deduced from the emotional and intellectual responses to them which the individual sonnets record. The sonnet is an introspective, witty, cerebral form of verse in which the momentary response is analysed or played with in terms of a conceit, and for this reason the individual sonnet is complete in itself and can stand alone, independent of the rest of the cycle. The difference, indeed, between a genuine sonnet cycle and a mere sequence of sonnets depends upon the ability of the poet to impose a common structure or tone upon a collection of individual units, and there are very few genuine cycles among the Elizabethans. Sidney and Shakespeare impose a dramatic unity upon their sequences, Spenser a common mood, Drayton a common quality of immediacy, but the rest are mostly memorable for good sonnets rather than for significant groupings. Spenser and Sidney never forget that the purpose of the sonnet is to woo and win the lady,

[1] Arber English Reprints, 1870.

and everything is related to the processes and pains of this central function. In *Amoretti* 68, for example, Spenser celebrates the Christian significance of Easter day as the expression of God's love, which he then uses in the last couplet as an argument to forward his own:

> So let us love, deare love, lyke as we ought:
> Love is the lesson which the lord us taught.

The most elaborate conceits of Sidney's sonnets often spring out of the frustrations of Astrophel which can find no satisfaction except in words. In sonnet 61, the lover laments that he has besieged Stella with sighs and tears, with words and even silences, but her reply is always that if he truly loves her, he will respect her chaste desires and withdraw his attentions. In this dilemma, Astrophel can only appeal hopelessly to Cupid for help, for what possible solution can there be to the paradox that he can only prove his love by ceasing to love, 'That I love not, without I leave to love'? There is at least a bitter-sweet satisfaction in the formulation of the paradox, as Astrophel gets some of his sufferings off his chest by means of wit. In this way the conceit takes on a dramatic function and the individual sonnet, while complete in itself, can yet form part of the larger unit. For this reason, too, in spite of its basically unhappy subject-matter, the sonnet is one of the lightest and most scintillating forms of verse.

One further general point needs to be made, namely, that the sonnet is the 'personal kind' in the Elizabethan poetic hierarchy, the type of verse in which the poet is expected to speak *in propria persona*. This, however, must not be taken too literally. Petrarch had written in the first person as of his own love, but it is far from certain that the Laura of his poems corresponded to any Laura in real life; and the association of the laurel with the poetic 'bays' led to all kinds of allegorical interpretations which Sidney, for example, shows himself aware of in sonnet 90. In his preface to *Licia*, Giles Fletcher warns his reader:

If thou muse what my Licia is, take her to be some Diana, at the

least chaste, or some Minerva, no Venus, fairer farre: it may be shee
is Learnings image, or some heavenlie woonder . . . perhaps under
that name I have shadowed Discipline . . . it may bee some Colledge;
it may bee my conceit, and portends nothing . . .[1]

This, I think, is nearer to the Elizabethan conception of the sonnet
mistress than much of the modern biographical research into the
private lives of Stella or the dark lady. Many of the sonnet personae
resemble their poet creators, and many of the sonnet ladies were
explicitly identified with contemporary figures; yet the fact that all
the sonnet sequences with the exception of Shakespeare's tell
substantially the same story and fill it out with the same detail
should put us on our guard against a simple biographical approach.
Astrophel has much in common with Sidney, and Stella was known
by everyone to be Penelope Devereux, yet there is no historical
evidence to suggest that Sidney's life followed the pattern of his
hero's or that he ever fell in love with Penelope, to whom incidentally, Constable also dedicated Petrarchan sonnets. The 'personal'
mode of poetry represents for the Elizabethans a dramatic exercise
in first-person writing rather than the exposure of the poet's own
bleeding heart, and unlike romantic poetry, the object of the sonnet
is ritual and ceremonial rather than autobiographical. A sonnet
sequence may be anything from a humanist exercise in the fashionable mode of love poetry to a public compliment paid to a patroness
or a friend or even, in the case of Spenser, to his own wife.

Sidney bases his defence of poetry on the argument that it is by
definition a form of fiction, and discusses the use of proper names
in this connection. He compares them to the generic names such as
John a Stile and John a Noakes in hypothetical legal cases and adds,
'Their naming of men is but to make their picture the more lively,
and not to build any history: painting men, they cannot leave men
nameless' (*Defence*, p. 124).[2] *Astrophel and Stella* was written as a
poetic fiction, a tragedy in three acts, and it is possible that Sidney
was making his fictional characters more lively (and, incidentally,
following the example of Petrarch) by giving them real identities.

[1] ed. Lloyd E. Berry. University of Wisconsin, 1964.
[2] ed. Geoffrey Shepperd. Nelson, 1965.

He is alluding to the ambiguous relationship between fact and fiction in poetry in sonnet 45 when Astrophel argues that since Stella is more moved by a story of lovers which she is reading than by the reality of his love, let her remember that poetry is fiction and respond to his sonnets accordingly:

> Then thinke my deare, that you in me do read
> > Of Lover's ruine some sad Tragedie:
> > I am not I, pitie the tale of me.

II

I pass now from the sonnet in general to those sonnets which make up this anthology. The term 'sonnet' was used very loosely in the period to describe almost any short love poem, as can be seen in Donne's *Songs and Sonets* for example: there are sonnets of fifteen lines, as in Barnes, or of eighteen, in Watson, and the type goes under a variety of names — Canzoni in *Zepheria*, Passions in Watson's *Passionate Centurie*, Amours in Drayton's *Idea*. In this anthology, with the exception of two fifteen-line sonnets by Barnes, I restrict myself to the strict quatorzain which was always the dominant form. Wyatt and Surrey had made brilliant translations and adaptations of Petrarch in sonnet form as far back as the reign of Henry VIII, and these had been widely circulated through the many editions of *Tottel's Miscellany* throughout the second half of the sixteenth century. The great burst of sonneteering in the 1590s, however, was sparked off by the work of Sidney, a pioneer in this as in so many other fields. His *Astrophel and Stella*, written about 1582 and circulated in manuscript until the pirated editions of 1591, created the taste and set the fashion going. Between 1591 and the end of the decade there were sonnet cycles by Daniel, Constable, Barnes, Drayton, Lodge, Percy, the anonymous author of *Zepheria*, Griffin, Smith, Tofte, Lynche, to mention only those reprinted by Sidney Lee in the two volumes of his *Elizabethan Sonnets* (1904). He does not include those of Shakespeare and Spenser and a host of very minor writers. The sonnet was the bow of Ulysses which every established or would-be poet, every young man of the Inns of Court with a literary taste, felt it his duty to bend.

This anthology prints the four major sequences of the period, excluding that of Shakespeare, with a brief selection from the minor sonneteers to give some idea of the normal level which the form achieved and the extravagances of which it was capable. Shakespeare is not included because he is easily accessible elsewhere, but he should nevertheless be considered in the context of the Elizabethan sonnet. His cycle is revolutionary in that it stands the conventional Petrarchan situation on its head, turning the sonnet-lady into a whore and attaching all the idealized emotion to a young man. It offers a more complex analysis of the relationship between love and passion than that of any other writer, but also a more fragmented vision in that it turns its back on the attempts of most serious sonneteers to achieve some reconciliation between the two. Shakespeare's sonnet drama is most profitably approached, I think, through the orthodox petrarchism against which it is a reaction, and in terms of the contemporary sonnet conceit which it exploits to the full. To read Shakespeare's sonnets as though they were an isolated phenomenon is to ignore one of their major dimensions.

Of the sonnets in this collection, *Astrophel and Stella* is the only sequence to follow Petrarch in systematically interweaving songs with its sonnets and to form a complete organic whole. Sidney was a theorist of poetry as well as a poet, and his sonnets are as much a part of his humanist programme for the rehabilitation of English poetry as are his pastorals or his revised *Arcadia*. The sonnets themselves are full of references to literary theory and insist throughout that we read them from this perspective. In his survey of English poetry in his *Defence*, Sidney is especially scathing about the love poetry of the period:

But truly many of such writings as come under the banner of unresistible love, if I were a mistress, would never persuade me they were in love; so coldly they apply fiery speeches, as men that had rather read lovers' writings . . . than that in truth they feel those passions. (pp. 137-8)

He could be describing Watson's *Passionate Centurie of Love*; and in contrasting love poetry based on other love .poetry with that derived from the direct human experience, he raises a fundamental literary problem of Renaissance humanism — how to copy the best models from the past, and yet remain true to life. It is, in the final analysis, the conflict between Nature and Art, but more specifically, one between the two common conceptions of 'Imitation' as defined by Aristotle and Horace. Aristotle's *Poetics*, newly discovered in the sixteenth century and used by Sidney for his *Defence*, defines poetry as 'Mimesis', the imitation of human action through the medium of words. In this process, the irrelevances and imperfections are stripped off, and the representation of life which emerges is more intense, more universal, but in no way a falsification of reality. Horace's definition of Imitation in his so-called 'Art of poetry', however, and that to be found in all the rhetorical textbooks from Cicero and Quintilian onwards, is the imitation of the best models as a method of extending one's literary or oratorical techniques. It is the standard method in Renaissance schools of teaching children to write and speak well, as can be seen from the very full account in Ascham's *Scholemaster*, to name only one of many examples. It is by this kind of Imitation that Spenser and Sidney hoped to extend the bounds of English literature by introducing the classical modes which it lacked.

Ideally, of course, the two modes of Imitation are not in conflict: the writer imitates the form of the best literary model and puts into it the appropriate human experience. The classical forms were created as vehicles to express human behaviour and can still be made to perform their task. Where, however, a convention is highly mannered, it is inevitable that the hack writers will imitate the surface mannerisms and ignore the underlying content; and this is the cause of Sidney's criticism of contemporary love poetry. Generations of love poets following Petrarch have mechanically reproduced his 'long deceased woes' and made hackneyed imitations of his time-worn conceits of ice and fire, while in the process the love out of which all originally sprang has leaked away. Sidney is not therefore attacking the Petrarchan conventions but trying to put some blood back into them, to restore love to love poetry and heal the breach between Horace and Aristotle.

Astrophel and Stella is written explicitly with this object in view. The opening sonnets in particular are so packed with reference to critical theory that they form a manifesto of Sidney's intention, and are worth analysing in some detail for what they tell us about the way we ought to approach the sequence. We must remember that Sidney's poem is about a poet writing poems to his mistress, which provides him with the ideal cover for his own theories of poetry. In his first sonnet, Astrophel, 'Loving in truth' and not merely going through the fashionable poses, sits down with pen in hand to write a poem to Stella, since he knows, from his *Poetics*, that tragedy gives pleasure and so presumably may the account of his pains, and from his Horace, that pleasure may move her to read, to know, to pity and by this route to show grace. He seeks fit words, therefore, in which to present his grief in the pure and absolute form — 'the blackest face of woe' — which, according to Aristotle, Imitation alone makes possible; but he has been thinking along Horatian lines so that his first impulse is to follow Horace's precepts and turn to other men's inventions for his models. 'Invention' is a complex word and one in process of transition at this period. It already has its modern meaning of things invented, things found out or made up by other people's wits, but it also carries for the Renaissance a traditional technical meaning which it has since lost. Invention is the first part of classic rhetoric, the process of finding out whatever materials are appropriate for a given task, whether one is making up an oration or writing a poem. Once the relevant materials have been chosen, the poet or orator proceeds to the second part of rhetoric, Disposition, the choice of the appropriate mode of presenting the material for the task in hand, and thence to Elocution, the third part, which is the selection of 'fit words'. It is interesting — and a point which an educated reader of Sidney's time would immediately recognize — that Astrophel approaches his composition in entirely the wrong order: he seeks fit words before he has chosen his basic materials or considered their presentation; he jumps straight to Elocution, leaving out Invention and Disposition, and this is why he finds it so hard to write. When he turns belatedly to Invention it is the wrong kind for this moment, Horatian: he seeks his materials in 'others' leaves' which can provide him with the proper form but not the proper materials for a love poem. He is, in fact, confusing Invention with Disposition. The true source of knowledge about love is not to be found in books but in the human heart, and it is to this source which his Muse therefore bids him turn. She is not telling him to write his own autobiography, but to look for the materials for a love poem in the proper place.

Astrophel immediately follows her advice in the very revolutionary second sonnet which presents love as it is in fact rather than as it has been represented in literature. In the medieval tradition of which Petrarch himself was only a late inheritor, literary lovers had always fallen in love at first sight — 'Whoever loved that loved not at first sight' — but Astrophel, when he looks into his own heart, finds that this does not tally with experience: he fell in love only gradually, without knowing what was happening, and when he discovered it, he resisted with all his might. Now he has reached the stage when he knows there is no escape and is trying to persuade himself that all is for the best, although he knows in his heart of hearts that it is not so. This sonnet challenges the centuries-old tradition of Courtly Love; and Astrophel, speaking with the voice of Sidney, draws attention to this in the next sonnet when he contrasts his own verse based on the reality of love — 'then all my deed / But copying is, what in her Nature writes' — with that of love poets who merely copy what has been written before. It is a theme to which Sidney returns continually — in sonnets 6, 15 and 55, for example, and a central point about the nature of love poetry which he uses his sonnet cycle to demonstrate.

The ape referred to in sonnet 3, with its capacity for mimicry, was a common Renaissance symbol for art; but Sidney is not anticipating Wordsworth's plea for a poetry of nature which shall reject all art. The philosophy of the period, which pictured even Nature herself as manifesting the art of God, involved too deep a reverence for good art for it ever to be repudiated. Stella's beauty in the third sonnet is, after all, 'what in her Nature *writes*'; and the poet is the most god-like among men because by means of his art he can recreate what God, the supreme artist, has already created. The art of true poetry is divine because it is based on Nature.

Yet when we look at the mass of sonnet conceits and patterns which make up *Astrophel and Stella*, our first impression is of a triumphant and self-sufficient art, though Astrophel denies that this is so throughout the sequence; and Sidney for once would have agreed with Watson in his notes to his Passion 40 which handles the time-honoured theme of the contradictory passions of love, 'I feare, and hope, I burne, yet freeze withall.' These paradoxes, says Watson, are in fact true to life:

The sense contained in this Sonnet will seeme straunge to such as never have acquainted themselves with Love and his Lawes, because of the contrarieties mentioned therein. But to such, as Love at any time hath had under his banner, all and every part of it will appeere to be a familiar truth.

Throughout all love poetry from Ovid to Yeats, lovers have gazed at the moon or tossed on their beds as Astrophel does in sonnets 31 and 39, and the great clichés of poetry correspond to the permanent patterns of human behaviour. More specifically, a witty man will be witty in his love, especially if he is a poet, and Astrophel's wit turns every occasion into a means of wooing Stella. He twists the double negative of her 'No, No,' into a grammatical affirmative (63), or turns her coat-of-arms into a compliment to her beauty (13), or his own into proof of a relationship with her (65). In the same way Donne turns his casual encounter with a flea into an argument for seduction. Even the traditional conceits about Cupid's bow and arrows (17, 20) become miniature pieces of Spenserean-type allegory and inner histories of his own soul wounded by the shafts of passion. Moreover, for the first part of the sequence at least, Astrophel is busily using the remnant of wit which love has left him 'To make myself beleeve that all is well'; and in his efforts to justify himself to himself and to the traditional rational 'friend' of love poetry, he drags in every argument, every support, every rag of philosophy that he can. Reason can be made to prove that love is better than reason (10); the fashionable Platonism of the time can be evoked in the defence of passion (5); even the astrological belief in the power of the stars can be brought in — not with entire flippancy in this period — to explain the irresistible power of Stella's eyes over him (26).

Sidney is in fact giving his sonnet conceits a dramatic justification. The whole witty structure of the poem is a dramatic projection of the character of Astrophel the poet, just as the characters of Richard II or Hamlet produce their own kinds of wit. These witty and conceited sonnets are natural from a lover such as Astrophel who, dramatically is nearly twenty years ahead of the times. A Hamlet with only love to plague him would behave as he does. There is nothing comparable to his wry, half-humorous self-awareness until we come to Shakespeare's plays. In the first sixty-three sonnets, he is torn between the claims of this highly inconvenient love and those of the active life for which he is trained; but his capacity for action is undermined even more by his consciousness of the slightly ridiculous figure he cuts as an unwilling lover, 'prauncing' in Mars' livery when he is really Cupid's man (53), or posing as the symbol of authority on his great horse when he himself is being ridden by Cupid (49). For a brief period his passion becomes strong enough to drive out all hesitation, and the insistent rhythms of the first song express a whole-heartedness in his approach which at once evokes a response from Stella: 'And do I see some cause a hope to feede . . .' (66). But Stella's love for him is coupled to an invincible chastity; and after a brief period of euphoric rapture, when continence seems a small price to pay for the joys of such platonic love, passion again cries for food (71) and the old conflicts are there once more in a new and more acute form. The poem moves to its predictable end as Stella sticks to her principles and Astrophel respects them, suffering in consequence moods of despair or taking refuge in erotic wishful-thinking in the tenth song — itself a thoroughly conventional erotic vision. It ends bleakly with the hint of a more willing mistress in the offing, and a request from Astrophel to be released so that he may get on with his duties for the state (107).

Sidney has written a new dramatic version of the old Petrarchan situation, with the central role filled by a modern lover whose particular character breathes new life into the old conventions. Sidney's dramatic power in this cannot be overstated, and the character he has created must never be confused with himself.

There is the clearest distinction in the first sonnet between the confused and pedantic Astrophel fumbling over his poem, and Sidney, the literary theorist, showing him how to do it; and throughout the cycle we are conscious of Sidney looking over Astrophel's shoulder with an amused detachment and doing things within the sonnet which undercut what Astrophel claims to be doing. In this way sonnet 34 presents a very unconfused description of a mind claiming itself to be in a state of utter confusion, while sonnet 35, professing the complete inadequacy of words to express the paradoxes of Stella's perfection, yet succeeds in expressing them through paradox itself. Sidney's control of his character, even when the character contains so much of himself, is much surer than, say, that of Byron with Childe Harold, and is capable of very subtle nuances. In sonnet 90, for example, in a supremely neat poem, Sidney makes Astrophel deny that he wishes to be thought a poet — which offers the same kind of complex perspective as we find in Shakespeare's plays, with boy actors playing the part of girls dressed up as boys.

The range and originality of Sidney's art is extraordinary, and he takes the English sonnet form at a bound virtually from birth to maturity. His favourite form is a Petrarchan one modified by a final couplet, but he experiments with a great variety of rhyme-schemes and with lines of varying lengths, and achieves remarkably different effects from the same basic patterns. His final couplet sometimes rounds off and neatly closes up the sonnet statement, sometimes explodes and stands the sonnet on its head (71, 72), sometimes introduces a note of ambiguity which leaves the mind wondering: is Stella or is she not the country to which our souls should move ?(5). Is virtue ungratefulness or ungratefulness virtue on the moon ?(31). Within the formal structure he can include with equal ease a process of argument (7), a comment on the contemporary scene (30), a vividly dramatic episode (47, 53) or a piece of animated dialogue (34, 54, 92). With Shakespeare the freer sonnet form can on occasion disappear altogether under the pressure of its content. The great sonnet on Lust, for example (sonnet 129) becomes an undivided unit of fourteen lines rather than a pattern of quatrains and couplets. This is never the case with Sidney. However colloquial and conversational the statement he is making or however compressed the thought, he always leaves us conscious of the sonnet form and aware of the individual tension between form and content. In this strait-jacket of the sonnet Sidney can move about with the ease of a Houdini.

The sonnets of Samuel Daniel, in contrast, are less dramatic in content and gentler in their appeal. In his *Elegie* to Henry Reynolds, Drayton says of Daniel that some consider him 'To be too much *Historian* in verse', and continues

> His rimes were smooth, his meeters well did close,
> But yet his maner better fitted prose.[1]

Such a comment would be quite inapplicable to Sidney with his artistic flamboyance, or to Drayton himself with his mastery of the decorum of so many different styles; but for Daniel it is not wholly inappropriate. He might even have taken it as a compliment, for he says, with reference to his own longer historical poems, 'I versify the truth not poetise'. He is here alluding to the common conception, held, as we have seen, by Sidney, that poetry is 'imitation', fiction, 'feigning', and he believes that truth is more important than poetry. The Renaissance literary theorists did not share the modern assumption that the form and the content of poetry are inseparable, but usually conceived of style and form as the clothes in which content is dressed up for a given occasion. In Daniel, this dichotomy is extreme. For him, the poetry *is* the content, it is the intensity and truth of the vision which makes the poetry. The style, though it may sometimes help to move and persuade, is more commonly something which distorts and gets in the way. Although his affection for rhyme makes him defend it as appropriate to English poetry against the claims of classical metres, he makes it clear that he considers both to be merely superficial matters of local fashion, and that only the truth within is important:

Eloquence and gay wordes are not of the Substance of wit, it is but the garnish of a nice time, the Ornaments that doe but decke the

---

[1] *Works of Michael Drayton*, ed. Hebel, vol. iii, p. 229.

house of a State. . . . Hunger is as well satisfied with meat served in pewter as silver. Discretion is the best measure, the rightest foote in what habit soever it runne. (*Defence of Ryme*, p. 145)

The pretty puns on foot and measure in the last line of this quotation suggest that as a poet Daniel was not quite so indifferent to the pleasure of verbal effects as he pretends, yet he is very conscious that they may get in the way. His own style shows the influence of this way of thought. At its best in his later poetry it has a transparency which forces us to ignore the outer cover and come to grips at once with the naked thought inside, as if we were reading very packed prose, although paradoxically it is the poetic technique itself which creates this illusion.

Daniel's belief in the pre-eminence of content in poetry makes him more dependent on his subject-matter than is the case with most of his contemporaries. Unlike Sidney and most of the son-neteers, he cannot make poetry out of the sheer excitement and pleasure of rhetorical or metrical virtuosity, nor can he trifle elegantly in the fashions of the day: his writing achieves greatness only when he has a subject about which he cares and has thought deeply. For this reason he is not wholly at home in the sonnet convention, although as a young and budding poet he felt the need to try his hand at the genre, and as a result, *Delia* is very uneven in its quality. A large number of the sonnets are what the anti-Petrarchan satirists at the end of the century called 'whining sonnets' — numbers 2, 4, 20, 21, 29 exemplify the 'wayling' and 'plaintive' modes to which they took exception — and they are often obscure, clumsy or even flabby in their diction, suggesting that Daniel had no great taste for what he was doing. The conceits have not the audacity of Sidney's, though Sidney's influence is apparent in the elaborate patterning of 11 and 14, for example. The control of the sonnet form and the matching of it to the sonnet argument are at times inadequate. The most successful are perhaps those like 13 or 31 which are organized around a central metaphor taken from a classical myth; and in this respect Daniel goes beyond Sidney in moving outside the range of Cupid-Venus conceits on which Sidney mainly relied. In subsequent editions Daniel revised his sonnets extensively and attempted to eliminate their weaknesses — he has, as he says in the 1607 preface, 'Repaird some parts defective here and there' — but this mainly took the form of cutting feminine endings and omitting the more plaintive of the sonnets. He often tinkers without improving or making less obscure, as in 21 line 4, where the relative immediacy of 1592 'Whilst my best blood my younge desiers sealeth' is replaced in 1594 by the cliché 'Whilst age upon my wasted body steales'; or in 40, where the difficult line 12 of 1592, 'Which shall instarre the needle and the trayle' is altered to the no less obscure 'Which must instarre the needle and the raile' of 1594. Unlike Drayton, Daniel's sonnets changed but did not improve with his age, and the greater poetic maturity of his other poetry does not show itself here.

This, however, is only true when Daniel is handling the conventional sonnet situation. Whenever he finds an important theme to deal with within the sonnet, his verse rises magnificently to the challenge, and the sequence of sonnets, 32-8 and 45, all dealing with the decay of beauty, are among the greatest in the language. Mortality and change haunted Daniel's consciousness, and the great commonplaces, the passing from spring to winter, the flowers of beauty born only to wither and die, ring out in his poetry with an authority equal to that of Shakespeare, though with less than Shakespeare's certainty that his sonnets are strong enough to keep that beauty ever young. There is nothing in Daniel quite so triumphant as Shakespeare's 'Not marble nor the guilded monuments' (55). The nearest he ever gets to it is in sonnets 40 and 50, but number 38 is more typical, where he laments that 'thou a Laura hast no Petrarch found'. Daniel's faith in the divinity not merely of his own but of all poetry was harder won than that of Shakespeare or Sidney, and his need to justify poetry in the modern world more anxious and acute. He was only too conscious that the Philistines can get on very well without the help of poetry:

> How many thousands never heard the name
> Of Sydney, or of Spenser, or their bookes?
> And yet brave fellowes, and presume of fame . . .
>
> (*Musophilus*, 440-2)[1]

[1] *Poems and a Defence of Ryme,* ed. Sprague.

Daniel's wrestling with the problem and his eventual justification to himself of the fact that he is a poet is finely worked out in his great poem of philosophical self revelation, *Musophilus*; and in the end, it is by an act of faith that he finds comfort, rather than by the argument that poetry can confer immortality or persuade to virtue:

> This is the thing that I was borne to do,
> This is my Scene, this part I must fulfill.
>
> (*Musophilus*, 577-8)

Like Daniel, Michael Drayton was very conscious that he was born to be a poet. As he writes in his *Elegie* to Henry Reynolds:

> From my cradle (you must know) that I
> Was still inclin'd to noble Poesie (Hebel, vol. iii, p. 226)

but he never doubted his calling. Drayton, after Spenser, is the arch-poet of his period, the true professional who systematically covers the whole range of literary 'kinds' from pastoral through to heroic and satiric, taking in the sonnet on the way in his *Ideas Mirrour* of 1594 which, like Daniel, he revised continually until its final appearance as *Idea* in 1619. His revisions in part consist in the rejection of the more extravagantly conceited of the earlier sonnets, but there is little real consistency in his method. He retains number 40, based on the old heart/anvil image, from 1594, but he rejects the wittier Amour 11 dealing with the alphabet of love. The 1619 version, indeed, has a new line of conceits of its own, more knotty and cerebral than those of the earlier version, but not essentially different. The play on 'I' and 'Aye' in sonnet 5, or the sophisticated logic of sonnet 26 are cases in point. As in Daniel, so Drayton's later versions include fewer of the 'whining' sonnets, a point to which the poet alludes in his sonnet 'To the Reader of these Sonnets' prefacing the 1619 edition:

> No farre-fetch'd Sigh shall ever wound my Brest,
> Love from mine Eye a Teare shall never wring,
> Nor in Ah-mees my whyning Sonnets drest.

In this vein, and following Sidney, Drayton compliments himself in sonnet 24 on his ability to conceal his feelings under a show of wit. Indeed, his debt to Sidney is very great, increasing with each revision; and it is paradoxical that the claim to originality with which he concludes his dedicatory sonnet to the edition of 1594 should explicitly echo Sidney's own claim to originality in sonnet 74 of *Astrophel and Stella*:

> Divine Syr Phillip, I avouch thy writ,
> I am no Pickpurse of anothers wit.
>
> (Hebel, vol. i, *Ideas Mirrour*)

There is a superficial similarity between Drayton's sonnet 24 and Sidney's 54; between his 38 and Sidney's 10; his 39 and 15; his 51 and 30, and many others. But the debt is deeper than this: the two poets have the same range of conversational tones, the same involvement in contemporary affairs and critical debates. Like the sonnets of Sidney but unlike those of Daniel and Spenser, Drayton's sonnets do not exist in a world of which love is the only dimension and where the function of the sonnet is to look inward into the private and traditional sufferings of the heart. Drayton's sonnets look outwards and in their imagery acknowledge the existence of a social situation and of other activities going on outside. Sonnets 2, 7, 10, 21, 28, 50, to name only a few, share this extrovert quality with *Astrophel and Stella*, and their conceits draw on the world of everyday experience, on the law, on bankruptcy, on the behaviour of spendthrift young men or the practises of the medical profession. From this fact, they gain a quality of realism which makes a heightened dramatic impact. *Idea* has no overall dramatic structure and development such as we find in Sidney, but of all the Elizabethan sonneteers, including even Shakespeare, Drayton is the master in the presentation of what Daniel calls 'a present passion' (*Defence*, 138). The famous anthology pieces 'Since ther's no helpe' (61), or 'You not alone' (11), or 'How many paltry, foolish, painted things' (6), or 'An evill spirit' (20), have a passionate intensity which no one but Shakespeare can rival in the sonnet. Moreover, this quality often appears in conjunction with the most elaborate conceit: 'You not alone, when You are still alone' (11), is based on the same kind of word play as the much slighter 'No and I' sonnet (5), the difference being that in sonnet 11, the wit is a means of analysing passion rather than an end in itself. In *Idea,* the sonnet comes nearest to the poetry of the Metaphysicals, and some of Drayton's sonnets, notably 8, 15, 52, are very close to Donne's anti-Petrarchan poems.

With Spenser's *Amoretti*, we are back once more, though with a difference, in the charmed circle of sonnet love. Where Sidney and Drayton allow the sonnet to spill over into everyday life and attract to itself the whole range of contemporary imagery and allusion, Spenser observes the strictest decorum of the amorous mode and excludes everything which is not a part of love's poetic world. The language itself is consciously poetical, never colloquial, and it is apparent in the *Amoretti* as in *The Faerie Queene* that we are dealing with a poet who, in Ben Jonson's sense of the words, 'writ no language'. The vocabulary is as archaic, the syntax as uncolloquial as anything in the heroic poem. Spenser creates structures of words which justify themselves as patterns in relation to each other rather than as accurate and precise reporting. One cannot imagine Sidney or Drayton getting away with words such as 'dumpish' (4,4), or 'portly' (5,2), unless they used them satirically; or using words as Spenser does in lines *10-12* of his sonnet 15 which have no other function than to sustain a structural pattern of anaphora, rhyme and poetic diction. The opening sonnet with its highly formal pattern of 'Happy leaves', 'happy lines', 'happy rhymes', concentrates the attention on the fact of the poetry itself and is a manifesto of the poetic diction to come. Spenser is the poet's poet in every sense; and the fact that the first sonnet may originally have been written as an introduction to *The Faerie Queene* itself only serves to emphasize this common quality shared by Spenser's different poetic modes.

Within the limits which he sets himself, however, Spenser finds room for a surprising degree of freedom and unorthodoxy. At the local level this appears in the liberties, greater than in any other sonnet writer, which he takes with the classical myths he uses so freely. Sonnets 23, 24, 28, 38, for example, show him changing the basic stories to suit his own purposes. But the originality goes deeper than this. The *Amoretti* is thoroughly orthodox in its central situation and story line: the lady is firmly on her pedestal and the sonnets are devoted to her praises more completely than, say, Astrophel's, which are mainly preoccupied with his own states of mind. Spenser's lady is described in all her beauty and her cruelty; and though she appears to relent from sonnets 65—78, a 'Venemous toung' has confounded the relationship once more by 86. Yet the prevalent state of mind is neither one of frustration nor of the platonic idealization of forced abstinence, the two normal responses to the Petrarchan dilemma. Instead, the *Amoretti* offers a paeon in praise of sexual love in the context of Christian marriage, which goes serenely on, often in opposition to the story line or in a way which makes it irrelevant. The classical properties are consistently Christianized, as in sonnet 1 where Helicon is peopled with angels; or 9, where the divinity of the lady is almost blasphemously equated with that of God himself; or 22, where love's altar becomes the high altar at Easter day; or 15 and 70 with their unmistakable allusions to the Song of Songs. The shame which afflicts Shakespeare's sonnet lover in the presence of lust, and drives Astrophel to try and platonize away the hunger of the flesh, seems to present Spenser with no problem, as the contrast between his sonnet 84 and Sidney's 71 or 72 reveals. The only exception is perhaps *Amoretti* 72, which suggests some degree of moral ambiguity. Otherwise, Spenser consistently stresses the moral goodness of sexual love in Christian marriage and it is easy to miss the precision with which the Christian context is defined. In *Amoretti* 55, for example, after eliminating the four material elements as fit substances from which his lady could be created, Spenser is left with only the celestial fifth element, the sky, out of which she could be formed. Having established his hyperbolic compliment, he then turns it neatly in the last couplet into a plea for mercy:

> Then sith to heaven ye lykened are the best,
>   be lyke in mercy as in all the rest.

The 'mercy' to which he is referring, however, is not merely that which the medieval lover implores from his mistress, nor is it the mercy of God in general terms: Spenser is also alluding to the specific manifestation of that mercy in the form of the Incarnation, and he is pleading with the lady to take on human flesh as Christ did. The Incarnation is the basis of Spenser's belief in the holiness of sex and the human body, as expressed in Books III and IV of *The Faerie Queene* and in the *Epithalamion*. It dictates also the dominant tone of the *Amoretti* and causes him to Christianize the Petrarchan love sonnet as he Christianized the heroic poem.

For this reason many critics have complained, with justification, that the *Amoretti* is self contradictory, and that the Petrarchan motif is at odds with the un-Petrarchan theme. This, I think, is true: the sonnet conventions ran counter to Spenser's basic sexual attitudes, and his awareness of this fact is apparent in his treatment of Britomart, Amoret and the two Florimels in *The Faerie Queene*, Books III and IV. What is interesting about the *Amoretti*, however, is how, having undertaken a Petrarchan cycle, Spenser sets about papering over the cracks. The lady's cruelty, for example, is softened by being described in mock heroic terms:

> See how the Tyrannesse doth joy to see
> the huge massacres which her eyes do make: (10)

and there is a similar flippancy in the address to his poems which she has torn up:

> Innocent paper, whom too cruell hand
> did make the matter to avenge her yre (48)

In this case the normal poetic diction of the *Amoretti* is exploited to give a touch of comedy to the situation. But the most potent force in the *Amoretti* is the Spenserean sonnet form itself with its interlocking quatrains used consistently throughout the whole sequence. The effect is to carry the statement forward without a break, and in this way to discourage the possibility of drama and play down the sense of conflict. By this means the whole cycle takes on a deceptive unity of tone not unlike that of Tennyson's *In*

Memoriam, and for the same reasons. Spenser's sonnet drama comes out as a sustained piece of lyric with its discordant elements scarcely apparent.

For this reason, the conjunction of the *Amoretti* with the *Epithalamion* seems to me right, though technically they belong to opposing genres; and the legend that Spenser wrote both of them as a wedding present to his new wife is a reasonable one. The evidence of the sonnets suggests that he felt that she, too, deserved her proper tribute of a sonnet cycle, however inappropriate a poem of frustration might be to a happy marriage; and though, as a passionate humanist, he was not prepared to reshape the genre in a fundamental way, he did his best to turn it into something not wholly unsuitable to the situation. The result is a brilliant and strongly individual hybrid.

There is no need to say more than has been said in the notes about the shorter Petrarchan sequences included in this volume, but a further comment may be added on the *Gullinge Sonnets* of Sir John Davies, since these represent a major shift in taste at the end of the century. A form as idiosyncratic and a fashion as rampant as that of the sonnet inevitably lead to parody in the end, especially when more erotic modes of love poetry exist and at times even infiltrate the sonnet itself. *Hero and Leander* or *Venus and Adonis* represent a very different tradition in love, and their values can be seen in Barnes's sonnet 63 or Griffin's number 3, for example. Sidney's attack on the sonnet of his own times from the start set the precedent for further appeals for a return to nature, and Shakespeare's sonnet against sonnet hyperbole, 'My mistress' eyes are nothing like the sun' (130), is in the Sidneyan tradition, not to mention the Bastard's outburst against the Dauphin's wooing of Blanche in sonnet terms — 'Drawn in the flattering table of her eye' (King John, II, *i*), or the whole of *Love's Labours Lost*. Shakespeare was anti-Petrarchan from the beginning, but by the late 1590s everyone felt that way, and the satirists such as Hall and Marston were in full cry against the sonneteers:

Then poures he forth in patched Sonettings

His love, his lust, and loathsome flatterings: . . .
Then can he terme his durtie ill-fac'd bride
Lady and Queene and Virgin deifide. . .

(Hall, *Virgidemiarum,* I,7)

It is easier, however, to denounce the sonnet than to parody it, since a pyrotechnic display of rhetoric is part of the sonnet's quality, and its very excesses can be its virtues. Davies's legal conceits (7, 8, 9), are less extravagant and far less interesting than those of *Zepheria* which he sets out to parody, just as number 5 is less elaborate than some of the poems in the *Old Arcadia*. He is at his best when he finds a common sonnet conceit which it is still possible to stretch further than ever before, as in the case of 3 and 6.

The reader who hopes to taste the full flavour of the minor Elizabethan sonnet should read the exquisite miniature editions of the 1590s in the British Museum. The arbitrary nature of the spelling and punctuation, generally attributable to the compositor rather than the author himself; the elegance of the printing, the elaborate capitals and decorative patterns of lay out, give a stronger sense of the individuality of each than any modern edition can hope to do. I have tried to retain something of that flavour by avoiding a standardized and uniform presentation of the varying texts; but the reader who takes one of the original octavos in his hand will feel something of the excitement which a new book of poems must have produced in the relative infancy of printing, and be unusually conscious that he is handling an artefact. It is an experience peculiarly relevant to the reading of the sonnet.

1977   Maurice Evans

Sonnet to the Reader

Thou find'st not heere, neither the furious alarmes,
Of the pride of Spaine, or subtilnes of France:
Nor of the rude English, or mutine Almanes:
Nor neither of Naples, noble men of armes.
No, an Infant, and that yet surmounteth Knights:
Hath both vanquished me, and also my Muse,
And were it not: this is a lawfull excuse.
If thou hearst not the report, of their great fights,
Thou shalt see no death of any valiant soldier,
And yet I sing the beauty of a fierce warrier.
And amore alone I must strike on my Leer,
And but Eroto I knowe no other Muse.
And harke all you that are lyke us amourous.
And you that are not, goe read some otherwhere.

K. Soowthern
Sonnets to his mystresse Diana, 1584

Sir Philip Sidney

Astrophel and Stella

1   Loving in truth, and faine in verse my love to show,
That she (deare she) might take some pleasure of my paine;
Pleasure might cause her reade, reading might make her know,
Knowledge might pitie winne, and pitie grace obtaine,
I sought fit words to paint the blackest face of woe,
Studying inventions fine her wits to entertaine;
Oft turning others' leaves, to see if thence would flow
Some fresh and fruitfull showers upon my sunne-burn'd braine.
    But words came halting forth, wanting Invention's stay;
Invention, Nature's child, fled step-dame Studie's blowes,
And others' feete still seem'd but strangers in my way.
Thus great with child to speake, and helplesse in my throwes,
    Biting my trewand pen, beating my selfe for spite,
    'Foole,' said my Muse to me, 'looke in thy heart and write.'

2   Not at the first sight, nor with a dribbed shot
    Love gave the wound, which while I breathe will bleed:
    But knowne worth did in mine of time proceed,
Till by degrees it had full conquest got.
I saw and liked, I liked but loved not,
    I loved, but straight did not what *Love* decreed:
    At length to *Love's* decrees I, forc'd, agreed,
Yet with repining at so partiall lot.
    Now even that footstep of lost libertie
Is gone, and now like slave-borne *Muscovite*,
I call it praise to suffer Tyrannie;

2

And now employ the remnant of my wit
    To make my selfe beleeve that all is well,
    While with a feeling skill I paint my hell.

3   Let daintie wits crie on the Sisters nine,
    That bravely maskt, their fancies may be told:
    Or *Pindare's* Apes, flaunt they in phrases fine,
    Enam'ling with pied flowers their thoughts of gold:
    Or else let them in statelier glorie shine,
    Ennobling new found Tropes with problemes old:
    Or with strange similies enrich each line,
    Of herbes or beastes, which *Inde* or *Afrike* hold.
      For me in sooth, no Muse but one I know:
      Phrases and Problemes from my reach do grow,
    And strange things cost too deare for my poore sprites.
      How then? Even thus: in *Stella's* face I reed
      What Love and Beautie be; then all my deed
    But Copying is what in her Nature writes.

4   *Vertue*, alas, now let me take some rest,
    Thou setst a bate betweene my will and wit:
    If vaine love have my simple soule opprest,
    Leave what thou likest not, deale not thou with it.
    Thy scepter use in some old *Catoe's* brest;
    Churches or schooles are for thy seate more fit:
    I do confesse; pardon a fault confest:
    My mouth too tender is for thy hard bit.
      But if that needs thou wilt usurping be
      The litle reason that is left in me,
    And stil th'effect of thy perswasions prove,
      I sweare, my heart such one shall shew to thee
      That shrines in flesh so true a Deitie,
    That, *Vertue*, thou thy selfe shalt be in love.

5   It is most true that eyes are form'd to serve
    The inward light, and that the heavenly part
    Ought to be king, from whose rules who do swerve,

Rebels to Nature, strive for their owne smart.
It is most true, what we call *Cupid's* dart,
An image is, which for our selves we carve,
And, fooles, adore in temple of our hart,
Till that good God make Church and Churchman starve.
True, that true Beautie Vertue is indeed,
Whereof this Beautie can be but a shade
Which elements with mortall mixture breed:
True, that on earth we are but pilgrims made,
And should in soule up to our countrey move:
True, and yet true that I must *Stella* love.

6 Some Lovers speake when they their Muses entertaine,
Of hopes begot by feare, of wot not what desires;
Of force of heav'nly beames, infusing hellish paine;
Of living deaths, deare wounds, faire stormes and freesing fires:
Some one his song in *Jove*, and *Jove's* strange tales attires,
Brodered with buls and swans, powdred with golden raine:
Another humbler wit to shepheard's pipe retires,
Yet hiding royall bloud full oft in rurall vaine.
To some a sweetest plaint a sweetest stile affords,
While teares powre out his inke, and sighs breathe out his words:
His paper, pale dispaire, and paine his pen doth move.
I can speake what I feele, and feele as much as they,
But thinke that all the Map of my state I display,
When trembling voice brings forth that I do *Stella* love.

7 When Nature made her chief worke, *Stella's* eyes,
In colour blacke why wrapt she beames so bright?
Would she in beamie blacke, like painter wise,
Frame daintiest lustre, mixt of shades and light?
Or did she else that sober hue devise
In object best to knit and strength our sight,
Least if no vaile these brave gleames did diguise,
They sun-like should more dazle then delight?
Or would she her miraculous power show,
That whereas blacke seemes Beautie's contrary,

She even in blacke doth make all beauties flow?
Both so and thus: she, minding love should be
    Placed ever there, gave him this mourning weed,
    To honor all their deaths who for her bleed.

8 *Love* borne in *Greece,* of late fled from his native place,
    Forc'd by a tedious proofe that Turkish hardned hart
    Is no fit marke to pierce with his fine pointed dart;
And pleasd with our soft peace, staid here his flying race.
But finding these North clymes do coldly him embrace,
    Not usde to frozen clips, he strave to find some part
    Where with most ease and warmth he night employ his art:
At length he perch'd himself in *Stella's* joyfull face,
    Whose faire skin, beamy eyes, like morning sun on snow,
Deceiv'd the quaking boy, who thought from so pure light
Effects of lively heat must needs in nature grow.
But she, most faire, most cold, made him thence take his flight
    To my close heart, where while some firebrands he did lay,
    He burnt unwares his wings, and cannot fly away.

9 Queene *Vertue's* court, which some call *Stella's* face,
    Prepar'd by Nature's choisest furniture,
    Hath his front built of Alablaster pure;
Gold is the covering of that stately place.
The doore, by which sometimes comes forth her Grace,
    Red Porphir is, which locke of pearle makes sure;
    Whose porches rich (which name of cheekes endure)
Marble mixt red and white do enterlace.
    The windowes now through which this heav'nly guest
Looks over the world, and can find nothing such
Which dare claime from those lights the name of best,
Of touch they are that without touch doth touch,
    Which *Cupid's* selfe from Beautie's mine did draw:
    Of touch they are, and poore I am their straw.

10 Reason, in faith thou art well serv'd, that still
    Wouldst brabling be with sence and love in me:
    I rather wisht thee clime the Muses' hill,

Or reach the fruite of Nature's choisest tree,
Or seeke heavn's course, or heavn's inside to see:
Why shouldst thou toyle our thornie soile to till?
Leave sense, and those which sense's objects be:
Deale thou with powers of thoughts; leave love to will.
But thou wouldst needs fight both with love and sence,
With sword of wit giving wounds of dispraise,
Till downe-right blowes did foyle thy cunning fence:
For soone as they strake thee with *Stella's* rayes,
Reason, thou kneel'dst, and offeredst straight to prove
By reason good, good reason her to love.

11   In truth, O love, with what a boyish kind
Thou doest proceed in thy most serious wayes:
That when the heav'n to thee his best displayes,
Yet of that best thou leav'st the best behind.
For like a child that some faire booke doth find,
With guilded leaves or colour Velume playes,
Or at the most on some fine picture stayes,
But never heeds the fruit of writer's mind:
So when thou saw'st in Nature's cabinet
Stella, thou straight lookst babies in her eyes,
In her cheeke's pit thou didst thy pitfould set,
And in her breast bopeepe or couching lyes,
Playing and shining in each outward part:
But, foole, seekst not to get into her hart.

12   *Cupid,* because thou shin'st in *Stella's* eyes,
That from her lockes, thy day-nets, none scapes free,
That those lips swell, so full of thee they bee,
That her sweete breath makes oft thy flames to rise,
That in her breast thy pap well sugred lies,
That her Grace gracious makes thy wrongs, that she,
What words so ere she speake, perswades for thee,
That her cleare voyce lifts thy fame to the skies;
Thou countest *Stella* thine, like those whose powers
Having got up a breach by fighting well,

Crie, 'Victorie, this faire day all is ours.'
O no, her heart is such a Cittadell,
    So fortified with wit, stor'd with disdaine,
    That to win it is all the skill and paine.

13 *Phœbus* was Judge betweene *Jove, Mars,* and *Love,*
    Of those three gods, whose armes the fairest were:
  Jove's golden shield did Eagle sables beare,
    Whose talents held young *Ganimed* above:
    But in Vert field *Mars* bare a golden speare,
  Which through a bleeding heart his point did shove:
  Each had his creast: *Mars* caried *Venus'* glove;
    Jove on his helme the thunderbolt did reare.
  Cupid then smiles, for on his crest there lies
    Stella's faire haire; her face he makes his shield,
    Where roses gueuls are borne in silver field.
  Phœbus drew wide the curtaines of the skies
    To blaze these last, and sware devoutly then,
    The first, thus matcht, were scantly Gentlemen.

14 Alas have I not paine enough, my friend,
    Upon whose breast a fiercer Gripe doth tire
    Then did on him who first stale downe the fire,
  While *Love* on me doth all his quiver spend,
  But with your Rubarb words you must contend
    To grieve me worse, in saying that Desire
    Doth plunge my wel-form'd soule even in the mire
  Of sinfull thoughts, which do in ruine end?
    If that be sinne which doth the maners frame,
  Well staid with truth in word and faith of deed,
  Readie of wit and fearing nought but shame:
  If that be sinne which in fixt hearts doth breed
    A loathing of all loose unchastitie,
    Then Love is sinne, and let me sinfull be.

15 You that do search for everie purling spring
    Which from the ribs of old *Parnassus* flowes,
    And everie floure, not sweet perhaps, which growes

Neare thereabouts, into your Poesie wring;
You that do Dictionaries' methode bring
    Into your rimes, running in ratling rowes:
    You that poore *Petrarch's* long deceased woes,
With new-borne sighes and denisend wit do sing;
    You take wrong waies; those far-fet helpes be such
    As do bewray a want of inward tuch;
And sure at length stolne goods do come to light.
    But if (both for your love and skill) your name
    You seeke to nurse at fullest breasts of Fame,
Stella behold, and then begin to endite.

16   In nature apt to like when I did see
    Beauties, which were of manie Carrets fine,
    My boiling sprites did thither soone incline,
And, Love, I thought that I was full of thee:
But finding not those restlesse flames in me
    Which others said did make their soules to pine,
    I thought those babes of some pinne's hurt did whine,
By my soule judging what Love's paine might be.
    But while I thus with this young Lyon plaid,
Mine eyes (shall I say curst or blest?) beheld
Stella: now she is nam'd, need more be said?
In her sight I a lesson new have speld;
    I now have learn'd Love right, and learn'd even so,
    As who by being poisond doth poison know.

17   His mother deare *Cupid* offended late,
    Because that *Mars*, growne slacker in her love,
    With pricking shot he did not throughly move
To keepe the pace of their first loving state.
The boy refusde for feare of *Marse's* hate,
    Who threatned stripes, if he his wrath did prove:
    But she in chafe him from her lap did shove,
Brake bow, brake shafts, while *Cupid* weeping sate:
    Till that his grandame *Nature* pittying it,

8

Of *Stella's* browes made him two better bowes,
And in her eyes of arrowes infinit.
O how for joy he leapes, O how he crowes,
  And straight therewith, like wags new got to play,
  Fals to shrewd turnes, and I was in his way.

18   With what sharpe checkes I in my selfe am shent,
       When into Reason's audite I do go,
       And by just counts my selfe a banckrout know
     Of all those goods, which heav'n to me hath lent;
     Unable quite to pay even Nature's rent,
       Which unto it by birthright I do ow:
       And which is worse, no good excuse can show,
     But that my wealth I have most idly spent.
       My youth doth waste, my knowledge brings forth toyes;
     My wit doth strive those passions to defend
     Which for reward spoile it with vaine annoyes.
     I see my course to loose my selfe doth bend:
       I see and yet no greater sorrow take
       Then that I loose no more for *Stella's* sake.

19   On *Cupid's* bow how are my heart-strings bent,
       That see my wracke, and yet embrace the same!
       When most I glorie, then I feele most shame:
     I willing run, yet while I run, repent.
     My best wits still their owne disgrace invent:
       My veries inke turnes straight to *Stella's* name;
       And yet my words, as them my pen doth frame,
     Avise themselves that they are vainely spent.
       For though she passe all things, yet what is all
     That unto me, who fare like him that both
     Lookes to the skies, and in a ditch doth fall?
     O let me prop my mind, yet in his growth,
       And not in Nature for best fruits unfit:
       'Scholler,' saith *Love*, 'bend hitherward your wit.'

20 Flie, fly, my friends, I have my death wound; fly,
    See there that boy, that murthring boy, I say,
    Who like a theefe, hid in darke bush doth ly,
    Till bloudie bullet get him wrongfull pray.
    So Tyran he no fitter place could spie,
    Nor so faire levell in so secret stay,
    As that sweete blacke which vailes the heav'nly eye:
    There himselfe with his shot he close doth lay.
        Poore passenger, passe now thereby I did,
    And staid pleasd with the prospect of the place,
    While that blacke hue from me the bad guest hid:
    But straight I saw motions of lightning grace,
        And then descried the glistring of his dart:
        But ere I could flie thence, it pierc'd my heart.

21 Your words, my friend (right healthfull caustiks) blame
        My young mind marde, whom *Love* doth windlas so,
        That mine owne writings like bad servants show
    My wits, quicke in vaine thoughts, in vertue lame;
    That *Plato* I read for nought, but if he tame
        Such coltish gyres; that to my birth I owe
        Nobler desires, least else that friendly foe,
    Great expectation, weare a traine of shame.
        For since mad March great promise made of me,
    If now the May of my yeares much decline,
    What can be hoped my harvest time will be?
    Sure you say well; your wisdome's golden mine
        Dig deepe with learning's spade; now tell me this,
        Hath this world ought so faire as *Stella* is?

22 In highest way of heav'n the Sunne did ride,
        Progressing then from faire twinnes' gold'n place;
        Having no scarfe of clowds before his face,
    But shining forth of heate in his chiefe pride;
    When some faire Ladies, by hard promise tied,
        On horsebacke met him in his furious race,
        Yet each prepar'd, with fanne's wel-shading grace,

From that foe's wounds their tender skinnes to hide.
Stella alone with face unarmed marcht,
   Either to do like him, which open shone,
   Or carelesse of the wealth because her owne:
Yet where the hid and meaner beauties parcht,
   Her daintiest bare went free; the cause was this,
   The Sunne, which others burn'd, did her but kisse.

23   The curious wits, seeing dull pensivenesse
     Bewray it selfe in my long setled eyes,
     Whence those same fumes of melancholy rise
   With idle paines, and missing ayme, do guesse.
Some that know how my spring I did addresse,
     Deem that my Muse some fruit of knowledge plies:
     Others, because the Prince my service tries,
   Thinke that I thinke state errours to redresse.
     But harder Judges judge ambition's rage,
   Scourge of it selfe, still climing slipprie place,
   Holds my young braine captiv'd in golden cage.
   O fooles, or over-wise, alas the race
     Of all my thoughts hath neither stop nor start,
     But only *Stella's* eyes and *Stella's* hart.

24   Rich fooles there be, whose base and filthy hart
   Lies hatching still the goods wherein they flow;
   And damning their owne selves to *Tantal's* smart,
   Wealth breeding want, more blist, more wretched grow.
   Yet to those fooles heav'n such wit doth impart,
   As what their hands do hold, their heads do know,
   And knowing, love, and loving, lay apart
   As sacred things, far from all daunger's show.
     But that rich foole, who by blind Fortune's lot
   The richest gemme of Love and life enjoyes,
   And can with foule abuse such beauties blot;
   Let him, deprived of sweet but unfelt joyes,
     (Exil'd for ay from those high treasures, which
     He knowes not) grow in only follie rich.

25   The wisest scholler of the wight most wise,
By *Phœbus'* doome, with sugred sentence sayes
That Vertue, if it once met with our eyes,
Strange flames of *Love* it in our soules would raise;
But for that man with paine this truth descries,
Whiles he each thing in sense's ballance wayes,
And so nor will, nor can, behold those skies
Which inward sunne to *Heroicke* minde displaies,
    Vertue of late, with vertuous care to ster
Love of her selfe, tooke *Stella's* shape, that she
To mortall eyes might sweetly shine in her.
It is most true, for since I her did see,
    Vertue's great beautie in that face I prove,
    And find th'effect, for I do burne in love.

26   Though dustie wits dare scorne Astrologie,
And fooles can thinke those Lampes of purest light,
Whose numbers, wayes, greatnesse, eternitie,
Promising wonders, wonder do invite,
To have for no cause birthright in the skie,
But for to spangle the blacke weeds of night;
Or for some brawle, which in that chamber hie,
They should still daunce to please a gazer's sight:
    For me, I do Nature unidle know,
And know great causes great effects procure:
And know those Bodies high raigne on the low.
And if these rules did faile, proofe makes me sure,
    Who oft fore-judge my after-following race
    By only those two starres in *Stella's* face.

27   Because I oft in darke abstracted guise
    Seeme most alone in greatest companie,
    With dearth of words, or answers quite awrie,
To them that would make speech of speech arise,
They deeme, and of their doome the rumour flies,
    That poison foule of bubling pride doth lie
    So in my swelling breast that only I

Fawne on my self, and others do despise:
    Yet pride I thinke doth not my soule possesse,
Which lookes too oft in his unflattring glasse:
But one worse fault, *Ambition,* I confesse,
That makes me oft my best friends overpasse,
    Unseene, unheard, while thought to highest place
    Bends all his powers, even unto *Stella's* grace.

28   You that with allegorie's curious frame
    Of others' children changelings use to make,
    With me those paines for God's sake do not take:
I list not dig so deepe for brasen fame.
When I say *'Stella',* I do meane the same
    Princesse of Beautie, for whose only sake
    The raines of *Love* I love, though never slake,
And joy therein, though Nations count it shame.
    I beg no subject to use eloquence,
Nor in hid wayes do guide Philosophie:
Looke at my hands for no such quintessence;
But know that I, in pure simplicitie,
    Breathe out the flames which burne within my heart,
    Love onely reading unto me this art.

29   Like some weake Lords, neighbord by mighty kings,
    To keepe themselves and their chiefe cities free,
    Do easly yeeld that all their coasts may be
Ready to store their campes of needfull things;
So *Stella's* heart, finding what power *Love* brings,
    To keepe it selfe in life and liberty
    Doth willing graunt that in the frontiers he
Use all, to helpe his other conquerings:
    And thus her heart escapes, but thus her eyes
Serve him with shot, her lips his heralds arre,
Her breasts his tents, legs his triumphall carre,
Her flesh his food, her skin his armour brave;
    And I, but for because my prospect lies
Upon that coast, am giv'n up for a slave.

30   Whether the Turkish new-moone minded be
      To fill his hornes this yeare on Christian coast;
      How *Poles'* right king meanes, without leave of hoast,
  To warme with ill-made fire cold *Moscovy*:
  If French can yet three parts in one agree;
      What now the Dutch in their full diets boast;
      How *Holland* hearts, now so good townes be lost,
  Trust in the shade of pleasing *Orange* tree;
      How *Ulster* likes of that same golden bit,
  Wherewith my father once made it halfe tame;
  If in the Scottishe Court be weltring yet;
  These questions busie wits to me do frame;
      I, cumbred with good maners, answer do,
      But know not how, for still I thinke of you.

31   With how sad steps, O Moone, thou climb'st the skies,
      How silently, and with how wanne a face;
      What, may it be that even in heav'nly place
  That busie archer his sharpe arrowes tries?
  Sure, if that long-with-*Love*-acquainted eyes
      Can judge of *Love*, thou feel'st a Lover's case;
      I reade it in thy lookes; thy languisht grace
  To me that feele the like, thy state descries.
      Then ev'n of fellowship, O Moone, tell me
  Is constant *Love* deem'd there but want of wit?
  Are Beauties there as proud as here they be?
  Do they above love to be lov'd, and yet
      Those Lovers scorne whom that *Love* doth possesse?
      Do they call *Vertue* there ungratefulnesse?

32   *Morpheus*, the lively sonne of deadly sleepe,
      Witnesse of life to them that living die;
      A Prophet oft, and oft an historie,
  A poet eke, as humours fly or creepe;
  Since thou in me so sure a power doest keepe,
      That never I with clos'd-up sense do lie,
      But by thy worke my *Stella* I descrie,

Teaching blind eyes both how to smile and weepe,
   Vouchsafe of all acquaintance this to tell,
Whence hast thou Ivorie, Rubies, pearle and gold,
To shew her skin, lips, teeth and head so well?
'Foole,' answers he, 'no *Indes* such treasures hold,
    But from thy heart, while my sire charmeth thee,
    Sweet *Stella's* image I do steale to mee.'

33   I might, unhappie word, O me, I might,
And then would not, or could not see my blisse:
Till now, wrapt in a most infernall night,
I find how heav'nly day, wretch, I did misse.
Hart, rent thy selfe, thou doest thy selfe but right;
No lovely *Paris* made thy *Hellen* his:
No force, no fraud, robd thee of thy delight,
Nor Fortune of thy fortune author is:
    But to my selfe my selfe did give the blow,
While too much wit (forsooth) so troubled me,
That I respects for both our sakes must show:
And yet could not by rising Morne foresee
    How faire a day was neare. O punisht eyes,
    That I had bene more foolish or more wise.

34   Come let me write. 'And to what end?' To ease
    A burthned hart. 'How can words ease, which are
    The glasses of thy dayly vexing care?'
Oft cruell fights well pictured forth do please.
'Art not asham'd to publish thy disease?'
    Nay, that may breed my fame, it is so rare.
    'But will not wise men thinke thy words fond ware?'
Then be they close, and so none shall displease.
    'What idler thing then speake and not be hard?'
What harder thing then smart and not to speake?
Peace, foolish wit, with wit my wit is mard.
Thus write I while I doubt to write, and wreake
    My harmes on Ink's poore losse: perhaps some find
    Stella's great powrs, that so confuse my mind.

35 What may words say, or what may words not say,
    Where truth it selfe must speake like flatterie?
    Within what bounds can one his liking stay,
    Where Nature doth with infinite agree?
    What *Nestor's* counsell can my flames alay,
    Since Reason's selfe doth blow the cole in me?
    And ah, what hope that hope should once see day,
    Where *Cupid* is sworne page to Chastity?
        Honour is honour'd that thou doest possesse
    Him as thy slave, and now long needy Fame
    Doth even grow rich, naming my *Stella's* name.
        Wit learnes in thee perfection to expresse:
    Not thou by praise, but praise in thee is raisde:
    It is a praise to praise, when thou art praisde.

36 *Stella*, whence doth this new assault arise,
    A conquerd, yelden, ransackt heart to winne?
    Whereto long since, through my long-battred eyes,
    Whole armies of thy beauties entred in.
    And there long since, *Love* thy Lieutenant lies,
    My forces razde, thy banners raisd within:
    Of conquest, do not these effects suffice,
    But wilt now warre upon thine owne begin?
        With so sweete voice, and by sweete Nature so,
    In sweetest strength, so sweetly skild withall,
    In all sweete stratagems sweete Arte can show,
    That not my soule, which at thy foot did fall,
        Long since forc'd by thy beames, but stone nor tree
        By Sence's priviledge, can scape from thee.

37 My mouth doth water, and my breast doth swell,
      My tongue doth itch, my thoughts in labour be:
      Listen then, Lordings, with good eare to me,
    For of my life I must a riddle tell.
    Towardes *Aurora's* Court a Nymph doth dwell,
      Rich in all beauties which man's eye can see;
      Beauties so farre from reach of words, that we

Abase her praise, saying she doth excell:
    Rich in the treasure of deserv'd renowne,
Rich in the riches of a royall hart,
Rich in those gifts which give th'eternall crowne;
Who, though most rich in these and everie part
    Which make the patents of true wordly blisse,
    Hath no misfortune, but that Rich she is.

38   This night, while sleepe begins with heavy wings
        To hatch mine eyes, and that unbitted thought
        Doth fall to stray, and my chiefe powres are brought
    To leave the scepter of all subject things,
    The first that straight my fancie's error brings
        Unto my mind is *Stella's* image, wrought
        By *Love's* owne selfe, but with so curious drought,
    That she, me thinks, not onely shines but sings
        I start, looke, hearke, but what in closde-up sence
    Was held, in opend sense it flies away,
    Leaving me nought but wailing eloquence:
    I, seeing better sights in sight's decay,
        Cald it anew, and wooed sleepe againe:
        But him, her host, that unkind guest had slaine.

39   Come sleepe, O sleepe, the certaine knot of peace,
    The baiting place of wit, the balme of woe,
    The poore man's wealth, the prisoner's release,
    Th'indifferent Judge betweene the high and low;
    With shield of proofe shield me from out the prease
    Of those fierce darts dispaire at me doth throw:
    O make in me those civill warres to cease;
    I will good tribute pay if thou do so.
        Take thou of me smooth pillowes, sweetest bed,
    A chamber deafe to noise, and blind to light;
    A rosie garland, and a wearie hed;
    And if these things, as being thine by right,
        Move not thy heavy grace, thou shalt in me,
        Livelier then else-where, *Stella's* image see.

40   As good to write as for to lie and grone.
        O *Stella* deare, how much thy power hath wrought,
        That hast my mind, none of the basest, brought
    My still kept course, while others sleepe, to mone.
    Alas, if from the height of Vertue's throne
        Thou canst vouchsafe the influence of a thought
        Upon a wretch that long thy grace hath sought,
    Weigh then how I by thee am overthrowne:
        And then, thinke thus: although thy beautie be
        Made manifest by such a victorie,
    Yet noblest Conquerours do wreckes avoid.
        Since then thou hast so farre subdued me
        That in my heart I offer still to thee,
    O do not let thy Temple be destroyd.

41   Having this day my horse, my hand, my launce
        Guided so well that I obtain'd the prize,
        Both by the judgement of the English eyes,
    And of some sent from that sweet enemie *Fraunce*;
    Horsemen my skill in horsmanship advaunce,
        Towne-folkes my strength; a daintier judge applies
        His praise to sleight, which from good use doth rise:
    Some luckie wits impute it but to chaunce:
        Others, because of both sides I do take
    My bloud from them, who did excell in this,
    Thinke Nature me a man of armes did make.
    How farre they shoote awrie! The true cause is
        Stella lookt on, and from her heav'nly face
        Sent forth the beames which made so faire my race.

42   O eyes, which do the Spheares of beautie move,
    Whose beames be joyes, whose joyes all vertues be,
    Who while they make *Love* conquer, conquer *Love*,
    The schooles where *Venus* hath learn'd Chastitie:
    O eyes, where humble lookes most glorious prove,
    Only lov'd Tyrants just in cruelty,
    Do not, O do not from poore me remove;

Keepe still my Zenith, ever shine on me.
   For though I never see them, but straight wayes
My life forgets to nourish languisht sprites,
Yet still on me, O eyes, dart downe your rayes;
And if from Majestie of sacred lights,
   Oppressing mortall sense, my death proceed,
   Wrackes Triumphs be, which *Love* (high set) doth breed.

43   Faire eyes, sweet lips, deare heart, that foolish I
Could hope by *Cupid's* helpe on you to pray,
Since to himselfe he doth your gifts apply
   As his maine force, choise sport, and easefull stay.
   For when he will see who dare him gainesay,
Then with those eyes he lookes: lo by and by
Each soule doth at *Love's* feet his weapons lay,
Glad if for her he give them leave to die.
   When he will play, then in her lips he is,
Where blushing red, that *Love's* selfe them doth love,
With either lip he doth the other kisse:
But when he will for quiet's sake remove
   From all the world, her heart is then his rome,
   Where well he knowes no man to him can come.

44   My words I know do well set forth my mind;
   My mind bemones his sense of inward smart;
   Such smart may pitie claime of any hart;
Her heart, sweete heart, is of no Tygre's kind:
And yet she heares, and yet no pitie I find;
   But more I crie, lesse grace she doth impart.
   Alas, what cause is there so overthwart,
That Noblenesse it selfe makes thus unkind?
   I much do guesse, yet find no truth save this,
That when the breath of my complaints doth tuch
Those daintie dores unto the Court of blisse,
The heav'nly nature of that place is such,
   That once come there, the sobs of mine annoyes
   Are metamorphosd straight to tunes of joyes.

45   *Stella* oft sees the verie face of wo
      Painted in my beclowded stormie face;
      But cannot skill to pitie my disgrace,
  Not though thereof the cause her selfe she know:
  Yet hearing late a fable, which did show
      Of Lovers never knowne a grievous case,
      Pitie thereof gate in her breast such place
  That, from that sea deriv'd, teares' spring did flow.
      Alas, if Fancy drawne by imag'd things,
  Though false, yet with free scope more grace doth breed
  Then servant's wracke where new doubts honor brings,
  Then thinke, my deare, that you in me do reed
      Of Lover's ruine some sad Tragedie:
      I am not I; pitie the tale of me.

46   I curst thee oft, I pitie now thy case,
      Blind-hitting boy, since she that thee and me
      Rules with a becke, so tyrannizeth thee,
  That thou must want or food, or dwelling place.
  For she protests to banish thee her face:
      Her face? O *Love*, a Rogue thou then shouldst be,
      If *Love* learne not alone to love and see,
  Without desire to feed of further grace.
      Alas poore wag, that now a scholler art
  To such a schoole-mistresse, whose lessons new
  Thou needs must misse, and so thou needs must smart.
  Yet Deare, let me this pardon get of you,
      So long (though he from booke myche to desire)
      Till without fewell you can make hot fire.

47   What, have I thus betrayed my libertie?
      Can those blacke beames such burning markes engrave
      In my free side? or am I borne a slave,
  Whose necke becomes such yoke of tyranny?
  Or want I sense to feele my miserie?
      Or sprite, disdaine of such disdaine to have,
      Who for long faith, tho dayly helpe I crave,

May get no almes but scorne of beggerie?
   Vertue awake; Beautie but beautie is:
I may, I must, I can, I will, I do
Leave following that, which it is gaine to misse.
Let her go. Soft, but here she comes. Go to,
   Unkind, I love you not: O me, that eye
   Doth make my heart give to my tongue the lie.

48   Soule's joy, bend not those morning starres from me,
   Where Vertue is made strong by Beautie's might,
   Where *Love* is chastnesse, Paine doth learne delight,
And Humblenesse growes one with Majestie.
What ever may ensue, O let me be
   Copartner of the riches of that sight:
   Let not mine eyes be hel-driv'n from that light:
O looke, O shine, O let me die and see.
   For though I oft my selfe of them bemone,
   That through my heart their beamie darts be gone,
Whose curelesse wounds even now most freshly bleed;
   Yet since my death-wound is already got,
   Deare Killer, spare not thy sweet cruell shot:
A kind of grace it is to slay with speed.

49   I on my horse, and *Love* on me doth trie
   Our horsmanships, while by strange worke I prove
   A horsman to my horse, a horse to *Love*;
And now man's wrongs in me, poore beast, descrie.
The raines wherewith my Rider doth me tie
   Are humbled thoughts, which bit of Reverence move,
   Curb'd in with feare, but with guilt bosse above
Of Hope, which makes it seeme faire to the eye.
   The Wand is Will; thou Fancie, Saddle art,
Girt fast by memorie, and while I spurre
My horse, he spurres with sharpe desire my hart:
He sits me fast, how ever I do sturre;
   And now hath made me to his hand so right,
   That in the Manage myselfe takes delight.

50   *Stella,* the fulnesse of my thoughts of thee
      Cannot be staid within my panting breast,
      But they do swell and struggle forth of me,
      Till that in words thy figure be exprest.
      And yet as soone as they so formed be,
      According to my Lord *Love's* owne behest,
      With sad eyes I their weake proportion see,
      To portrait that which in this world is best.
        So that I cannot chuse but write my mind,
      And cannot chuse but put out what I write,
      While those poore babes their death in birth do find:
      And now my pen these lines had dashed quite,
          But that they stopt his furie from the same,
          Because their forefront bare sweet *Stella's* name.

51   Pardon mine eares, both I and they do pray,
          So may your tongue still fluently proceed
          To them that do such entertainment need,
      So may you still have somewhat new to say.
      On silly me do not the burthen lay
          Of all the grave conceits your braine doth breed;
          But find some *Hercules* to beare, in steed
      Of *Atlas* tyr'd, your wisedome's heav'nly sway.
          For me, while you discourse of courtly tides,
      Of cunningst fishers in most troubled streames,
      Of straying wayes, when valiant errour guides;
      Meane while my heart confers with *Stella's* beames,
          And is even irkt that so sweet Comedie
          By such unsuted speech should hindred be.

52   A strife is growne between *Vertue* and *Love,*
          While each pretends that *Stella* must be his:
          Her eyes, her lips, her all, saith *Love,* do this,
      Since they do weare his badge, most firmely prove.
      But *Vertue* thus that title doth disprove:
          That *Stella* (O deare name) that *Stella* is
          That vertuous soule, sure heire of heav'nly blisse,

Not this faire outside, which our hearts doth move:
    And therefore, though her beautie and her grace
Be *Love's* indeed, in *Stella's* selfe he may
By no pretence claime any maner place.
Well *Love*, since this demurre our sute doth stay,
    Let *Vertue* have that *Stella's* selfe; yet thus,
    That *Vertue* but that body graunt to us.

53   In Martiall sports I had my cunning tride,
    And yet to breake more staves did me addresse,
    While with the people's shouts, I must confesse,
Youth, lucke, and praise, even fild my veines with pride;
When *Cupid*, having me, his slave, describe
    In *Marse's* liverie, prauncing in the presse,
    'What now, sir foole,' said he, 'I would no lesse:
Looke here, I say.' I look'd, and *Stella* spide,
    Who hard by made a window send forth light.
My heart then quak'd, then dazled were mine eyes,
One hand forgat to rule, th'other to fight.
Nor trumpets' sound I heard, nor friendly cries;
    My Foe came on, and beat the aire for me,
    Till that her blush taught me my shame to see.

54   Because I breathe not love to everie one,
    Nor do not use set colours for to weare,
    Nor nourish speciall lockes of vowed haire,
Nor give each speech a full point of a grone,
The courtly Nymphs, acquainted with the mone
    Of them, who in their lips *Love's* standerd beare,
    'What he?' say they of me, 'now I dare sweare,
He cannot love: no, no, let him alone.'
    And thinke so still, so *Stella* know my mind.
Professe in deed I do not *Cupid's* art;
But you, faire maides, at length this true shall find,
That his right badge is but worne in the hart:
    Dumbe Swannes, not chatring Pies, do Lovers prove;
    They love indeed who quake to say they love.

55 Muses, I oft invoked your holy ayde,
    With choisest flowers my speech to engarland so,
    That it, despisde in true but naked shew,
Might winne some grace in your sweet grace arraid;
And oft whole troupes of saddest words I staid,
    Striving abroad a-foraging to go,
    Untill by your inspiring I might know
How their blacke banner might be best displaid.
    But now I meane no more your helpe to trie,
Nor other sugring of my speech to prove,
But on her name incessantly to crie:
For let me but name her whom I do love,
    So sweete sounds straight mine eare and heart do hit,
    That I well find no eloquence like it.

56 Fy, schoole of Patience, Fy, you lesson is
    Far far too long to learne it without booke:
    What, a whole weeke without one peece of looke,
And thinke I should not your large precepts misse?
When I might reade those letters faire of blisse,
    Which in her face teach vertue, I could brooke
    Somewhat thy lead'n counsels, which I tooke
As of a friend that meant not much amisse:
    But now that I, alas, do want her sight,
What, dost thou thinke that I can ever take
In thy cold stuffe a flegmatike delight?
No, Patience, if thou wilt my good, then make
    Her come and heare with patience my desire,
    And then with patience bid me beare my fire.

57 Wo, having made with many fights his owne
    Each sence of mine, each gift, each power of mind,
    Growne now his slaves, he forst them out to find
The thorowest words, fit for woe's selfe to grone,
Hoping that when they might find *Stella* alone,
    Before she could prepare to be unkind,
    Her soule, arm'd but with such a dainty rind,

Should soone be pierc'd with sharpnesse of the mone.
   She heard my plaints, and did not only heare,
But them (so sweete is she) most sweetly sing,
With that faire breast making woe's darknesse cleare:
A prety case! I hoped her to bring
   To feele my griefes, and she with face and voice
   So sweets my paines that my paines me rejoyce.

58   Doubt there hath bene, when with his golden chaine
   The Oratour so farre men's harts doth bind,
   That no pace else their guided steps can find
But as he them more short or slacke doth raine,
Whether with words this soveraignty he gaine,
   Cloth'd with fine tropes, with strongest reasons lin'd,
   Or else pronouncing grace, wherewith his mind
Prints his owne lively forme in rudest braine.
   Now judge by this: in piercing phrases late,
   Th'anatomy of all my woes I wrate;
Stella's sweete breath the same to me did reed.
   O voice, O face, maugre my speeche's might
   Which wooed wo, most ravishing delight
Even those sad words even in sad me did breed.

59   Deare, why make you more of a dog then me?
   If he do love, I burne, I burne in love:
   If he waite well, I never thence would move:
If he be faire, yet but a dog can be.
Litle he is, so litle worth is he;
   He barks; my songs thine owne voyce oft doth prove:
   Bid'n, perhaps he fetcheth thee a glove,
But I, unbid, fetch even my soule to thee.
   Yet while I languish, him that bosome clips,
That lap doth lap, nay lets, in spite of spite,
This sowre-breath'd mate tast of those sugred lips.
Alas, if you graunt only such delight
   To witlesse things, then *Love* I hope (since wit
   Becomes a clog) will soone ease me of it.

60 When my good Angell guides me to the place,
      Where all my good I do in *Stella* see,
      That heav'n of joyes throwes onely downe on me
    Thundred disdaines and lightnings of disgrace:
    But when the ruggedst step of Fortune's race
      Makes me fall from her sight, then sweetly she
      With words, wherein the Muses' treasures be,
    Shewes love and pitie to my absent case.
      Now I, wit-beaten long by hardest Fate,
    So dull am that I cannot looke into
    The ground of this fierce *Love* and lovely hate:
    Then some good body tell me how I do,
      Whose presence, absence, absence presence is;
      Blist in my curse, and cursed in my blisse.

61 Oft with true sighes, oft with uncalled teares,
    Now with slow words, now with dumbe eloquence
    I *Stella's* eyes assayll, invade her eares;
    But this at last is her sweet breath'd defence:
    That who indeed infelt affection beares
    So captives to his Saint both soule and sence
    That, wholly hers, all selfnesse he forbeares;
    Thence his desires he learnes, his live's course thence.
      Now since her chast mind hates this love in me,
      With chastned mind, I straight must shew that she
    Shall quickly me from what she hates remove.
      O Doctor *Cupid*, thou for me reply,
      Driv'n else to graunt by Angel's sophistrie,
    That I love not, without I leave to love.

62 Late tyr'd with wo, even ready for to pine
    With rage of *Love*, I cald my Love unkind;
    She in whose eyes *Love*, though unfelt, doth shine,
    Sweet said that I true love in her should find.
    I joyed, but straight thus watred was my wine,
    That love she did, but loved a Love not blind,
    Which would not let me, whom she loved, decline

From nobler course, fit for my birth and mind:
    And therefore by her Love's authority,
    Wild me these tempests of vaine love to flie,
And anchor fast my selfe on *Vertue's* shore.
    Alas, if this the only mettall be
    Of *Love*, new-coind to helpe my beggery,
Deare, love me not, that you may love me more.

63 O Grammer rules, O now your vertues show;
    So children still reade you with awfull eyes,
    As my young Dove may, in your precepts wise,
Her graunt to me by her owne vertue know.
For late with heart most high, with eyes most low,
    I crav'd the thing which ever she denies:
    She, lightning *Love*, displaying *Venus'* skies,
Least once should not be heard, twise said, 'No, No.'
    Sing then, my Muse, now *Io Pean* sing;
    Heav'ns, envy not at my high triumphing,
But Grammer's force with sweet successe confirme;
    For Grammer sayes (O this, deare *Stella,* weighe,)
    For Grammer sayes (to Grammer who sayes nay?)
That in one speech two Negatives affirme.

First song

Doubt you to whom my Muse these notes entendeth,
Which now my breast orecharg'd to Musicke lendeth?
To you, to you, all song of praise is due,
Only in you my song begins and endeth.

Who hath the eyes which marrie state with pleasure,
Who keepes the key of Nature's chiefest treasure?
To you, to you, all song of praise is due,
Only for you the heav'n forgate all measure.

Who hath the lips, where wit in fairenesse raigneth,
Who womankind at once both deckes and stayneth?

27

To you, to you, all song of praise is due,
Onely by you *Cupid* his crowne maintaineth.

Who hath the feet, whose step all sweetnesse planteth,
Who else for whom *Fame* worthy trumpets wanteth?
To you, to you, all song of praise is due,
Onely to you her Scepter *Venus* granteth.

Who hath the breast whose milke doth passions nourish,
Whose grace is such, that when it chides doth cherish?
To you, to you, all song of praise is due,
Onelie through you the tree of life doth flourish.

Who hath the hand which without stroke subdueth,
Who long dead beautie with increase reneweth?
To you, to you, all song of praise is due,
Onely at you all envie hopelesse rueth.

Who hath the haire which, loosest, fastest tieth,
Who makes a man live then glad when he dieth?
To you, to you, all song of praise is due:
Only of you the flatterer never lieth.

Who hath the voyce, which soule from sences sunders,
Whose force but yours the bolts of beautie thunders?
To you, to you, all song of praise is due:
Only with you not miracles are wonders.

Doubt you to whom my Muse these notes intendeth,
Which now my breast orecharg'd to Musicke lendeth?
To you, to you, all song of praise is due:
Only in you my song begins and endeth.

64 No more, my deare, no more these counsels trie,
      O give my passions leave to run their race:
      Let Fortune lay on me her worst disgrace,
    Let folke orecharg'd with braine against me crie;

Let clouds bedimme my face, breake in mine eye,
    Let me no steps but of lost labour trace;
    Let all the earth with scorne recount my case,
But do not will me from my *Love* to flie.
    I do not envie *Aristotle's* wit,
Nor do aspire to *Cæsar's* bleeding fame,
Nor ought do care, though some above me sit,
Nor hope, nor wishe another course to frame,
    But that which once may win thy cruell hart:
    Thou art my Wit, and thou my Vertue art.

65   Love, by sure proofe I may call thee unkind,
    That giv'st no better eare to my just cries;
    Thou whom to me such my good turnes should bind,
As I may well recount, but none can prize:
    For when, nak'd boy, thou couldst no harbour find
In this old world, growne now so too too wise,
I lodg'd thee in my heart, and being blind
By Nature borne, I gave to thee mine eyes:
    Mine eyes, my light, my heart, my life, alas:
If so great services may scorned be,
Yet let this thought thy tygrish courage passe,
That I perhaps am somewhat kinne to thee;
    Since in thine armes, if learnd fame truth hath spread,
    Thou bear'st the arrow, I the arrow head.

66   And do I see some cause a hope to feede,
    Or doth the tedious burd'n of long wo
    In weakened minds quicke apprehending breed
Of everie image which may comfort show?
    I cannot brag of word, much lesse of deed;
Fortune wheeles still with me in one sort slow,
My wealth no more, and no whit lesse my need;
Desire still on the stilts of feare doth go.
    And yet amid all feares a hope there is
Stolne to my heart, since last faire night, nay day,
Stella's eyes sent to me the beames of blisse,

Looking on me, while I lookt other way:
　　But when mine eyes backe to their heav'n did move,
　　They fled with blush, which guiltie seem'd of love.

67　Hope, art thou true, or doest thou flatter me?
　　　Doth *Stella* now begin with piteous eye
　　　The ruines of her conquest to espie?
　　Will she take time, before all wracked be?
　　Her eye's-speech is translated thus by thee:
　　　But failst thou not in phrase so heav'nly hie?
　　　Looke on again, the faire text better trie:
　　What blushing notes doest thou in margine see?
　　　What sighes stolne out, or kild before full borne?
　　Hast thou found such and such like arguments?
　　Or art thou else to comfort me forsworne?
　　Well, how so thou interpret the contents,
　　　I am resolv'd thy errour to maintaine,
　　　Rather then by more truth to get more paine.

68　*Stella,* the onely Planet of my light,
　　　Light of my life, and life of my desire,
　　　Chiefe good, whereto my hope doth only aspire,
　　World of my wealth, and heav'n of my delight;
　　Why doest thou spend the treasures of thy sprite,
　　　With voice more fit to wed *Amphion's* lyre,
　　　Seeking to quench in me the noble fire,
　　Fed by thy worth, and kindled by thy sight?
　　　And all in vaine, for while thy breath most sweet,
　　With choisest words, thy words with reasons rare,
　　Thy reasons firmly set on *Vertue's* feet,
　　Labour to kill in me this killing care,
　　　O thinke I then, what paradise of joy
　　　It is, so faire a Vertue to enjoy.

69　O joy, too high for my low stile to show:
　　　O blisse, fit for a nobler state then me:
　　　Envie, put out thine eyes, least thou do see

What Oceans of delight in me do flow.
My friend, that oft saw through all maskes my wo,
    Come, come, and let me powre my selfe on thee;
    Gone is the winter of my miserie,
My spring appeares; O see what here doth grow.
    For *Stella* hath with words where faith doth shine,
Of her high heart giv'n me the monarchie:
I, I, O I may say that she is mine.
And though she give but thus conditionly
    This realme of blisse, while vertuous course I take,
    No kings be crown'd, but they some covenants make.

70   My Muse may well grudge at my heavn'ly joy,
If still I force her in sad rimes to creepe:
She oft hath drunke my teares, now hopes to enjoy
Nectar of Mirth, since I *Jove's* cup do keepe.
Sonets be not bound prentise to annoy:
Trebles sing high, as well as bases deepe:
Griefe but *Love's* winter liverie is; the Boy
Hath cheekes to smile, as well as eyes to weepe.
    Come then my Muse, shew thou height of delight
In well raisde notes; my pen the best it may
Shall paint out joy, though but in blacke and white.
Cease, eager Muse; peace pen, for my sake stay;
    I give you here my hand for truth of this,
    Wise silence is best musicke unto blisse.

71   Who will in fairest booke of Nature know
    How Vertue may best lodg'd in beautie be,
    Let him but learne of *Love* to reade in thee,
Stella, those faire lines which true goodnesse show.
There shall he find all vices' overthrow,
    Not by rude force, but sweetest soveraigntie
    Of reason, from whose light those night-birds flie,
That inward sunne in thine eyes shineth so:
    And not content to be Perfection's heire
Thy selfe, doest strive all minds that way to move,

Who marke in thee what is in thee most faire.
So while thy beautie drawes the heart to love,
   As fast thy Vertue bends that love to good:
   'But ah,' Desire still cries, 'give me some food.'

72   Desire, though thou my old companion art,
     And oft so clings to my pure Love, that I
     One from the other scarcely can descrie,
While each doth blow the fier of my hart;
Now from thy fellowship I needs must part;
   Venus is taught with *Dian's* wings to flie:
   I must no more in thy sweet passions lie:
Vertue's gold now must head my *Cupid's* dart.
   Service and Honor, wonder with delight,
Feare to offend, will worthie to appeare,
Care shining in mine eyes, faith in my sprite,
These things are left me by my only Deare;
   But thou, Desire, because thou wouldst have all,
   Now banisht art, but yet alas how shall?

Second song

Have I caught my heav'nly jewell,
Teaching sleepe most faire to be?
Now will I teach her that she,
When she wakes, is too too cruell.

Since sweet sleep her eyes hath charmed,
The two only darts of *Love*,
Now will I with that boy prove
Some play, while he is disarmed.

Her tongue waking still refuseth,
Giving frankly niggard 'No':
Now will I attempt to know,
What 'No' her tongue sleeping useth.

See the hand which waking gardeth,
Sleeping, grants a free resort:
Now will I invade the fort;
Cowards *Love* with losse rewardeth.

But O foole, thinke of the danger
Of her just and high disdaine:
Now will I alas refraine;
Love feares nothing else but anger.

Yet those lips so sweetly swelling,
Do invite a stealing kisse:
Now will I but venture this:
Who will read must first learne spelling.

Oh sweet kisse, but ah she is waking;
Lowring beautie chastens me:
Now will I away hence flee:
Foole, more foole, for no more taking.

73   *Love* still a boy, and oft a wanton is,
School'd onely by his mother's tender eye:
What wonder then if he his lesson misse,
When for so soft a rod deare play he trie?
And yet, my Starre, because a sugred kisse
In sport I suckt, while she asleepe did lie,
Doth lowre, nay, chide; nay, threat for only this:
Sweet, it was saucie *Love,* not humble I.
    But no scuse serves, she makes her wrath appeare
    In Beautie's throne; see now who dares come neare
Those scarlet judges, threatning bloudy paine?
    O heav'nly foole, thy most kisse-worthie face
    Anger invests with such a lovely grace,
That Anger' selfe I needs must kisse againe.

74 I never dranke of *Aganippe* well,
Nor ever did in shade of *Tempe* sit:
And Muses scorne with vulgar braines to dwell;
Poor Layman I, for sacred rites unfit.
Some do I heare of Poets' furie tell,
But (God wot) wot not what they meane by it:
And this I sweare by blackest brooke of hell,
I am no pick-purse of another's wit.
    How falles it then, that with so smooth an ease
My thoughts I speake, and what I speake doth flow
In verse, and that my verse best wits doth please?
Guesse we the cause: 'What, is it thus?' Fie no:
'Or so?' Much lesse: 'How then?' Sure thus it is:
    My lips are sweet, inspired with *Stella's* kisse.

75 Of all the kings that ever here did raigne,
Edward named fourth, as first in praise I name,
Not for his faire outside, nor well-lined braine,
    Although lesse gifts impe feathers oft on Fame;
    Nor that he could young-wise, wise-valiant frame
His Sire's revenge, joyn'd with a kingdome's gaine
And gain'd by *Mars,* could yet mad *Mars* so tame,
That Ballance weigh'd what sword did late obtaine;
    Nor that he made the Flouredeluce so fraid,
Though strongly hedg'd of bloudy Lyon's pawes,
That wittie *Lewis* to him a tribute paid:
Nor this, nor that, nor any such small cause,
    But only for this worthy knight durst prove
    To lose his Crowne, rather then faile his Love.

76 She comes, and streight therewith her shining twins do move
    Their rayes to me, who in her tedious absence lay
    Benighted in cold wo, but now appeares my day,
The onely light of joy, the onely warmth of *Love.*
She comes with light and warmth, which like *Aurora* prove
    Of gentle force, so that mine eyes dare gladly play
    With such a rosie morne, whose beames most freshly gay

Scortch not, but onely do darke chilling sprites remove.
   But lo, while I do speake, it groweth noone with me;
Her flamie glistring lights increase with time and place;
My heart cries 'ah, it burnes'; mine eyes now dazled be:
No wind, no shade can coole; what helpe then in my case,
    But with short breath, long lookes, staid feet and walking hed,
    Pray that my sunne go downe with meeker beames to bed.

77   Those lookes, whose beames be joy, whose motion is delight,
    That face, whose lecture shewes what perfect beautie is;
    That presence, which doth give darke hearts a living light;
    That grace, which *Venus* weepes that she her selfe doth misse;
    That hand, which without touch holds more then *Atlas* might;
    Those lips, which make death's pay a meane price for a kisse;
    That skin, whose passe-praise hue scorns this poore terme of white;
    Those words, which do sublime the quintessence of blisse;
      That voyce, which makes the soule plant himselfe in the eares;
    That conversation sweet, where such high comforts be,
As consterd in true speech, the name of heav'n it beares,
Makes me in my best thoughts and quietst judgement see
      That in no more but these I might be fully blest:
      Yet ah, my Mayd'n Muse doth blush to tell the best.

78   O how the pleasant aires of true love be
    Infected by those vapours, which arise
    Frome out that noysome gulfe, which gaping lies
Betweene the jawes of hellish Jealousie.
A monster, others' harme, selfe-miserie,
    Beautie's plague, Vertue's scourge, succour of lies;
    Who his owne joy to his owne hurt applies,
And onely cherish doth with injurie;
    Who since he hath, by Nature's speciall grace,
    So piercing pawes as spoyle when they embrace,
So nimble feet as stirre still, though on thornes;
    So manie eyes ay seeking their owne woe,
    So ample eares as never good newes know:
It is not evill that such a Devill wants hornes?

79   Sweet kisse, thy sweets I faine would sweetly endite,
      Which even of sweetnesse sweetest sweetner art:
      Pleasingst consort, where each sence holds a part,
  Which, coupling Doves, guides *Venus'* chariot right;
  Best charge, and bravest retrait in *Cupid's* fight,
      A double key, which opens to the heart,
      Most rich, when most his riches it impart;
  Neast of young joyes, schoolmaster of delight,
      Teaching the meane at once to take and give;
  The friendly fray, where blowes both wound and heale,
  The prettie death, while each in other live;
  Poore hope's first wealth, ostage of promist weale,
      Breakefast of *Love* — but lo, lo, where she is:
      Cease we to praise, now pray we for a kisse.

80   Sweet swelling lip, well maist thou swell in pride,
      Since best wits thinke it wit thee to admire;
      Nature's praise, Vertue's stall, *Cupid's* cold fire,
  Whence words, not words, but heav'nly graces slide:
  The new *Pernassus,* where the Muses bide,
      Sweetner of musicke, wisedome's beautifier:
      Breather of life, and fastner of desire,
  Where Beautie's blush in Honour's graine is dide.
      Thus much my heart compeld my mouth to say,
      But now spite of my heart my mouth will stay,
  Loathing all lies, doubting this Flatterie is;
      And no spurre can his resty race renew,
      Without how farre this praise is short of you,
  Sweet lip, you teach my mouth with one sweet kisse.

81   O kisse, which doest those ruddie gemmes impart,
  Or gemmes, or frutes of new-found *Paradise,*
  Breathing all blisse and sweetning to the heart,
      Teaching dumbe lips a nobler exercise:
      O kisse, which soules, even soules together ties
  By linkes of *Love*, and only Nature's art;
  How faine would I paint thee to all men's eyes,

Or of thy gifts at least shade out some part.
    But she forbids; with blushing words, she sayes
    She builds her fame on higher seated praise:
But my heart burnes, I cannot silent be.
    Then since (deare life) you faine would have me peace,
    And I, mad with delight, want wit to cease,
Stop you my mouth with still still kissing me.

82   Nymph of the gard'n, where all beauties be;
    Beauties which do in excellencie passe
    His who till death lookt in a watrie glasse,
Of hers whom naked the *Trojan* boy did see:
Sweet gard'n Nymph, which keepes the Cherrie tree,
    Whose fruit doth farre th'*Esperian* tast surpasse:
    Most sweet-faire, most faire-sweet, do not, alas,
From comming neare those Cherries banish me:
    For though full of desire, emptie of wit,
Admitted late by your best-graced grace,
I caught at one of them a hungrie bit;
Pardon that fault, once more graunt me the place,
    And I do sweare even by the same delight,
    I will but kisse, I never more will bite.

83   Good brother *Philip*, I have borne you long;
    I was content you should in favour creepe,
    While craftily you seem'd your cut to keepe,
As though that faire soft hand did you great wrong.
I bare (with Envie) yet I bare your song,
    When in her necke you did *Love* ditties peepe;
    Nay, more foole I, oft suffered you to sleepe
In Lillies' neast, where *Love's* selfe lies along.
    What, doth high place ambitious thoughts augment?
Is sawcinesse reward of curtesie?
Cannot such grace your silly selfe content,
But you must needs with those lips billing be,
    And through those lips drinke Nectar from that toong?
    Leave that, sir *Phip*, least off your necke be wroong.

Third song

If *Orpheus'* voyce had force to breathe such musicke's love
Through pores of sencelesse tree, as it could make them move:
If stones good measure daunc'd, the *Theban* walles to build,
To cadence of the tunes, which *Amphyon's* lyre did yeeld,
More cause a like effect at leastwise bringeth:
O stones, O trees, learne hearing: *Stella* singeth.

If Love might sweet'n so a boy of shepheard' brood,
To make a Lyzard dull to taste Love's daintie food;
If Eagle fierce could so in *Grecian* Mayd delight,
As his light was her eyes, her death his endlesse night;
Earth gave that Love; heav'n, I trow, Love refineth:
O birds, O beasts, looke, love; lo, *Stella* shineth.

The birds, beasts, stones and trees feele this, and feeling, love:
And if the trees, nor stones stirre not the same to prove,
Nor beasts, nor birds do come unto this blessed gaze,
Know, that small Love is quicke, and great Love doth amaze:
They are amaz'd, but you with reason armed,
O eyes, O eares of men, how are you charmed!

84 Highway since you my chiefe *Pernassus* be,
      And that my Muse, to some eares not unsweet,
      Tempers her words to trampling horse's feet
More oft then to a chamber melodie;
Now blessed you, beare onward blessed me
      To her, where I my heart safeliest shall meet.
      My Muse and I must you of dutie greet
With thankes and wishes, wishing thankfully.
      Be you still faire, honoured by publike heed,
By no encrochment wrongd, nor time forgot;
Nor blam'd for bloud, nor sham'd for sinfull deed:
And that you know I envy you no lot
      Of highest wish, I wish you so much blisse,
      Hundreds of yeares you *Stella's* feet may kisse.

85   I see the house; my heart thy selfe containe;
      Beware full sailes drowne not thy tottring barge,
      Least joy, by Nature apt sprites to enlarge,
   Thee to thy wracke beyond thy limits straine:
   Nor do like Lords, whose weake confused braine,
      Not pointing to fit folkes each undercharge,
      While everie office themselves will discharge,
   With doing all, leave nothing done but paine.
      But give apt servants their due place, let eyes
   See Beautie's totall summe summ'd in her face;
   Let eares heare speech, which wit to wonder ties;
   Let breath sucke up those sweetes, let armes embrace
      The globe of weale, lips *Love's* indentures make:
      Thou but of all the kingly Tribute take.

Fourth song
Onely joy, now here you are,
Fit to heare and ease my care:
Let my whispering voyce obtaine
Sweete reward for sharpest paine:
Take me to thee, and thee to me.
'No, no, no, no, my Deare, let be.'

Night hath closd all in her cloke,
Twinckling starres Love-thoughts provoke:
Danger hence good care doth keepe,
Jealousie it selfe doth sleepe:
Take me to thee, and thee to me.
'No, no, no, no, my Deare, let be.'

Better place no wit can find,
Cupid's yoke to loose or bind:
These sweet flowers on fine bed too,
Us in their best language woo:
Take me to thee, and thee to me.
'No, no, no, no, my Deare, let be.'

This small light the Moone bestowes,
Serves thy beames but to disclose,
So to raise my hap more hie:
Feare not else, none can us spie:
Take me to thee, and thee to me.
'No, no, no, no, my Deare, let be.'

That you heard was but a Mouse,
Dumbe sleepe holdeth all the house:
Yet asleep, me thinkes they say,
Yong folkes, take time while you may:
Take me to thee, and thee to me.
'No, no, no, no, my Deare, let be.'

Niggard Time threats, if we misse
This large offer of our blisse,
Long stay ere he graunt the same:
Sweet then, while each thing doth frame,
Take me to thee, and thee to me.
'No, no, no, no, my Deare, let be.'

Your faire mother is a bed,
Candles out, and curtaines spread:
She thinkes you do letters write:
Write, but first let me endite:
Take me to thee, and thee to me.
'No, no, no, no, my Deare, let be.'

Sweet alas, why strive you thus?
Concord better fitteth us:
Leave to *Mars* the force of hands,
Your power in your beautie stands:
Take me to thee, and thee to me.
'No, no, no, no, my Deare, let be.'

Wo to me, and do you sweare
Me to hate, but I forbeare?
Cursed be my destines all
That brought me so high to fall:
Soone with my death I will please thee.
'No, no, no, no, my Deare, let be.'

86   Alas, whence came this change of lookes? If I
     Have chang'd desert, let mine owne conscience be
     A still felt plague, to selfe-condemning me:
Let wo gripe on my heart, shame loade mine eye.
But if all faith, like spotlesse Ermine ly
     Safe in my soule, which only doth to thee
     (As his sole object of felicitie)
With wings of *Love* in aire of wonder flie,
     O ease your hand, treate not so hard your slave;
In justice paines come not till faults do call:
Or if I needs (sweet Judge) must torments have,
Use something else to chast'n me withall
     Then those blest eyes, where all my hopes do dwell:
     No doome should make one's heav'n become his hell.

Fifth song   *Omitted*

Sixth song
O you that heare this voice,
O you that see this face,
Say whether of the choice
Deserves the former place:
Feare not to judge this bate,
For it is void of hate.

This side doth beauty take,
For that doth Musike speake,
Fit oratours to make

41

The strongest judgements weake:
The barre to plead their right,
Is only true delight.

Thus doth the voice and face,
These gentle Lawyers, wage,
Like loving brothers' case
For father's heritage,
That each, while each contends,
It selfe to other lends.

For beautie beautifies
With heavenly hew and grace
The heavenly harmonies;
And in this faultlesse face
The perfect beauties be
A perfect harmony.

Musicke more loftly swels
In speeches nobly placed:
Beauty as farre excels
In action aptly graced:
A friend each party drawes,
To continuance his cause:

Love more affected seemes
To beautie's lovely light,
And wonder more esteemes
Of Musick's wondrous might:
But both to both so bent,
As both in both are spent.

Musike doth witnesse call
The eare, his truth to trie:
Beauty brings to the hall
The judgement of the eye;
Both in their objects such,
As no exceptions tutch.

The common sence, which might
Be Arbiter of this,
To be, forsooth, upright,
To both sides partiall is:
He layes on this chiefe praise,
Chiefe praise on that he laies.

Then reason, Princesse hy,
Whose throne is in the mind,
Which Musicke can in sky
And hidden beauties find,
Say whether thou wilt crowne
With limitlesse renowne.

Seventh song
Whose senses in so evill consort their stepdame Nature laies,
That ravishing delight in them most sweete tunes do not raise;
Or if they do delight therein, yet are so closde with wit,
As with sententious lips to set a title vaine on it:
O let them heare these sacred tunes, and learne in wonder's schooles,
To be, in things past bounds of wit, fooles, if they be not fooles.

Who have so leaden eyes as not to see sweet beautie's show,
Or seeing, have so wodden wits as not that worth to know;
Or knowing, have so muddy minds as not to be in love;
Or loving, have so frothy thoughts as easly thence to move:
O let them see these heavenly beames, and in faire letters reede
A lesson fit, both sight and skill, love and firme love to breed.

Heare then, but then with wonder heare; see, but adoring see,
No mortall gifts, no earthly fruites now here descended be:
See, do you see this face? A face? Nay image of the skies,
Of which the two life-giving lights are figured in her eyes:
Heare you this soule-invading voice, and count it but a voice?
The very essence of their tunes, when Angels do rejoyce.

Eighth song

In a grove most rich of shade,
Where birds wanton musicke made,
May then yong his pide weedes showing,
New perfumed with flowers fresh growing,

Astrophel with *Stella* sweete,
Did for mutuall comfort meete,
Both within themselves oppressed,
But each in the other blessed.

Him great harmes had taught much care,
Her faire necke a foule yoke bare;
But her sight his cares did banish,
In his sight her yoke did vanish.

Wept they had, alas the while,
But now teares themselves did smile,
While their eyes by love directed,
Enterchangeably reflected.

Sigh they did, but now betwixt
Sighs of woes were glad sighs mixt,
With armes crost, yet testifying
Restlesse rest, and living dying.

Their eares hungry of each word
Which the deere tongue would afford,
But their tongues restrained from walking,
Till their harts had ended talking.

But when their tongues could not speake,
Love it selfe did silence breake;
Love did set his lips asunder,
Thus to speake in love and wonder:

'*Stella,* soveraigne of my joy,
Faire triumpher of annoy,

Stella, starre of heavenly fier,
Stella, loadstar of desier.

'*Stella,* in whose shining eyes
Are the lights of *Cupid's* skies,
Whose beames, where they once are darted,
Love therewith is streight imparted.

'*Stella,* whose voice when it speakes,
Senses all asunder breakes;
Stella, whose voice when it singeth,
Angels to acquaintance bringeth.

'*Stella,* in whose body is
Writ each character of blisse,
Whose face all, all beauty passeth,
Save thy mind which yet surpasseth:

'Graunt, O graunt — but speech, alas,
Failes me, fearing on to passe;
Graunt — O me, what am I saying?
But no fault there is in praying.

'Graunt, O deere, on knees I pray,'
(Knees on ground he then did stay)
That not I, but since I love you,
Time and place for me may move you.

'Never season was more fit,
Never roome more apt for it;
Smiling ayre allowes my reason,
These birds sing, "Now use the season."

'This small wind which so sweete is,
See how it the leaves doth kisse,
Ech tree in his best attiring,
Sense of love to love inspiring.

'Love makes earth the water drinke,
Love to earth makes water sinke;
And if dumbe things be so witty,
Shall a heavenly grace want pitty?'

There his hands in their speech, faine
Would have made tongue's language plaine;
But her hands his hands repelling,
Gave repulse all grace excelling.

Then she spake; her speech was such
As not eares but hart did tuch,
While such wise she love denied
As yet love she signified.

'*Astrophel*' sayd she, 'my love
Cease in these effects to prove:
Now be still, yet still beleeve me,
Thy griefe more than death would grieve me.

'If that any thought in me
Can tast comfort but of thee,
Let me, fed with hellish anguish,
Joylesse, hopelesse, endlesse languish.

'If those eyes you praised be
Half so deere as you to me,
Let me home returne, starke blinded
Of those eyes, and blinder minded.

'If to secret of my hart
I do any wish impart
Where thou art not formost placed,
Be both wish and I defaced.

'If more may be sayd, I say,
All my blisse in thee I lay;

If thou love, my love content thee,
For all love, all faith is meant thee.

'Trust me, while I thee deny,
In my selfe the smart I try;
Tyran honour doth thus use thee;
Stella's selfe might not refuse thee.

'Therefore, Deere, this no more move,
Least, though I leave not thy love
Which too deep in me is framed,
I should blush when thou art named.'

Therewithall away she went,
Leaving him so passion rent
With what she had done and spoken,
That therewith my song is broken.

Ninth song
Go my flocke, go get you hence,
Seeke a better place of feeding,
Where you may have some defence
From the stormes in my breast breeding,
And showers from mine eyes proceeding.

Leave a wretch, in whom all wo
Can abide to keepe no measure;
Merry flocke, such one forgo,
Unto whom mirth is displeasure,
Only rich in mischiefe's treasure.

Yet alas before you go,
Heare your wofull maister's story,
Which to stones I els would show
Sorrow onely then hath glory,
When tis excellently sory.

47

Stella fiercest shepherdesse,
Fiercest but yet fairest ever;
Stella whom, O heavens, do blesse,
Tho against me shee persever,
Tho I blisse enherit never;

Stella hath refused me,
Stella who more love hath proved
In this caitife hart to be
Then can in good eawes be moved
Toward *Lamkins* best beloved.

Stella hath refused me:
Astrophel, that so wel served,
In this pleasant spring must see,
While in pride flowers be preserved,
Himselfe onely winter-sterved.

Why alas doth she then sweare
That she loveth me so dearely,
Seing me so long to beare
Coles of love that burne so clearely,
And yet leave me helplesse meerely?

Is that love? Forsooth I trow,
If I saw my good dog grieved,
And a helpe for him did know,
My love should not be beleeved
But he were by me releeved.

No, she hates me, wellaway,
Faining love, somewhat to please me;
For she knowes, if she display
All her hate, death soone would seaze me,
And of hideous torments ease me.

Then adieu, deere flocke, adieu:
But alas, if in your straying
Heavenly *Stella* meete with you,
Tell her in your piteous blaying,
Her poore slave's unjust decaying.

87 When I was forst from *Stella* ever deere,
   Stella food of my thoughts, hart of my hart,
   Stella whose eyes make all my tempests cleere,
     By iron lawes of duty to depart;
     Alas I found, that she with me did smart;
   I saw that teares did in her eyes appeare;
   I saw that sighes her sweetest lips did part,
   And her sad words my saddest sence did heare.
     For me, I wept to see pearles scattered so,
     I sighd her sighes, and wailed for her wo,
   Yet swam in joy, such love in her was seene.
     Thus while th' effect most bitter was to me,
     And nothing then the cause more sweet could be,
   I had bene vext, if vext I had not beene.

88 Out, traytour absence, darest thou counsell me
   From my deare Captainnesse to run away,
   Because in brave array heere marcheth she,
   That to win me oft shewes a present pay?
   Is faith so weake? Or is such force in thee?
   When Sun is hid, can starres such beames display?
   Cannot heavn's food, once felt, keepe stomakes free
   From base desire on earthly cates to pray?
     Tush, absence; while thy mistes eclipse that light,
     My Orphan sence flies to the inward sight,
   Where memory sets foorth the beames of love;
     That where before hart loved and eyes did see,
     In hart both sight and love now coupled be;
   United powers make each the stronger prove.

89 Now that of absence the most irksome night
     With darkest shade doth overcome my day;
     Since *Stella's* eyes, wont to give me my day,
  Leaving my Hemisphere, leave me in night,
  Each day seemes long, and longs for long-staid night;
     The night, as tedious, wooes th'approch of day;
     Tired with the dusty toiles of busie day,
  Languisht with horrors of the silent night,
  Suffering the evils both of the day and night,
     While no night is more darke then is my day,
  Nor no day hath lesse quiet then my night;
     With such bad mixture of my night and day,
  That living thus in blackest winter night,
     I feele the flames of hottest sommer day.

90 *Stella,* thinke not that I by verse seeke fame,
     Who seeke, who hope, who love, who live but thee;
     Thine eyes my pride, thy lips my history:
  If thou praise not, all other praise is shame.
  Nor so ambitious am I, as to frame
     A nest for my yong praise in Lawrell tree:
     In truth I sweare, I wish not there should be
  Graved in mine Epitaph a Poet's name:
     Ne if I would, could I just title make,
  That any laud to me thereof should grow,
  Without my plumes from others' wings I take.
  For nothing from my wit or will doth flow,
     Since all my words thy beauty doth endite,
     And love doth hold my hand, and makes me write.

91 *Stella,* while now by honour's cruell might
     I am from you, light of my life, mis-led,
     And that faire you, my Sunne, thus overspred
  With absence' Vaile, I live in Sorowe's night;
  If this darke place yet shew, like candle light,
     Some beautie's peece, as amber-coloured hed,
     Milke hands, rose cheeks, or lips more sweet, more red,

Or seeing jets, blacke, but in blacknesse bright:
    They please, I do confesse, they please mine eyes,
But why? Because of you they models be,
Models such be wood-globes of glistring skies.
Deere, therefore be not jealous over me,
    If you heare that they seeme my hart to move;
    Not them, O no, but you in them I love.

92   Be your words made (good Sir) of Indian ware,
    That you allow me them by so small rate?
    Or do you cutted Spartanes imitate?
Or do you meane my tender eares to spare,
That to my questions you so totall are?
    When I demaund of *Phenix Stella's* state,
    You say, forsooth, you left her well of late.
O God, thinke you that satisfies my care?
    I would know whether she did sit or walke,
How cloth'd, how waited on, sighd she or smilde,
Whereof, with whom, how often did she talke,
With what pastime time's journey she beguilde,
    If her lips daignd to sweeten my poore name.
    Say all, and all well sayd, still say the same.

Tenth song

O Deare life, when shall it be
    That mine eyes thine eyes may see?
    And in them thy mind discover
    Whether absence have had force
    Thy remembrance to divorce
    From the image of thy lover?

O if I my selfe find not
    After parting ought forgot,
    Nor debard from beautie's treasure,
    Let no tongue aspire to tell
    In what high joyes I shall dwell;
    Only thought aymes at the pleasure.

Thought therefore I will send thee
    To take up the place for me;
    Long I will not after tary.
    There unseene thou maist be bold
    Those faire wonders to behold,
    Which in them my hopes do cary.

Thought, see thou no place forbeare;
    Enter bravely every where;
    Seaze on all to her belonging;
    But if thou wouldst garded be,
    Fearing her beames, take with thee
    Strength of liking, rage of longing.

Think of that most gratefull time,
    When my leaping hart will clime
    In my lips to have his biding,
    There those roses for to kisse
    Which do breath a sugred blisse,
    Opening rubies, pearles deviding.

Think of my most Princely power,
    When I blessed shall devower
    With my greedy licorous sences
    Beauty, musicke, sweetnesse, love,
    While she doth against me prove
    Her strong darts but weake defences.

Thinke, thinke of those dalyings,
    When with Dovelike murmurings,
    With glad moning passed anguish,
    We change eyes, and hart for hart,
    Each to other do depart,
    Joying till joy make us languish.

O my thought, my thoughts, surcease;
    Thy delights my woes increase,
    My life melts with too much thinking;

Thinke no more but die in me
Till thou shalt revived be,
At her lips my Nectar drinking.

93 O fate, O fault, O curse, child of my blisse,
    What sobs can give words grace my griefe to show?
    What inke is blacke inough to paint my wo?
Through me, wretch me, even *Stella* vexed is.
Yet truth (if Caitif's breath may call thee) this
    Witnesse with me, that my foule stumbling so
    From carelesnesse did in no maner grow,
But wit confus'd with too much care did misse.
    And do I then my selfe this vaine scuse give?
I have (live I and know this?) harmed thee;
Tho worlds quite me, shall I my selfe forgive?
Only with paines my paines thus eased be,
    That all thy hurts in my hart's wracke I reede;
    I cry thy sighs; my deere, thy teares I bleede.

94 Griefe, find the words, for thou hast made my braine
    So darke with misty vapors, which arise
    From out thy heavy mould, that inbent eyes
Can scarce discerne the shape of mine owne paine.
Do thou then (for thou canst) do thou complaine
    For my poore soule, which now that sicknesse tries
    Which even to sence, sence of it selfe denies,
Though harbengers of death lodge there his traine:
    Or if thy love of plaint yet mine forbeares,
As of a caitife worthy so to die,
Yet waile thy selfe, and waile with causefull teares
That though in wretchednesse thy life doth lie,
Yet growest more wretched then thy nature beares,
By being placed in such a wretch as I.

95 Yet sighs, deere sighs, indeede true friends you are,
    That do not leave your best friend at the wurst,
    But as you with my breast I oft have nurst,

So gratefull now you waite upon my care.
Faint coward joy no longer tarry dare,
   Seeing hope yeeld when this wo strake him furst:
   Delight protests he is not for the accurst,
Though oft himselfe my mate-in-armes he sware.
   Nay, sorrow comes with such maine rage, that he
Kils his owne children, teares, finding that they
By love were made apt to consort with me.
Only true sighs, you do not go away,
   Thanke may you have for such a thankfull part,
   Thanke-worthiest yet when you shall breake my hart.

96   Thought with good cause thou likest so well the night,
     Since kind or chance gives both one liverie;
     Both sadly blacke, both blackly darkned be,
   Night bard from Sun, thou from thy owne sunne's light;
   Silence in both displaies his sullen might,
     Slow heaviness in both holds one degree,
     That full of doubts, thou of perplexity;
   Thy teares expresse night's native moisture right:
     In both a mazefull solitarinesse:
   In night, of sprites the gastly powers stur,
   In thee, or sprites or sprited gastlinesse:
   But, but (alas) night's side the ods hath fur,
     For that at length yet doth invite some rest,
     Thou, though still tired, yet still doost it detest.

97   *Dian* that faine would cheare her friend the Night,
     Shewes her oft at the full her fairest face,
     Bringing with her those starry Nimphs, whose chace
   From heavenly standing hits each mortall wight.
   But ah, poore Night, in love with *Phœbus'* light,
     And endlesly dispairing of his grace,
     Her selfe (to shew no other joy hath place)
   Silent and sad in mourning weedes doth dight:
     Even so (alas) a Lady, *Dian's* peere,
   With choise delights and rarest company,

Would faine drive cloudes from out my heavy cheere.
But wo is me, though joy it selfe were she,
    She could not shew my blind braine waies of joy,
    While I dispaire my Sunne's sight to enjoy.

98   Ah bed, the field where joye's peace some do see,
      The field where all my thoughts to warre be traind,
      How is thy grace by my strange fortune staind!
How thy lee shores by my sighes stormed be!
With sweete soft shades thou oft invitest me
      To steale some rest, but wretch I am constraind,
      (Spurd with love's spur, though gald and shortly raind
With care's hard hand) to turne and tosse in thee,
      While the blacke horrors of the silent night
      Paint woe's blacke face so lively to my sight,
That tedious leasure marks each wrinckled line:
      But when *Aurora* leades out *Phœbus'* daunce,
      Mine eyes then only winke, for spite perchance,
That wormes should have their Sun, and I want mine.

99   When far spent night perswades each mortall eye,
      To whom nor art nor nature graunteth light,
      To lay his then marke-wanting shafts of sight,
Clos'd with their quivers, in sleep's armory;
With windowes ope then most my mind doth lie,
      Viewing the shape of darknesse and delight,
      Takes in that sad hue, which with th'inward night
Of his mazde powers keepes perfit harmony:
      But when birds charme, and that sweete aire, which is
Morne's messenger, with rose enameld skies
Cals each wight to salute the floure of blisse,
In tombe of lids then buried are mine eyes,
      Forst by their Lord, who is asham'd to find
      Such light in sense, with such a darkned mind.

100   O teares, no teares but raine from beautie's skies,
      Making those Lillies and those Roses grow,
      Which ay most faire, now more then most faire show,

While gracefull pitty beauty beautifies:
O honied sighs, which from that breast do rise,
    Whose pants do make unspilling creame to flow,
    Wing'd with whose breath so pleasing *Zephires* blow,
As can refresh the hell where my soule fries:
    O plaints conserv'd in such a sugred phraise,
    That eloquence it selfe envies your praise,
While sobd out words a perfect Musike give:
    Such teares, sighs, plaints, no sorrow is, but joy;
    Of if such heavenly signes must prove annoy,
All mirth farewell, let me in sorrow live.

101   *Stella* is sicke, and in that sicke bed lies
Sweetnesse, that breathes and pants as oft as she:
And grace, sicke too, such fine conclusions tries,
That sicknesse brags it selfe best graced to be.
Beauty is sicke, but sicke in so faire guise,
That in that palenesse beautie's white we see;
And joy, which is inseperate from those eyes,
Stella now learnes (strange case) to weepe in thee.
    Love moves thy paine, and like a faithfull page,
As thy lookes sturre, runs up and downe to make
All folkes prest at thy will thy paine to 'swage.
Nature with care sweates for her darling's sake,
    Knowing worlds passe, ere she enough can find
    Of such heaven stuffe to cloath so heavenly mynde.

102   Where be those Roses gone, which sweetned so our eyes?
    Where those red cheeks, which oft with faire encrease did frame
    The height of honor in the kindly badge of shame?
Who hath the crimson weeds stolne from my morning skies?
How doth the colour vade of those vermillion dies
    Which Nature' selfe did make, and selfe engraind the same?
    I would know by what right this palenesse overcame
That hue, whose force my hart still unto thraldome ties.
    Gallein's adoptive sonnes, who by a beaten way

Their judgements hackney on, the fault on sicknesse lay,
But feeling proofe makes me say they mistake it furre:
 It is but love, which makes his paper perfit white
 To write therein more fresh the story of delight,
While beautie's reddest inke *Venus* for him doth sturre.

103 O happie Tems, that didst my *Stella* beare,
 I saw thy selfe with many a smiling line
 Upon thy cheerefull face, joye's livery weare,
 While those faire planets on thy streames did shine.
 The bote for joy could not to daunce forbeare,
 While wanton winds with beauties so devine
 Ravisht, staid not, till in her golden haire
 They did themselves (O sweetest prison) twine.
  And faine those *Æeols'* youth there would their stay
 Have made, but forst by Nature still to flie,
 First did with puffing kisse those lockes display.
 She so discheveld, blusht; from window I
  With sight thereof cride out; 'O faire disgrace,
  Let honor's selfe to thee graunt highest place.'

104 Envious wits, what hath bene mine offence,
  That with such poysonous care my lookes you marke,
  That to each word, nay sigh of mine you harke,
 As grudging me my sorrowe's eloquence?
 Ah, is it not enough, that I am thence,
  Thence, so farre thence, that scarcely any sparke
  Of comfort dare come to this dungeon darke,
 Where rigour's exile lockes up all my sense?
  But if I by a happy window passe,
 If I but stars upon mine armour beare,
 Sicke, thirsty, glad (though but of empty glasse:)
 Your mortall notes straight my hid meaning teare
  From out my ribs, and puffing prove that I
  Do *Stella* love. Fooles, who doth it deny?

Eleventh song
'Who is it that this darke night,
Underneath my window playneth?'
It is one who from thy sight,
Being (ah) exild, disdayneth
Every other vulgar light.

'Why alas, and are you he?
Be not yet those fancies changed?'
Deere, when you find change in me,
Though from me you be estranged,
Let my chaunge to ruine be.

'Well in absence this will dy,
Leave to see, and leave to wonder.'
Absence sure will helpe, if I
Can learne how my selfe to sunder
From what in my hart doth ly.

'But time will these thoughts remove:
Time doth worke what no man knoweth.'
Time doth as the subject prove;
With time still th' affection groweth
In the faithfull Turtle dove.

'What if you new beauties see,
Will not they stir new affection?'
I will thinke theye pictures be,
(Image-like of Saints' perfection)
Poorely counterfeting thee.

'But your reason's purest light,
Bids you leave such minds to nourish.'
Deere, do reason no such spite,
Never doth thy beauty florish
More then in my reason's sight.

'But the wrongs love beares will make
Love at length leave undertaking.'
No, the more fooles it do shake,
In a ground of so firme making,
Deeper still they drive the stake.

'Peace, I thinke that some give eare:
Come no more, least I get anger.'
Blisse, I will my blisse forbeare,
Fearing (sweete) you to endanger,
But my soule shall harbour there.

'Well, be gone, be gone I say,
Lest that *Argus'* eyes perceive you.'
O unjustest fortune's sway,
Which can make me thus to leave you,
And from lowts to run away.

105   Unhappie sight, and hath she vanisht by
      So neere, in so good time, so free a place?
      Dead glasse, doost thou thy object so imbrace,
   As what my hart still sees thou canst not spie?
   I sweare by her I love and lacke, that I
      Was not in fault, who bent thy dazling race
      Onely unto the heav'n of *Stella's* face,
   Counting but dust what in the way did lie.
      But cease mine eyes, your teares do witnesse well
   That you, guiltlesse thereof, your Nectar mist:
   Curst be the page from whome the bad torch fell,
   Curst be the night which did your strife resist,
      Curst be the Cochman which did drive so fast,
      With no worse curse then absence makes me tast.

106   O absent presence! *Stella* is not here:
      False flattering hope, that with so faire a face
      Bare me in hand, that in this Orphane place
   Stella, I say, my *Stella,* should appeare;

What saist thou now, where is that dainty cheere
    Thou toldst mine eyes should helpe their famisht case?
    But thou art gone, now that selfe felt disgrace
Doth make me most to wish thy comfort neere.
    But heere I do store of faire Ladies meete,
    Who may with charme of conversation sweete
Make in my heavy mould new thoughts to grow:
    Sure they prevaile as much with me, as he
    That bad his friend, but then new maim'd, to be
Mery with him, and not thinke of his woe.

107   *Stella* since thou so right a Princesse art
    Of all the powers which life bestowes on me,
    That ere by them ought undertaken be,
They first resort unto that soveraigne part;
Sweete, for a while give respite to my hart,
    Which pants as though it still should leape to thee,
    And on my thoughts give thy Lieftenancy
To this great cause, which needs both use and art.
    And as a Queene, who from her presence sends
Whom she imployes, dismisse from thee my wit,
Till it have wrought what thy owne will attends.
On servants' shame oft Maister's blame doth sit;
    O let not fooles in me thy workes reprove,
    And scorning say, 'See, what it is to love!'

108   When sorrow (using mine owne fier's might)
    Melts downe his lead into my boyling brest,
    Through that darke fornace to my hart opprest,
There shines a joy from thee my only light;
But soone as thought of thee breeds my delight,
    And my yong soule flutters to thee, his nest,
    Most rude dispaire, my daily unbidden guest,
Clips streight my wings, streight wraps me in his night,
    And makes me then bow downe my head, and say,
'Ah, what doth *Phœbus'* gold that wretch availe,
Whom iron doores do keepe from use of day?'

So strangely (alas) thy works in me prevaile,
    That in my woes for thee thou art my joy,
    And in my joyes for thee my only annoy.

From Certaine Sonnets
Thou blind man's marke, thou foole's selfe chosen snare,
Fond fancie's scum, and dregs of scattred thought,
Band of all evils, cradle of causelesse care,
    Thou web of will, whose end is never wrought:
    Desire, desire I have too dearely bought
With price of mangled mind thy worthlesse ware:
Too long, too long asleepe thou hast me brought,
Who should my mind to higher things prepare.
But yet in vaine thou hast my ruine sought,
    In vaine thou madest me to vaine things aspire,
    In vaine thou kindlest all thy smokie fire;
For vertue hath this better lesson taught,
    Within my selfe to seeke my onelie hire,
    Desiring nought but how to kill desire.

Leave me, O Love, which reachest but to dust,
And thou, my mind, aspire to higher things:
Grow rich in that which never taketh rust:
What ever fades but fading pleasure brings.
    Draw in thy beames, and humble all thy might
To that sweet yoke, where lasting freedomes be,
Which breakes the clowdes and opens forth the light,
That doth both shine and give us sight to see.
    O take fast hold, let that light be thy guide,
In this small course which birth drawes out to death,
And thinke how evill becommeth him to slide,
Who seeketh heav'n, and comes of heav'nly breath.
    Then farewell world, thy uttermost I see:
    Eternall Love maintaine thy life in me.

Samuel Daniel

To Delia

Sonnet 1

Unto the boundles Ocean of thy beautie
   Runs this poore river, charg'd with streams of zeale,
   Returning thee the trybute of my duty,
   Which heere my love, my youth, my plaints reveale.
Heere I unclaspe the booke of my charg'd soule,
   Where I have cast th'accounts of all my care:
   Heere have I summ'd my sighes; heere I enrole
   How they were spent for thee; looke what they are.
Looke on the deere expences of my youth,
   And see how just I reckon with thine eyes:
   Examine well thy beauty with my truth,
   And crosse my cares ere greater summes arise.
Reade it (sweet maide) though it be doone but slightly:
Who can shew all his love, doth love but lightly.

Sonnet 2

Goe, wayling verse, the Infants of my love,
   Minerva-lyke, brought foorth without a mother:
   Present the Image of the cares I prove,
   Witnes your Father's griefe exceeds all other.
Sigh out a story of her cruell deedes,
   With interrupted accents of dispaire:
   A monument that whosoever reedes,
   May justly praise, and blame my loveless Fayre
Say her disdaine hath dryed up my blood,

And starved you, in succours still denying:
　　Presse to her eyes, importune me some good;
　　Waken her sleeping pitty with your crying.
Knock at her hard hart, beg till you have mov'd her,
And tell th'unkind, how deerely I have lov'd her.

Sonnet 3

If so it hap this of-spring of my care,
　　These fatall Antheames, sad and mournful songs,
　　Come to their view who like afflicted are,
　　Ah let them sigh theyr owne, and mone my wrongs.
But untoucht harts, with unaffected eye,
　　Approch not to behold so great distresse:
　　Cleer-sighted, you soone note what is awry,
　　Whilst blinded ones mine errours never gesse.
You blinded soules whom youth and errors leade,
　　You outcast Eaglets, dazeled with your sunne,
　　Ah you, and none but you my sorrowes reade,
　　You best can judge the wrongs that she hath done:
That she had done, the motive of my paine,
Who whilst I love, doth kill me with disdaine.

Sonnet 4

These plaintive verse, the Posts of my desire,
　　Which haste for succour to her slowe regard,
　　Beare not report of any slender fire,
　　Forging a griefe to winne a fame's reward.
Nor are my passions lymned for outward hewe,
　　For that no colours can depaint my sorrows:
　　Delia her selfe, and all the world, may view
　　Best in my face, where cares hath till'd deepe furrows.
No Bayes I seeke to deck my mourning brow,
　　O cleer-eyde Rector of the holy Hill:
　　My humble accents beare the Olive bough
　　Of intercession to a tyrant's will.
These lines I use, t'unburthen mine owne hart;
My love affects no fame, nor steemes of art.

Sonnet 5

Whilst youth and error led my wandring minde,
    And sette my thoughts in heedles waies to range,
    All unawares a Goddesse chaste I finde,
    (*Diana*-like) to worke my suddaine change.
For her no sooner had mine eye bewraid,
    But with disdaine to see me in that place,
    With fairest hand, the sweet unkindest maid
    Casts water-cold disdaine upon my face:
Which turn'd my sport into a Hart's despaire,
    Which still is chac'd, while I have any breath,
    By mine owne thoughts, sette on mee by my faire;
    My thoughts (like houndes) pursue me to my death.
Those that I fostred of mine owne accord
Are made by her to murder thus theyr Lord.

Sonnet 6

Fayre is my love, and cruell as sh'is fayre;
    Her brow shades frowns, althogh her eyes are sunny;
    Her smyles are lightning, though her pride, dispaire;
    And her disdaines are gall, her favours hunny.
A modest mayde, deckt with a blush of honour,
    Whose feete do tread greene pathes of youth and love;
    The wonder of all eyes that looke upon her:
    Sacred on earth, design'd a Saint above.
Chastity and Beauty, which were deadly foes,
    Live reconciled friends within her brow:
    And had she pitty to conjoyne with those,
    Then who had heard the plaints I utter now?
O had she not been fayre, and thus unkind,
My Muse had slept, and none had knowne my minde.

Sonnet 7

O had shee not beene faire and thus unkind,
    Then had no finger pointed at my lightnes:
    The world had never knowne what I doe finde,
    And clowdes obscure had shaded stil her brightnes.

Then had no Censor's eye these lynes survaide,
   Nor graver browes have judg'd my Muse so vaine;
   No sunne my blush and errour had bewraid,
   Nor yet the world had heard of such disdaine.
Then had I walkt with bold erected face;
   No down-cast looke had signified my misse:
   But my degraded hopes, with such disgrace
   Did force me grone out griefes, and utter this.
For being full, should I not then have spoken,
My sence, oppress'd, had faild, and hart had broken.

Sonnet 8

Thou poore hart, sacrifiz'd unto the fairest,
   Hast sent the incens of thy sighes to heaven;
   And still against her frownes fresh vowes repayrest,
   And made thy passions with her beauty even.
And you, mine eyes, the agents of my hart,
   Told the dumbe message of my hidden griefe;
   And oft with carefull turnes, with silent Arte,
   Did treate the cruell Fayre to yeeld reliefe.
And you, my verse, the Advocates of love,
   Have followed hard the processe of my case,
   And urg'd that tytle which doth plainly prove
   My faith should win, if justice might have place.
Yet though I see that nought we doe can move her,
Tis not disdaine must make me cease to love her.

Sonnet 9

If thys be love, to draw a weary breath,
   Paint on floods, till the shore, cry to th'ayre;
   With downward lookes still reading on the earth
   The sad memorials of my love's despayre:
If this be love, to warre against my soule,
   Lye downe to waile, rise up to sigh and grieve;
   The never-resting stone of care to roule,
   Still to complaine my griefes, whilst none relieve:
If this be love, to cloathe me with darke thoughts,

Haunting untroden pathes to waile apart;
My pleasures, horror; Musique, tragick notes;
Teares in mine eyes, and sorrow at my hart:
If thys be love, to live a living death,
O then love I, and draw this weary breath.

Sonnet 10

O then love I, and draw this weary breath
For her, the cruell Fayre, within whose brow
I written finde the sentence of my death,
In unkinde letters, wrought she cares not how.
O thou that rul'st the confines of the night,
Laughter-loving goddesse, worldly plesures' Queen,
Intenerat that hart that sets so light
The truest love that ever yet was seene;
And cause her leave to tryumph in this wise
Uppon the prostrate spoyle of that poore hart
That serves a Trophey to her conquering eyes,
And must theyr glory to the world impart.
Once let her know, sh'hath done enough to prove me,
And let her pitty if she cannot love me.

Sonnet 11

Teares, vowes, and prayers winne the hardest hart;
Teares, vowes, and prayers have I spent in vaine:
Teares cannot soften Flint, nor vowes convart;
Prayers prevaile not with a quaint disdaine.
I lose my teares, where I have lost my love;
I vowe my faith, where faith is not regarded;
I pray in vaine, a merciles to move:
So rare a faith ought better be rewarded.
Yet though I cannot win her will with teares,
Though my soule's Idoll scorneth all my vowes,
Though all my prayers be to so deafe eares,
No favour though the cruell faire allowes;
Yet will I weepe, vowe, pray to cruell shee;
Flint, frost, disdaine, weares, melts, and yeelds, we see.

Sonnet 12

My spotlesse love hoovers with purest wings
    About the temple of the proudest frame,
      Where blaze those lights, fayrest of earthly things,
      Which cleer our clowdded world with brightest flame.
M'ambitious thoughts, confined in her face,
    Affect no honour but what she can give:
      My hopes doe rest in limits of her grace;
      I weigh no comfort unlesse she relieve.
For she that can my hart imparadize,
    Holds in her fairest hand what deerest is:
      My fortune's wheele's the circle of her eyes,
      Whose rowling grace deigne once a turne of blis.
All my live's sweet consists in her alone,
So much I love the most unloving one.

Sonnet 13

Behold what hap *Pigmalion* had to frame
    And carve his propper griefe upon a stone:
      My heavie fortune is much like the same;
      I worke on Flint, and that's the cause I mone.
For haplesse loe, even with mine owne desires,
    I figured on the Table of mine hart
      The fairest forme that all the world admires,
      And so did perrish by my proper arte.
And still I toyle to change the Marble breast
    Of her, whose sweetest grace I doe adore,
      Yet cannot finde her breathe unto my rest;
      Hard is her hart and woe is me therefore.
O happie he that joy'd his stone and arte;
Unhappy I, to love a stony harte.

Sonnet 14

Those snary locks are those same nets (my Deere)
    Where-with my libertie thou didst surprize:
      Love was the flame that fired me so neere;
      The Dart transpearsing were those Christall eyes.

Strong is the net and fervent is the flame;
    Deepe is the wounde, my sighes doe well report:
    Yet doe I love, adore, and praise the same
    That holds, that burnes, that wounds me in this sort.
And list not seeke to breake, to quench, to heale,
    The bonde, the flame, the wound that festreth so,
    By knife, by liquor, or by salve to deale;
    So much I please to perrish in my woe.
Yet least long travailes be above my strength,
Good *Delia,* lose, quench, heale me now at length.

Sonnet 15

If that a loyall hart and fayth unfained,
    If a sweete languish with a chast desire,
    If hunger-starven thoughts so long retained,
    Fed but with smoake, and cherisht but with fire,
And if a brow with cares' characters painted,
    Bewraies my love, with broken words halfe spoken,
    To her that sits in my thought's Temple sainted,
    And layes to view my Vultur-gnawne hart open:
If I have done due homage to her eyes,
    And had my sighes styll tending on her name,
    If on her love my life and honour lyes,
    And shee (th'unkindest mayd) still scornes the same;
Let this suffice, that all the world may see
The fault is hers, though mine the hurt must bee.

Sonnet 16

Happy in sleepe, waking content to languish,
    Imbracing clowdes by night, in day time mourne,
    My joyes but shadowes, touch of truth my anguish,
    Griefes ever springing, comforts never borne:
And still expecting when she will relent,
    Growne hoarce with crying 'Mercy, mercy gyve';
    So many vowes and prayers having spent,
    That weary of myselfe, I loathe to lyve.
And yet the Hydra of my cares renewes

Still new-borne sorrowes of her fresh disdaine:
And still my hope the sommer windes pursues,
Finding no end nor period of my paine.
This is my state; my griefes doe touch so neerely,
And thus I live because I love her deerely.

Sonnet 17

Why should I sing in verse, why should I frame
These sad neglected notes for her deere sake?
Why should I offer up unto her name
The sweetest sacrifice my youth can make?
Why should I strive to make her live for ever,
That never deignes to give me joy to live?
Why should m'afflicted Muse so much endevour
Such honour unto crueltie to give?
If her defects have purchast her this fame,
What should her vertues doe, her smiles, her love?
If this her worst, how should her best inflame?
What passions would her milder favours move?
Favours (I thinke) would sence quite over-come,
And that makes happy Lovers ever dombe.

Sonnet 18

Since the first looke that led me to this error,
To this thoughts-maze, to my confusion tending,
Still have I liv'd in griefe, in hope, in terror,
The circle of my sorrowes never ending,
Yet cannot leave her love that holds me hatefull;
Her eyes exact it, though her hart disdaines me:
See what reward he hath that serves th'ungratefull;
So true and loyall love no favour gaines mee.
Still must I whet my young desires abated
Upon the Flint of such a hart rebelling;
And all in vaine; her pride is so innated,
She yeeldes no place at all for pittye's dwelling.
Oft have I tolde her that my soule did love her,
(And that with teares) yet all this will not move her.

Sonnet 19

Restore thy tresses to the golden Ore,
    Yeeld *Citherea's* sonne those Arkes of love;
    Bequeath the heavens the starrs that I adore,
    And to th'Orient doe thy Pearles remove.
Yeeld thy hands' pride unto th'Ivory white,
    T'*Arabian* odors give thy breathing sweet:
    Restore thy blush unto *Aurora* bright,
    To *Thetis* give the honour of thy feete.
Let *Venus* have thy graces, her resign'd,
    And thy sweete voyce give backe unto the Spheares:
    But yet restore thy fierce and cruell minde
    To *Hyrcan* Tygers, and to ruthles Beares.
Yeelde to the Marble thy hard hart againe;
So shalt thou cease to plague, and I to paine.

Sonnet 20

If Beauty thus be clowded with a frowne,
    That pitty shines no comfort to my blis,
    And vapours of disdaine so over-growne
    That my live's light thus wholy darkned is,
Why should I more molest the world with cryes,
    The ayre with sighes, the earth below with teares,
    Sith I live hatefull to those ruthlesse eyes,
    Vexing with untun'd moane her dainty eares?
If I have lov'd her deerer then my breath,
    My breath that calls the heavens to witnes it,
    And still must holde her deere till after death,
    And if that all this cannot move a whit,
Yet let her say that she hath done me wrong
To use me thus and know I lov'd so long.

Sonnet 21

Come Death, the anchor-hold of all my thoughts,
    My last resort whereto my soule appeales,
    For all too-long on earth my fancy dotes,
    Whilst age upon my wasted body steales.

That hart, being made the prospective of horror,
    That honored hath the cruelst faire that lives,
    The cruelst faire, that sees I languish for her,
    Yet never mercy to my merrite gives:
Thys is her Lawrell and her triumphe's prize,
    To tread me downe with foote of her disgrace,
    Whilst I did builde my fortune in her eyes,
    And layd my live's rest on so faire a face:
Which rest I lost, my love, my life and all:
So high attempts to low disgraces fall.

Sonnet 22

These sorrowing sighes, the smoakes of mine annoy,
    These teares, which heate of sacred flame distils,
    Are those due tributes that my faith doth pay
    Unto the Tyrant whose unkindnes kils.
I sacrifize my youth and blooming yeeres
    At her proude feete, and she respects not it:
    My flowre untimely's withred with my teares,
    And Winter woes, for spring of youth unfit.
She thinkes a looke may recompence my care,
    And so with lookes prolongs my long-lookt ease:
    As short that blisse, so is the comfort rare,
    Yet must that blisse my hungry thoughts appease.
Thus she returnes my hopes so fruitlesse ever:
Once let her love indeede, or eye me never.

Sonnet 23

False hope prolongs my ever certaine griefe,
    Traytour to me and faithfull to my Love:
    A thousand times it promis'd me reliefe,
    Yet never any true effect I prove.
Oft when I finde in her no truth at all,
    I bannish her, and blame her trecherie;
    Yet soone againe I must her backe recall,
    As one that dyes without her companie.
Thus often as I chase my hope from mee,

      Straight way she hastes her unto *Delia's* eyes;
      Fed with some pleasing looke there shall she bee,
      And so sent backe, and thus my fortune lyes.
Lookes feede my Hope, Hope fosters me in vaine;
Hopes are unsure, when certaine is my paine.

Sonnet 24

Looke in my griefes, and blame me not to mourne,
      From care to care that leades a life so bad;
      Th'Orphan of Fortune, borne to be her scorne,
      Whose clowded brow doth make my dayes so sad.
Long are their nights whose cares doe never sleepe,
      Lothsome their dayes, whome no sunne ever joyd:
      Her fairest eyes doe penetrate so deepe,
      That thus I live both day and night annoyd.
But sith the sweetest roote doth yeeld thus much,
      Her praise from my complaint I may not part:
      I love th'effect for that the cause is such;
      I'le praise her face, and blame her flinty hart;
Whilst that wee make the world admire at us,
Her for disdaine, and me for loving thus.

Sonnet 25

Raigne in my thoughts, faire hande, sweete eye, rare voyce,
      Posses me whole, my hart's triumvirate:
      Yet heavy hart to make so hard a choyse
      Of such as spoile thy poore afflicted state.
For whilst they strive which shall be Lord of all,
      All my poore life by them is troden downe:
      They all erect their Trophies on my fall,
      And yeeld me nought that gives them their renowne.
When backe I looke, I sigh my freedome past,
      And waile the state wherein I present stand;
      And see my fortune ever like to last,
      Finding me rain'd with such a heavie hand.
What can I do but yeeld? And yeeld I doo,
And serve all three, and yet they spoyle me too.

Sonnet 26

*Alluding to the sparrow pursued by a Hauke that flew
into the bosome of Zenocrates*

Whilst by her eyes pursu'd, my poore hart flew it
   Into the sacred bosome of my deerest,
   She there in that sweete sanctuarie slew it,
   Where it presum'd his safetie to be neerest.
My priviledge of faith could not protect it,
   That was with blood and three yeres' witnes signed;
   In all which time she never could suspect it,
   For well she sawe my love, and how I pined.
And yet no comfort would her brow reveale mee,
   No lightning looke, which falling hopes erecteth:
   What bootes to lawes of succour to appeale mee?
   Ladies and Tyrants never lawes respecteth.
Then there I die, where hop'd I to have liven,
And by that hand, which better might have given.

Sonnet 27

Still in the trace of my tormented thought,
   My ceaseless cares must martch on to my death:
   Thy least regarde too deerelie have I bought,
   Who to my comfort never deign'st a breath.
Why should'st thou stop thine eares now to my cryes,
   Whose eyes were open, ready to oppresse me?
   Why shutt'st thou not the cause whence al did rise,
   Or heare me now, and seeke how to redress me?
Injurious *Delia,* yet I'le love thee still,
   Whilst that I breathe in sorrow of my smart:
   I'le tell the world that I deserv'd but ill,
   And blame my selfe for to excuse thy hart.
Then judge who sinnes the greater of us twaine,
I in my love, or thou in thy disdaine.

Sonnet 28

Oft do I mervaile, whether *Delia's* eyes
   Are eyes, or else two radiant starres that shine:

For how could Nature ever thus devise
Of earth on earth a substance so divine?
Starrs sure they are, whose motions rule desires,
    And calme and tempest follow their aspects:
    Their sweet appearing still such power inspires,
    That makes the world admire so strange effects.
Yet whether fixt or wandring starrs are they,
    Whose influence rule the Orbe of my poore hart,
    Fixt sure they are, but wandring make me stray,
    In endles errors whence I cannot part.
Starrs then, not eyes, move you with milder view
Your sweet aspect on him that honours you.

Sonnet 29

The starre of my mishap impos'd this paine,
    To spend the Aprill of my yeeres in wayling,
    That ever found my fortune on the wayne,
    With still fresh cares my present woes assayling.
Yet her I blame not, though for her 'tis done,
    But my desire's wings so high aspyring,
    Which now are melted by that glorious Sunne,
    That makes me fall from off my hie desiring.
And in my fall, I cry for helpe with speed:
    No pittying eye lookes backe upon my mourning;
    No succour finde I now when most I need;
    Th'Ocean of my teares must drowne me burning;
Whilst my distress shall christen her anew,
And give the *Cruell Fayre* this title due.

Sonnet 30

And yet I cannot reprehend the flight,
    Or blame th'attempt presuming so to sore:
    The mounting venter for a high delight
    Did make the honour of the fall the more.
For who gets wealth that puts not from the shore?
    Daunger hath honour, great designes their fame,
    Glorie doth follow, courage goes before.

And though th'event oft aunswers not the same,
Suffise that high attempts have never shame.
    The Meane-observer, (whom base Safety keepes,)
    Lives without honour, dies without a name,
    And in eternall darkness ever sleepes.
And therefore, Delia, 'tis to me no blot
To have attempted, though attain'd thee not.

Sonnet 31

Raysing my hopes on hills of high desire,
    Thinking to scale the heaven of her hart,
    My slender meanes presum'd too high a part;
    Her thunder of disdaine forst me retyre,
And threw mee downe to paine in all this fire,
    Where, loe, I languish in so heavie smart,
    Because th'attempt was farre above my arte:
    Her pride brook'd not poore soules shold come so nie her.
Yet I protest my high aspyring will
    Was not to dispossesse her of her right:
    Her soveraignty should have remained still,
    I onely sought the blisse to have her sight.
Her sight, contented thus to see me spill,
Fram'd my desires fit for her eyes to kill.

Sonnet 32

O why doth *Delia* credite so her glasse,
    Gazing her beautie deign'd her by the skyes,
    And doth not rather looke on him (alas)
    Whose state best shewes the force of murthering eyes?
The broken tops of loftie trees declare
    The furie of a mercy-wanting storme;
    And of what force your wounding graces are,
    Upon my selfe you best may finde the forme.
Then leave your glasse, and gaze your selfe on mee:
    That Mirror shewes what power is in your face:
    To view your forme too much may daunger bee;

75

Narcissus chang'd t'a flower in such a case.
And you are chang'd, but not t'a Hiacint;
I feare your eye hath turn'd your hart to flint.

Sonnet 33

I once may see when yeres shall wreck my wrong,
    When golden hayres shall change to silver wier:
    And those bright rayes that kindle all this fire
    Shall faile in force, their working not so stronge;
Then beautie (now the burthen of my song)
    Whose glorious blaze the world doth so admire,
    Must yeeld up all to tyrant Time's desire:
    Then fade those flowers that deckt her pride so long:
When, if she grieve to gaze her in the glasse,
    Which then presents her winter-withered hew,
    Goe you, my verse, goe tell her what she was,
    For what shee was shee best shall finde in you.
Your fierie heate lets not her glorie passe,
But (Phenix-like) shall make her live anew.

Sonnet 34

Looke, *Delia*, how wee steeme the half-blowne Rose,
    The image of thy blush, and Sommer's honour,
    Whilst in her tender greene shee doth inclose
    The pure sweet beauty Time bestowes upon her:
No sooner spreades her glory in the ayre,
    But straight her ful-blowne pride is in declining;
    Shee then is scorn'd, that late adorn'd the fayre:
    So clowdes thy beautie, after fairest shining.
No Aprill can revive thy withred flowers,
    Whose blooming grace adornes thy glory now:
    Swift speedy Time, feathred with flying howers,
    Dissolves the beautie of the fairest brow.
O let not then such riches waste in vaine;
But love whilst that thou maist be lov'd againe.

Sonnet 35

But love whilst that thou maist be lov'd againe,
   Now whilst thy May hath fill'd thy lap with flowers,
   Now whilst thy beauty beares without a staine,
   Now use thy Sommer smiles ere Winter lowers.
And whilst thou spread'st unto the rysing sunne
   The fairest flowre that ever sawe the light,
   Now joy thy time before thy sweet be done,
   And *(Delia)* thinke thy morning must have night;
And that thy brightnes sets at length to West,
   When thou wilt close up that which now thou showest;
   And thinke the same becomes thy fading best,
   Which then shall hide it most, and cover lowest.
Men doe not wey the stalke for that it was,
When once they finde her flowre, her glory passe.

Sonnet 36

When men shall finde thy flower, thy glory passe,
   And thou with carefull brow sitting alone
   Received hast this message from thy glasse,
   That tells the truth, and saies that all is gone;
Fresh shalt thou see in mee the wounds thou madest,
   Though spent thy flame, in mee the heate remaining:
   I that have lov'd thee thus before thou fadest,
   My faith shall waxe, when thou art in thy waining.
The world shall finde this myracle in mee,
   That fire can burne, when all the matter's spent:
   Then what my faith hath beene thy selfe shalt see,
   And that thou wast unkind thou maist repent.
Thou maist repent that thou hast scorn'd my teares,
When winter snowes upon thy golden haires.

Sonnet 37

When Winter snowes upon thy golden haires,
   And frost of age hath nipt thy flowers neere,
   When dark shal seeme thy day that never cleeres,
   And all lies withred that was held so deere;

Then take this picture which I heere present thee,
    Limned with a Pensill not all unworthy:
    Heere see the gifts that God and nature lent thee;
    Heare reade thy selfe, and what I suffred for thee.
This may remaine thy lasting monument,
    Which happily posteritie may cherrish:
    These colours with thy fading are not spent;
    These may remaine, when thou and I shall perrish.
If they remaine, then thou shalt live thereby.
They will remaine, and so thou canst not die.

Sonnet 38

Thou canst not die whilst any zeale abound
    In feeling harts, that can conceive these lynes:
    Though thou a *Laura* hast no *Petrarch* found,
    In base attyre yet cleerely Beauty shines.
And I (though borne within a colder clime)
    Doe feele mine inward heat as great, (I knowe it):
    Hee never had more faith, although more rime;
    I love as well, though he could better show it.
But I may add one feather to thy fame,
    To helpe her flight throughout the fairest Ile;
    And if my pen could more enlarge thy name,
    Then shouldst thou live in an immortall stile.
For though that *Laura* better limned bee,
Suffice, thou shalt be lov'd as well as shee.

Sonnet 39

O be not griev'd that these my papers should
    Bewray unto the world how faire thou art,
    Or that my wits have shewed the best they could,
    (The chastest flame that ever warmed hart).
Thinke not (sweet *Delia*) this shall be thy shame
    My Muse should sound thy praise with mournefull warble:
    How many live, the glory of whose name
    Shall rest in Ise, when thine is grav'd in Marble.
Thou maist in after ages live esteem'd,

Unburied in these lines reserv'd in purenes;
These shall intombe those eyes that have redeem'd
Mee from the vulgar, thee from all obscurenes.
Although my carefull accents never moov'd thee,
Yet count it no disgrace that I have lov'd thee.

Sonnet 40

Delia, these eyes that so admireth thine
Have seene those walls the which ambition rear'd
To check the world, how they intombd have lyen
Within themselves, and on them ploughes have ear'd.
Yet found I that no barbarous hand attaind
The spoyle of fame deserv'd by vertuous men,
Whose glorious actions luckily had gaind
Th'eternall Annals of a happy pen.
Why then, though *Delia* fade, let that not move her,
Though time doe spoile her of the fairest vaile
That ever yet mortalitie did cover,
Which must instarre the needle and the Raile.
That grace, that vertue, all that serv'd t'in-woman,
Dooth her unto eternitie assommon.

Sonnet 41

Fayre and lovely mayde, looke from the shore,
See thy *Leander* striving in these waves,
Poore soule quite spent, whose force can do no more;
Now send forth hopes, for now calme pitty saves:
And waft him to thee with those lovely eyes,
A happy convoy to a holy Lande:
Now shewe thy power, and where thy vertue lyes;
To save thine owne, stretch out the fairest hand.
Stretch out the fairest hand, a pledge of peace;
That hand that dartes so right, and never misses:
I shall forget old wrongs, my griefes shall cease,
And that which gave me wounds, Ile give it kisses.
O then let th'Ocean of my care find shore,
That thou be pleas'd, and I may sigh no more.

Sonnet 42

Reade in my face a volume of dispayres,
    The wayling Iliads of my tragicke woe,
    Drawne with my blood, and printed with my cares,
    Wrought by her hand that I have honoured so:
Who whilst I burne, she sings at my soule's wrack,
    Looking aloft from Turret of her pride:
    There my soule's Tyrant joyes her, in the sack
    Of her owne seate, whereof I made her guide.
There doe these smoakes that from affliction rise
    Serve as an incense to a cruell Dame;
    A Sacrifice thrice-gratefull to her eyes,
    Because their powre serve to exact the same.
Thus ruines shee (to satisfie her will)
The Temple, where her name was honour'd still.

Sonnet 43

My *Delia* hath the waters of mine eyes
    The ready handmaids on her grace attending,
    That never fall to ebb, but ever rise,
    For to their flow she never grants an ending.
Th'Ocean never did attend more dulie
    Upon his soveraigne's course, the night's pale Queen,
    Nor paid the impost of his waves more truely
    Then mine unto her Deitie have been.
Yet nought the rock of that hard hart can move,
    Where beate these teares with zeale, and fury driveth:
    And yet I rather languish in her love
    Then I would joy the fairest shee that liveth.
I doubt to finde such pleasure in my gayning,
As now I taste in compasse of complayning.

Sonnet 44

How long shall I in mine affliction mourne,
    A burthen to my selfe, distrest in minde?
    When shall my interdicted hopes returne
    From out dispaire wherein they live confin'd?

When shall her troubled brow, charg'd with disdaine,
    Reveale the treasure which her smyles impart?
    When shall my faith the happines attaine,
    To breake the Ise that hath congeald her hart?
Unto herselfe, herselfe my love doth sommon,
    (If love in her hath any power to move)
    And let her tell me as shee is a woman,
    Whether my faith hath not deserv'd her love.
I know she cannot but must needs confesse it,
Yet deignes not with one simple signe t'expresse it.

Sonnet 45

Beautie (sweet Love) is like the morning dewe
    Whose short refresh upon the tender greene
    Cheeres for a time but till the Sunne doth shew,
    And straight tis gone as it had never beene.
Soone doth it fade that makes the fairest florish;
    Short is the glory of the blushing Rose:
    The hewe which thou so carefully dost nourish,
    Yet which at length thou must be forc'd to lose.
When thou surcharg'd with burthen of thy yeeres,
    Shalt bend thy wrinkles homeward to the earth;
    When time hath made a pasport for thy feares,
    Dated in age, the Kalends of our death —
But ah, no more, this hath beene often tolde,
And women grieve to thinke they must be olde.

Sonnet 46

I must not grieve my Love, whose eyes would reede
    Lynes of delight, whereon her youth might smyle:
    Flowers have a tyme before they come to seed,
    And shee is young and now must sport the while.
Ah sport (sweet Maide) in season of these yeeres,
    And learne to gather flowers before they wither:
    And where the sweetest blossoms first appeares,
    Let love and youth conduct thy pleasures thither.
Lighten forth smyles to cleere the clowded ayre,

And calme the tempest which my sighes do rayse:
Pittie and smiles doe best become the faire,
Pittie and smiles shall yeeld thee lasting praise.
I hope to say, when all my griefes are gone,
Happie the hart that sigh'd for such a one.

Sonnet 47   *At the Author's going into Italie.*
O Whether (poore forsaken) wilt thou goe,
    To goe from sorrow, and thine owne distresse,
    When every place presents like face of woe,
    And no remove can make thy sorrowes lesse?
Yet goe (forsaken,) leave these woods, these playnes,
    Leave her and all, and all for her that leaves
    Thee and thy love forlorne, and both disdaines;
    And of both, wrongfull deemes, and ill conceaves.
Seeke out some place, and see if any place
    Can give the least release unto they griefe:
    Convay thee from the thought of thy disgrace,
    Steale from thy selfe, and be thy care's own thiefe.
But yet what comfort shall I heereby gaine?
Bearing the wound, I needs must feele the paine.

Sonnet 48   *This Sonnet was made at the Author's being in Italie.*
Drawne with th'attractive vertue of her eyes,
    My toucht hart turnes it to that happie cost,
    My joyfull North, where all my fortune lyes,
    The levell of my hopes desired most;
There, where my *Delia,* fairer than the Sunne,
    Deckt with her youth wheron the world doth smile,
    Joyes in that honour which her eyes have wonne,
    Th'eternall wonder of our happy Ile.
Florish, faire, *Albion,* glorie of the North,
    Neptune's best darling held betweene his armes,
    Devided from the world as better worth,
    Kept for himselfe, defended from all harmes.
Still let disarmed peace decke her and thee;
And Muse-foe *Mars* abroade farre fostred bee.

Sonnet 49

Care-charmer Sleepe, sonne of the sable Night,
    Brother to death, in silent darknes borne;
    Relieve my languish, and restore the light,
    With darke forgetting of my care's returne:
And let the day be time enough to mourne
    The shipwrack of my ill-adventred youth:
    Let waking eyes suffice to waile their scorne,
    Without the torment of the night's untruth.
Cease dreames, th'imag'ry of our day desires,
    To modell forth the passions of the morrow:
    Never let rysing Sunne approve you lyers,
    To adde more griefe to agravate my sorrow.
Still let me sleepe, imbracing clowdes in vaine,
And never wake to feele the daye's disdayne.

Sonnet 50

Let others sing of Knights and Palladines
    In aged accents and untimely words,
    Paint shadowes in imaginarie lines,
    Which wel the reach of their high wits records:
But I must sing of thee and those faire eyes;
    Autentique shall my verse in time to come,
    When yet th'unborne shall say, 'Loe, where she lyes,
    Whose beauty made him speak that else was dombe.
These are the Arkes, the Trophies I erect,
    That fortifie thy name against old age;
    And these thy sacred vertues must protect
    Against the darke, and Time's consuming rage.
Though th'error of my youth they shall discover,
Suffice, they shew I liv'd and was thy lover.

Sonnet 51

As to the Roman that would free his Land,
    His error was his honour and renowne;
    And more the fame of his mistaking hand,
    Then if he had the Tyrant over-throwne:

So *Delia,* hath mine errour made me knowne,
 And my deceiv'd attempt deserv'd more fame
 Then if I had the victory mine owne,
 And thy hard hart had yeelded up the same:
And so likewise, renowned is thy blame,
 Thy crueltie, thy glorie. O strange case,
 That errours should be grac'd that merrite shame,
 And sinne of frownes bring honor to the face.
Yet happy *Delia* that thou wast unkind,
But happier yet, if thou wouldst change thy minde.

Sonnet 52

Like as the Lute that joyes or els dislikes,
 As is his arte that playes upon the same,
 So sounds my Muse according as shee strikes
 On my hart strings, high tun'd unto her fame.
Her touch doth cause the warble of the sound,
 Which heere I yeeld in lamentable wise,
 A wailing deskant on the sweetest ground,
 Whose due reports give honour to her eyes.
Els harshe my stile, untunable my Muse,
 Hoarce sounds the voyce that praiseth not her name:
 If any pleasing relish heere I use,
 Then judge the world her beauty gives the same.
O happie ground that makes the musique such,
And blessed hand that gives so sweet a touch.

Sonnet 53

None other fame myne unambitious Muse
 Affected ever but t'eternize thee:
 All other honours doe my hopes refuse,
 Which meaner priz'd and momentarie be.
For God forbid I should my papers blot,
 With mercynarie lines, with servile pen;
 Praysing vertues in them that have them not,
 Basely attending on the hopes of men.

No, no, my verse respects nor Thames nor Theaters,
    Nor seekes it to be knowne unto the great:
    But *Avon* poore in fame, and poore in waters,
    Shall have my song, where *Delia* hath her seate.
Avon shall be my Thames, and shee my song;
I'le sound her name the River all along.

Sonnet 54

Unhappy pen and ill accepted papers,
    That intimate in vaine my chast desires,
    My chast desires, (the ever burning Tapers)
    Inkindled by her eyes' celestiall fires:
Celestiall fires and unrespecting powers,
    That deigne not viewe the glory of your might,
    In humble lines the worke of carefull howres,
    The sacrifice I offer to her sight.
But sith she scornes her owne, this rests for mee,
    I'le mone my selfe, and hide the wrong I have;
    And so content mee that her frownes should be
    To m'infant stile the cradle, and the grave.
What though my selfe no honour get thereby,
Each byrd sings to herselfe, and so will I.

Sonnet 55

Loe heere the impost of a faith unfayning,
    That love hath paid, and her disdaine extorted:
    Behold the message of my just complaining,
    That shewes the world how much my griefe imported.
These tributarie plaints fraught with desire
    I send those eyes, the cabinets of love,
    The Paradice whereto my hopes aspire,
    From out this hell, which mine afflictions prove:
Wherein I thus doe live cast downe from myrth,
    Pensive alone, none but dispaire about mee;
    My joyes abortive, perrisht at their birth,

My cares long liv'd, and will not die without mee.
This is my state, and *Delia's* hart is such;
I say no more, I feare I said too much.

FINIS

Michael Drayton

TO THE READER OF THESE SONNETS

Into these Loves, who but for Passion lookes,
At this first sight, here let him lay them by,
And seeke else-where, in turning other Bookes,
Which better may his labour satisfie.
No farre-fetch'd Sigh shall ever wound my Brest,
Love from mine Eye a Teare shall never wring,
Nor in Ah-mees my whyning Sonnets drest,
(A Libertine) fantastickly I sing:
My Verse is the true image of my Mind,
Ever in motion, still desiring change;
And as thus to Varietie inclin'd,
So in all Humors sportively I range:
   My Muse is rightly of the English straine,
   That cannot long one Fashion intertaine.

Idea

1 Like an adventurous Sea-farer am I
   Who hath some long and dang'rous Voyage beene,
   And call'd to tell of his Discoverie,
   How farre he sayl'd, what Countries he had seene,
   Proceeding from the Port whence he put forth,
   Shewes by his Compasse how his Course he steer'd,
   When East, when West, when South, and when by North,
   As how the Pole to ev'ry place was rear'd;
   What Capes he doubled, of what Continent

The Gulphes and Straits that strangely he had past,
Where most becalm'd, where with foule Weather spent,
And on what Rocks in perill to be cast:
    Thus in my Love, Time calls me to relate
    My tedious Travels and oft-varying Fate.

2   My heart was slaine, and none but you and I:
Who should I thinke the Murther should commit?
Since, but your selfe, there was no Creature by,
But onely I, guiltlesse of murth'ring it.
It slew it selfe: the Verdict on the view
Doe quit the dead, and me not accessarie:
Well, well, I feare it will be prov'd by you,
Th'evidence so great a proofe doth carrie.
But O, see, see, we need inquire no further;
Upon your Lips the scarlet drops are found,
And in your Eye, the Boy that did the Murther,
Your Cheekes yet pale, since first he gave the Wound.
    By this I see, how-ever things be past,
    Yet Heav'n will still have Murther out at last.

3   Taking my Penne, with Words to cast my Woe,
Duely to count the summe of all my cares,
I finde, my Griefes innumerable growe,
The reck'nings rise to millions of Despaires;
And thus dividing of my fatall Houres,
The paiments of my Love I read, and crosse;
Substracting, set my Sweets unto my Sowres;
My Joyes' arrerage leades me to my losse.
And thus mine Eies a debtor to thine Eye
Which by Extortion gaineth all their lookes;
My heart hath paid such grievous Usurie,
That all their Wealth lies in thy beautie's Bookes,
    And all is Thine which hath been due to Me,
    And I a Bankrupt, quite undone by Thee.

4   Bright starre of Beauty, on whose eye-lids sit
     A thousand Nimph-like and inamor'd Graces,
     The Goddesses of Memory and Wit,
     Which there in order take their severall places;
     In whose deare Bosome, sweet delicious Love
     Layes downe his Quiver, which he once did beare:
     Since he that blessed Paradise did prove,
     And leaves his Mother's lap to sport him there,
     Let others strive to entertaine with Words;
     My Soule is of a braver Mettle made;
     I hold that vile, which Vulgar wit affords;
     In Me's that Faith which Time cannot invade.
        Let what I praise be still made good by you:
        Be you most worthy, whilst I am most true.

5   Nothing but No and I, and I and No:
     How fals it out so strangely you reply?
     I tell yee (Faire) I'le not be answered so,
     With this affirming No, denying I.
     I say, 'I Love'; you sleightly answere 'I':
     I say, 'You Love'; you peule me out a No:
     I say, 'I Die'; you Eccho me with 'I':
     'Save mee', I Crie; you sigh me out a No.
     Must Woe and I have naught but No and I?
     No I am I, if I no more can have:
     Answere no more; with Silence make reply,
     And let me take my selfe what I doe crave;
        Let No and I with I and you be so:
        Then answere No and I, and I and No.

6   How many paltry, foolish, painted things,
     That now in Coaches trouble ev'ry Street,
     Shall be forgotten, whom no Poet sings,
     Ere they be well wrap'd in their winding Sheet!
     Where I to thee Eternitie shall give,
     When nothing else remayneth of these dayes,
     And Queenes hereafter shall be glad to live

Upon the Almes of thy superfluous prayse:
Virgins and Matrons reading these my Rimes,
Shall be so much delighted with thy story,
That they shall grieve they liv'd not in these Times,
To have seene thee, their Sexe's onely glory:
   So shalt thou flye above the vulgar Throng,
   Still to survive in my immortall Song.

7   Love, in a Humor, play'd the Prodigall,
And bad my Senses to a solemne Feast;
Yet more to grace the Company withall,
Invites my Heart to be the chiefest Ghest:
No other Drinke would serve this Glutton's turne
But precious Teares distilling from mine Eyne,
Which with my Sighes this Epicure doth burne,
Quaffing Carowses in this costly Wine;
Where, in his Cups o'rcome with foule Excesse,
Straightwayes he plays a swagg'ring Ruffin's part,
And at the Banquet, in his Drunkennesse,
Slew his deare Friend, my kind and truest Heart:
   A gentle warning (Friends) thus may you see,
   What 'tis to keepe a Drunkard companie.

8   There's nothing grieves me, but that Age should haste,
That in my dayes I may not see thee old;
That where those two cleare sparkling Eyes are plac'd,
Onely two Loope-holes then I might behold.
That lovely, arched, yvorie, pollish'd Brow,
Defac'd with Wrinkles, that I might but see;
Thy daintie Hayre, so curl'd, and crisped now,
Like grizzled Mosse upon some aged Tree;
Thy Cheeke, now flush with Roses, sunke, and leane,
Thy Lips, with age, as any Wafer thinne;
Thy Pearly Teeth out of thy Head so cleane,
That when thou feed'st, thy Nose shall touch thy Chinne:
   These Lines that now thou scorn'st, which should delight thee,
   Then would I make thee read but to despight thee.

9   As other Men, so I my selfe doe Muse,
     Why in this sort I wrest Invention so,
     And why these giddy Metaphors I use,
     Leaving the Path the greater part doe goe.
     I will resolve you; I am Lunaticke,
     And ever this in Mad-men you shall finde,
     What they last thought of, when the Braine grew sicke,
     In most distraction they keepe that in Minde.
     Thus talking idly in this Bedlam fit,
     Reason and I (you must conceive) are twaine;
     'Tis nine yeeres now since first I lost my Wit;
     Beare with Me then, though troubled be my Braine:
        With Diet and Correction Men distraught
        (Not too farre past) may to their Wits be brought.

10 To nothing fitter can I Thee compare
     Then to the Sonne of some rich Penny-father,
     Who having now brought on his end with Care,
     Leaves to his Sonne all he had heap'd together.
     This new rich Novice, lavish of his chest,
     To one Man gives, doth on another spend,
     Then heere he riots, yet amongst the rest
     Haps to lend some to one true honest Friend.
     Thy Gifts thou in Obscuritie doest waste,
     False Friends thy kindnesse, borne but to deceive Thee,
     Thy Love, that is on the unworthy plac'd;
     Time hath thy Beautie, which with Age will leave thee;
        Onely that little which to Me was lent
        I give Thee backe, when all the rest is spent.

11 You not alone, when You are still alone,
     O God from You, that I could private be;
     Since You one were, I never since was one;
     Since You in Me, my selfe since out of Me,
     Transported from my Selfe, into Your being;
     Though either distant, present yet to either,
     Senselesse with too much Joy, each other seeing,

And onely absent, when Wee are together.
Give Me my Selfe, and take your Selfe againe;
Devise some meanes but how I may forsake You;
So much is Mine, that doth with You remaine,
That taking what is Mine, with Me I take You;
    You doe bewitch Me: O that I could flie,
      From my Selfe You, or from your owne Selfe I.

To the Soule

12 That learned Father, which so firmely proves
    The Soule of Man immortall and divine,
    And doth the sev'rall Offices define,

Anima	Gives her that Name, as she the Body moves;
Amor	Then is she Love, imbracing Charitie;
Animus	Moving a Will in us, it is the Mind;
Mens	Retayning Knowledge, still the same in kind;
Memoria	As intellectuall, it is Memorie;
Ratio	In judging, Reason onely is her Name;
Sensus	In speedie apprehension, it is Sense;
Conscientia	In Right or Wrong, they call her Conscience;
Spiritus	The Spirit, when it to God-ward doth inflame.

    These of the Soule the sev'rall Functions bee,
    Which my Heart, lightned by thy Love, doth see.

To the Shadow

13 Letters and Lines we see are soone defaced,
    Metals doe waste, and fret with Canker's Rust,
    The Diamond shall once consume to Dust,
    And freshest Colours with foule staynes disgraced;
    Paper and Inke can paint but naked Words;
    To write with Bloud of force offends the Sight,
    And if with Teares, I find them all too light,
    And Sighes and Signes a silly Hope affords.
    O sweetest Shadow, how thou serv'st my turne,
    Which still shalt be, as long as there is Sunne;

Nor whilst the World is, never shall be done,
Whilst Moone shall shine, or any Fire shall burne:
    That ev'ry thing whence Shadow doth proceed,
    May in his Shadow my Love's storie read.

14   If he, from Heav'n that filch'd that living Fire,
    Condemn'd by JOVE to endlesse Torment bee,
    I greatly marvell, how you still goe free,
    That farre beyond PROMETHEUS did aspire:
    The Fire he stole, although of Heav'nly kind,
    Which from above he craftily did take,
    Of livelesse Clods us living Men to make,
    He did bestow in temper of the Mind.
    But you broke into Heav'n's immortall store,
    Where Vertue, Honour, Wit, and Beautie lay;
    Which taking thence, you have escap'd away,
    Yet stand as free as ere you did before:
        Yet old PROMETHEUS punish'd for his Rape.
        Thus poore Theeves suffer, when the greater scape.

His Remedie for Love

15   Since to obtaine thee nothing me will sted,
    I have a Med'cine that shall cure my Love:
    The powder of her Heart dry'd, when she is dead,
    That Gold nor Honour ne'r had pow'r to move;
    Mix'd with her Teares, that ne'r her true-Love crost,
    Nor at Fifteene ne'r long'd to be a Bride;
    Boyl'd with her Sighes, in giving up the Ghost,
    That for her late deceased Husband dy'd:
    Into the same then let a Woman breathe,
    That being chid, did never word replie,
    With one thrice-marry'd's Pray'rs, that did bequeath
    A Legacie to stale Virginitie.
        If this Receit have not the pow'r to winne me,
        Little I'le say, but thinke the Devill's in me.

An Allusion to the Phœnix

16 'Mongst all the Creatures in this spacious Round,
Of the Birds' kind, the Phœnix is alone,
Which best by you, of living Things, is knowne:
None like to that, none like to you is found:
Your Beautie is the hot and splend'rous Sunne;
The precious Spices be your chaste Desire,
Which being kindled by that heav'nly fire,
Your Life so like the Phœnix's begun;
Your selfe thus burned in that sacred flame,
With so rare sweetnesse all the Heav'ns perfuming,
Againe increasing as you are consuming,
Onely by dying, borne the very same:
    And wing'd by Fame, you to the Starres ascend,
    So you of Time shall live beyond the End.

To Time

17 Stay, speedy Time, behold, before thou passe,
From Age to Age what thou hast sought to see,
One, in whom all the Excellencies be,
In whom, Heav'n lookes it selfe as in a Glasse:
Time, looke thou too, in this Tralucent Glasse,
And thy Youth past in this pure Mirrour see,
As the World's Beautie in his Infancie,
What it was then, and thou before it was;
Passe on, and to Posteritie tell this,
Yet see thou tell, but truly, what hath beene;
Say to our Nephewes that thou once hast seene,
In perfect humane shape, all heav'nly Blisse;
    And bid them mourne, nay more, despaire with thee,
    That she is gone, her like againe to see.

To the Celestiall Numbers

18 To this our World, to Learning, and to Heaven,
Three Nines there are, to every one a Nine,
One number of the Earth, the other both Divine:
One Woman now makes three odde Numbers even

Nine orders first of Angels be in Heaven;
Nine Muses doe with Learning still frequent,
These with the Gods are ever resident;
Nine worthie Women to the World were given:
My worthy, One to these Nine Worthies addeth,
And my faire Muse, one Muse unto the Nine,
And my good Angell (in my Soule divine)
With one more Order these nine Orders gladdeth:
    My Muse, my Worthy, and my Angel then
    Makes every One of these three Nines a Ten.

To Humour

19 You cannot love, my prettie Heart, and why?
There was a time, You told Me that you would,
But now againe You will the same denie;
If it might please You, would to God You could:
What, will You hate? Nay that You will not neither?
Nor Love, nor Hate, how then? What will You doe?
What, will You keepe a meane then betwixt either?
Or will You love Me, and yet hate Me too?
Yet serves not This. What next, what other Shift?
You Will, and Will not: what a coyle is here!
I see Your craft, now I perceive Your drift,
And all this while, I was mistaken there:
    Your Love and Hate is this, I now doe prove You,
    You love in Hate, by Hate to make Me love You.

20 An evill spirit, your beautie haunts Me still,
Where with (alas) I have beene long possest,
Which ceaseth not to tempt Me to each Ill,
Nor gives Me once but one poore minute's rest:
In Me it speakes, whether I Sleepe or Wake,
And when by Meanes to drive it out I try,
With greater Torments then it Me doth take,
And tortures Me in most extremity:
Before my Face it layes downe my Despaires,
And hastes Me on unto a sudden Death,

Now tempting Me to drowne my Selfe in teares,
And then in sighing, to give up my breath:
 Thus am I still provok'd to every Evill
 By this good wicked Spirit, sweet Angell Devill.

21 A witlesse Gallant a young Wench that woo'd,
(Yet his dull Spirit her not one jot could move)
Intreated me, as e'r I wish'd his good,
To write him but one Sonnet to his Love:
When I, as fast as e'r my Penne could trot,
Powr'd out what first from quicke Invention came,
Nor never stood one word thereof to blot,
Much like his Wit, that was to use the same:
But with my Verses he his Mistres wonne,
Who doted on the Dolt beyond all measure.
But see, for you to Heav'n for Phraze I runne,
And ransacke all APOLLO's golden Treasure;
 Yet by my Froth, this Foole his Love obtaines,
 And I lose you, for all my Wit and Paines.

To Folly

22 With Fooles and Children good Discretion beares;
Then honest People, beare with Love and Me,
Nor older yet, nor wiser made by yeeres,
Amongst the rest of Fooles and Children be:
Love still a Baby, playes with Gawdes and Toyes,
And like a Wanton, sports with every Fether;
And Ideots still are running after Boyes,
Then Fooles and Children fitt'st to goe together:
He still as young as when he first was borne,
No wiser I then when as young as he.
You that behold us, laugh us not to scorne;
Give Nature thankes, you are not such as we:
 Yet Fooles and Children sometimes tell in play
 Some wise in shew, more Fooles indeed then they.

23   Love banish'd Heav'n, in Earth was held in scorne,
       Wand'ring abroad in Need and Beggerie;
       And wanting Friends, though of a Goddesse borne,
       Yet crav'd the Almes of such as passed by:
       I, like a Man devout and charitable,
       Clothed the Naked, lodg'd this wand'ring Ghest,
       With Sighes and Teares still furnishing his Table,
       With what might make the Miserable blest.
       But this ungratefull, for my good desert,
       Intic'd my Thoughts against me to conspire,
       Who gave consent to steale away my Heart,
       And set my Brest, his Lodging, on a fire.
          Well, well, my Friends, when Beggers grow thus bold,
          No marvell then though Charitie grow cold.

24   I heare some say, 'This Man is not in love:
       Who? Can he love? A likely thing!' they say;
       'Reade but his Verse, and it will eas'ly prove.'
       O, judge not rashly (gentle Sir) I pray:
       Because I loosely trifle in this sort,
       As one that faine his Sorrowes would beguile,
       You now suppose me all this time in sport,
       And please your selfe with this Conceit the while:
       Yee shallow Censures, sometime see yee not
       In greatest Perils some Men pleasant be;
       Where Fame by Death is onely to be got,
       They resolute? So stands the case with me:
          Where other Men in depth of Passion crie,
          I laugh at Fortune, as in jest to die.

25   O, why should Nature niggardly restraine
       That Foraine Nations rellish not our Tongue!
       Else should my Lines glide on the Waves of *Rhene*,
       And crowne the *Piren's* with my living Song.
       But bounded thus, to *Scotland* get you forth,
       Thence take you Wing unto the *Orcades*;
       There let my Verse get glory in the North,

Making my Sighes to thaw the Frozen Seas:
And let the *Bards* within that *Irish* Ile,
To whom my Muse with fierie Wings shall passe,
Call backe the stiffe-neck'd Rebels from Exile,
And mollifie the slaught'ring *Galliglasse*;
    And when my flowing Numbers they rehearse,
    Let Wolves and Beares be charmed with my Verse.

To Despaire

26 I ever love where never Hope appeares,
Yet Hope drawes on my never-hoping Care,
And my Live's Hope would die but for Despaire.
My never-certaine Joy breeds ever-certaine Feares,
Uncertaine Dread gives Wings unto my Hope;
Yet my Hope's Wings are laden so with Feare,
As they cannot ascend to my Hope's Sphere:
Though Feare gives them more then a Heav'nly Scope,
Yet this large Roome is bounded with Despaire,
So my Love is still fett'red with vaine Hope,
And Liberty deprives him of his Scope,
And thus am I imprison'd in the Aire.
    Then, sweet Despaire, awhile hold up thy head,
    Or all my Hope for Sorrow will be dead.

27 Is not Love here as 'tis in other Clymes,
And diff'reth it as doe the sev'rall Nations?
Or hath it lost the Vertue with the Times,
Or in this Iland alt'reth with the Fashions?
Or have our Passions lesser pow'r then theirs
Who had lesse Art them lively to expresse?
Is Nature growne lesse pow'rfull in their Heires,
Or in our Fathers did she more transgresse?
I am sure my Sighes come from a Heart as true
As any Man's that Memory can boast,
And my Respects and Services to you
Equall with his that loves his Mistres most:
    Or Nature must be partiall in my Cause,
    Or onely you doe violate her Lawes.

28   To such as say Thy Love I over-prize,
     And doe not sticke to terme my Prayses folly,
     Against these Folkes, that thinke themselves so wise,
     I thus oppose my Reason's forces wholly:
     Though I give more then well affords my state,
     In which expence the most suppose me vaine,
     Which yeelds them nothing, at the easiest rate,
     Yet at this price returnes me treble gaine.
     They value not, unskilfull how to use,
     And I give much, because I gaine thereby:
     I that thus take, or they that thus refuse,
     Whether are these deceived then, or I?
        In ev'ry thing I hold this Maxim still,
        The Circumstance doth make it good, or ill.

To the Senses

29   When conqu'ring Love did first my Heart assayle,
     Unto mine aid I summon'd ev'ry Sense,
     Doubting, if that proud Tyrant should prevayle,
     My Heart should suffer for mine Eyes' Offence;
     But he with Beautie first corrupted Sight,
     My Hearing brib'd with her Tongue's Harmonie,
     My Taste by her sweet Lips drawne with Delight,
     My Smelling wonne with her Breath's Spicerie:
     But when my Touching came to play his part,
     (The King of Senses, greater then the rest)
     He yeelds Love up the Keyes unto my Heart,
     And tells the other how they should be blest.
        And thus by those of whom I hop'd for ayd
        To cruell Love my Soule was first betray'd.

To the Vestals

30   Those Priests which first the Vestall Fire begun,
     Which might be borrow'd from no Earthly flame,
     Devis'd a Vessell to receive the Sunne,
     Being stedfastly opposed to the same;
     Where, with sweet Wood, layd curiously by Art,

On which the Sunne might by reflection beat,
Receiving strength from ev'ry secret part,
The Fuell kindled with Celestiall Heat.
Thy blessed Eyes, the Sunne which lights this Fire;
My holy Thoughts, they be the Vestall flame;
The precious Odors be my chaste Desire;
My Brest's the Vessell which includes the same:
    Thou art my VESTA, thou my Goddesse art,
    Thy hallow'd Temple onely is my Heart.

To the Criticke

31 Methinkes I see some crooked Mimickejeere,
And taxe my Muse with this fantasticke Grace,
Turning my Papers, askes, 'What have we heere?'
Making withall some filthy Antike Face.
I feare no censure, nor what thou canst say,
Nor shall my Spirit one jot of vigour lose.
Think'st thou my Wit shall keepe the pack-Horse Way
That ev'ry Dudgen low Invention goes?
Since Sonnets thus in Bundles are imprest,
And ev'ry Drudge doth dull our satiate Eare,
Think'st thou my Love shall in those Ragges be drest
That ev'ry Dowdy, ev'ry Trull doth weare?
    Up, to my Pitch, no common Judgement flyes;
    I scorne all Earthly Dung-bred Scarabies.

To the River Ankor

32 Our Flouds-Queen *Thames* for Ships & Swans is crowned,
And stately *Severne* for her Shoare is praysed;
The Crystall *Trent*, for Foords and Fish renowned,
And *Avon's* Fame to *Albion's* Cliffes is raysed;
Carlegion Chester vaunts her holy *Dee*,
Yorke many Wonders of her *Owse* can tell,
The *Peake* her *Dove*, whose Bankes so fertile be,
And *Kent* will say her *Medway* doth excell;
Cotswold commends her *Isis* to the *Tame*,
Our Northerne Borders boast of *Tweed's* faire Floud,

Our Westerne Parts extoll their *Wili's* Fame,
And the old *Lea* brags of the *Danish* Bloud:
    Arden's sweet *Ankor*, let thy glory bee
    That faire *Idea* onely lives by thee.

To Imagination

33 Whilst yet mine Eyes doe surfet with Delight,
My wofull Heart, imprison'd in my Brest,
Wisheth to be transformed to my Sight,
That it, like those, by looking might be blest:
But whilst mine Eyes thus greedily doe gaze,
Finding their Objects over-soone depart,
These now the other's Happinesse doe prayse,
Wishing themselves that they had beene my Heart;
That Eyes were Heart, or that the Heart were Eyes,
As covetous the other's use to have:
But finding Nature their request denyes,
This to each other mutually they crave,
    That since the one cannot the other bee,
    That Eyes could thinke of that my Heart could see.

To Admiration

34 Marvell not, Love, though I thy pow'r admire,
Ravish'd a World beyond the farthest Thought,
And knowing more then ever hath beene taught,
That I am onely starv'd in my desire:
Marvell not, Love, though I thy pow'r admire,
Ayming at things exceeding all perfection,
To Wisedome's selfe to minister direction,
That I am onely starv'd in my desire:
Marvell not, Love, though I thy pow'r admire,
Though my Conceit I further seeme to bend
Then possibly Invention can extend,
And yet am onely starv'd in my desire:
    If thou wilt wonder, here's the wonder, Love,
    That this to me doth yet no wonder prove.

To Miracle

35 Some misbeleeving and prophane in Love,
When I doe speake of Miracles by thee,
May say that thou art flattered by mee,
Who onely write, my skill in Verse to prove.
See Miracles, ye unbeleeving, see:
A dumbe-borne Muse made to expresse the Mind,
A cripple Hand to write, yet lame by Kind,
One by thy Name, the other touching thee:
Blind were mine Eyes till they were seene of thine,
And mine Eares deafe by thy Fame healed bee,
My Vices cur'd by Vertues sprung from thee,
My Hopes reviv'd which long in Grave had lyne:
      All uncleane Thoughts, foule Spirits, cast out in mee,
      Onely by Vertue that proceeds from thee.

Cupid *conjured*

36 Thou purblind Boy, since thou hast beene so slacke
To wound her Heart, whose Eyes have wounded me,
And suff'red her to glory in my Wracke,
Thus to my aid, I lastly conjure thee:
By Hellish *Styx* (by which the THUND'RER sweares)
By thy faire Mother's unavoided Power,
By HECAT's Names, by PROSERPINE's sad Teares,
When she was rapt to the infernall Bower;
By thine owne loved PSYCHE's, by the Fires
Spent on thine Altars, flaming up to Heav'n;
By all true Lovers' Sighes, Vowes, and Desires,
By all the Wounds that ever thou hast giv'n;
      I conjure thee by all that I have nam'd,
      To make her love, or CUPID be thou damn'd.

37 Deare, why should you command me to my Rest,
When now the Night doth summon all to sleepe?
Me thinkes this Time becommeth Lovers best;
Night was ordayn'd together Friends to keepe.
How happy are all other living Things,

Which though the Day dis-joyne by sev'rall flight,
The quiet Ev'ning yet together brings,
And each returnes unto his Love at Night!
O, Thou that art so courteous else to all!
Why should'st thou, Night, abuse me onely thus,
That ev'ry Creature to his kind do'st call,
And yet 'tis thou do'st onely sever us?
    Well could I wish it would be ever Day,
    If when Night comes, you bid me goe away.

38   Sitting alone, Love bids me goe and write;
Reason plucks back, commanding me to stay,
Boasting that she doth still direct the way,
Or else Love were unable to indite:
Love growing angry, vexed at the Spleene,
And scorning Reason's maymed Argument,
Straight taxeth Reason wanting to invent
Where she with Love conversing hath not beene:
Reason, reproched with this coy Disdaine,
Despiteth Love, and laugheth at her Folly;
And Love, contemning Reason's reason wholly,
Thought it in weight too light by many a Graine:
    Reason, put back, doth out of sight remove,
    And Love alone picks reason out of love.

39   Some, when in Ryme they of their Loves doe tell,
With Flames and Lightnings their Exordiums paint;
Some call on Heaven, some invocate on Hell,
And Fates and Furies with their woes acquaint.
Elizium is too high a seate for Me,
I will not come in *Stix* or *Phlegeton*;
The thrice-three Muses but too wanton be;
Like they that Lust, I care not, I will none.
Spightfull ERINNIS frights Me with her Lookes;
My man-hood dares not with foule ATE mell;
I quake to looke on HECAT's charming Bookes;

I still feare Bug-beares in APOLLO's Cell.
   I passe not for MINERVA, nor ASTREA,
   Onely I call on my divine IDEA.

40   My Heart the Anvile where my Thoughts doe beate,
   My Words the Hammers, fashioning my desire,
   My Brest the Forge, including all the heate,
   Love is the Fewell, which maintaines the fire;
   My Sighes the Bellowes, which the Flame encreaseth,
   Filling mine Eares with Noise and Nightly groning;
   Toyling with Paine, my Labour never ceaseth,
   In grievous Passions my Woes still bemoning:
   My Eyes with Teares against the fire striving,
   Whose scorching gleed my heart to Cinders turneth;
   But with those Drops the Flame againe reviving,
   Still more and more it to my torment burneth:
      With SISIPHUS thus doe I role the stone,
      And turne the Wheele with damned IXION.

Love's Lunacie

41   Why doe I speake of Joy, or write of Love,
   When my Heart is the very Den of Horror,
   And in my Soule the paines of hell I prove,
   With all his Torments and Infernall terror?
   What should I say? What yet remaines to doe?
   My Braine is drie with weeping all too long;
   My Sighes be spent in utt'ring of my Woe,
   And I want words wherewith to tell my Wrong:
   But still distracted in Love's Lunacie,
   And Bedlam-like, thus raving in my Griefe,
   Now raile upon her Haire, then on her Eye;
   Now call her Goddesse, then I call her Thiefe;
      Now I deny Her, then I doe confesse Her,
      Now doe I curse Her, then againe I blesse Her.

42   Some Men there be which like my Method well,
And much commend the strangenesse of my Vaine:
Some say I have a passing pleasing Straine,
Some say That in my Humor I excell;
Some, who not kindly rellish my Conceit,
They say (As Poets doe) I use to faine,
And in bare words paint out my Passion's paine;
Thus sundry Men their sundry Minds repeat:
I passe not, I, how Men affected bee,
Nor who commends or discommends my Verse;
It pleaseth me if I my Woes rehearse,
And in my Lines if she my love may see:
    Onely my comfort still consists in this,
    Writing her prayse, I cannot write amisse.

43   Why should your faire Eyes with such sov'raigne grace
Disperse their Rayes on ev'ry vulgar Spirit,
Whilst I in darknesse, in the selfe-same place,
Get not one glance, to recompence my Merit?
So doth the Plow-man gaze the wand'ring Starre,
And onely rest contented with the Light,
That never learn'd what Constellations are
Beyond the bent of his unknowing Sight.
O, why should Beautie (Custome to obey)
To their grosse Sense apply her selfe so ill!
Would God I were as ignorant as they,
When I am made unhappy by my skill;
    Onely compell'd on this poore good to boast,
    Heav'ns are not kind to them that know them most.

44   Whilst thus my Pen strives to eternize thee,
Age rules my Lines with Wrinkles in my Face,
Where, in the Map of all my Miserie,
Is model'd out the World of my Disgrace;
Whilst in despite of tyrannizing Times,
MEDEA-like, I make thee young againe,
Proudly thou scorn'st my World-out-wearing Rimes,

And murther'st Vertue with thy coy disdaine:
And though in youth my Youth untimely perish,
To keepe Thee from Oblivion and the Grave,
Ensuing Ages yet my Rimes shall cherish,
Where I, intomb'd, my better part shall save;
    And though this Earthly Body fade and die,
    My Name shall mount upon Eternitie.

45   Muses which sadly sit about my Chayre,
    Drown'd in the Teares extorted by my Lines,
    With heavie Sighes whilst thus I breake the Ayre,
    Painting my Passions in these sad Designes;
    Since she disdaines to blesse my happie Verse,
    The strong-built Trophies to her living Fame,
    Ever henceforth my Bosome be your Hearse,
    Wherein the World shall now intombe her Name:
    Inclose my Musike, you poore senselesse Walls,
    Sith she is deafe, and will not heare my Mones;
    Soften your selves with ev'ry Teare that falls,
    Whilst I like ORPHEUS sing to Trees and Stones,
        Which with my plaint seeme yet with pittie moved,
        Kinder then she whom I so long have loved.

46   Plaine-path'd Experience, th'unlearned's guide,
    Her simple Followers evidently shewes
    Sometimes what Schoole-men scarcely can decide,
    Nor yet wise Reason absolutely knowes:
    In making tryall of a Murther wrought,
    If the vile actors of the heynous deed
    Neere the dead Body happily be brought,
    Oft't'ath been prov'd, the breathlesse Coarse will bleed.
    She comming neere, that my poore Heart hath slaine,
    Long since departed (to the World no more)
    Th'ancient Wounds no longer can containe,
    But fall to bleeding, as they did before:
        But what of this? Should she to death be led,
        If furthers Justice, but helpes not the dead.

47   In pride of Wit, when high desire of Fame
      Gave Life and Courage to my lab'ring Pen,
      And first the sound and vertue of my Name
      Wonne grace and credit in the Eares of Men;
      With those the thronged Theaters that presse,
      I in the Circuit for the Lawrell strove,
      Where the full Prayse, I freely must confesse,
      In heat of Bloud a modest Mind might move.
      With Showts and Claps at ev'ry little pawse,
      When the proud Round on ev'ry side hath rung
      Sadly I sit, unmov'd with the Applause,
      As though to me it nothing did belong:
          No publike Glorie vainely I pursue;
          All that I seeke is to enternize you.

48   Cupid, I hate thee, which I'de have thee know:
      A naked Starveling ever may'st thou be.
      Poore Rogue, goe pawne thy *Fascia* and thy Bow,
      For some few Ragges wherewith to cover thee:
      Or if thou'lt not, thy Archerie forbeare;
      To some base Rustick doe thy selfe preferre,
      And when Corne's sowne, or growne into the Eare,
      Practise thy Quiver, and turne Crow-keeper;
      Or being Blind (as fittest for the Trade)
      Goe hyre thy selfe some bungling Harper's Boy:
      They that are blind are Minstrels often made.
      So may'st thou live, to thy faire Mother's Joy;
          That whilst with MARS she holdeth her old Way,
          Thou, her blind Sonne, may'st sit by them, and play.

49   Thou Leaden Braine, which censur'st what I write,
      And say'st my Lines be dull and doe not move,
      I marvell not thou feel'st not my Delight,
      Which never felt'st my fierie touch of Love:
      But thou, whose Pen hath like a Packe-Horse serv'd,
      Whose Stomack unto Gall hath turn'd thy Food,
      Whose Senses, like poore Pris'ners, hunger-starv'd,

Whose Griefe hath parch'd thy Body, dry'd thy Blood;
Thou which hast scorned Life, and hated Death,
And in a moment Mad, Sober, Glad, and Sorrie;
Thou which hast bann'd thy Thoughts, and curst thy Birth,
With thousand Plagues more then in Purgatorie:
    Thou, thus whose Spirit Love in his fire refines,
    Come thou and reade, admire, applaud my Lines.

50 As in some Countries, farre remote from hence,
The wretched Creature destined to die,
Having the Judgement due to his Offence,
By Surgeons beg'd, their Art on him to trie,
Which on the Living worke without remorse,
First make incision on each mast'ring Veine,
Then stanch the bleeding, then trans-pierce the Coarse,
And with the Balmes recure the Wounds againe;
Then Poyson, and with Physike him restore:
Not that they feare the hope-lesse Man to kill,
But their Experience to increase the more:
Ev'n so my Mistres workes upon my Ill,
    By curing me and killing me each How'r,
    Onely to shew her Beautie's Sov'raigne Pow'r.

51 Calling to minde, since first my Love begun,
Th'incertaine Times oft varying in their Course,
How Things still unexpectedly have runne,
As't please the Fates by their resistlesse force:
Lastly, mine Eyes amazedly have seene
ESSEX' great fall, TYRONE his Peace to gaine,
The quiet end of that Long-living Queene,
This King's faire Entrance, and our Peace with *Spaine*,
We and the *Dutch* at length our Selves to sever:
Thus the World doth, and evermore shall Reele;
Yet to my Goddesse am I constant ever,
How e're blind Fortune turne her giddie Wheele:
    Though Heaven and Earth prove both to me untrue,
    Yet am I still inviolate to You.

52 What do'st thou meane to Cheate me of my Heart,
   To take all Mine, and give me none againe?
   Or have thine Eyes such Magike or that Art,
   That what They get They ever doe retaine?
   Play not the Tyrant, but take some Remorse;
   Rebate thy Spleene, if but for Pittie's sake;
   Or, Cruell, if thou can'st not, let us scorse,
   And for one piece of Thine, my whole heart take.
   But what of Pitty doe I speake to Thee,
   Whose Brest is proofe against Complaint or Prayer?
   Or can I thinke what my Reward shall be
   From that proud Beauty, which was my betrayer?
     What talke I of a Heart, when thou hast none,
     Or if thou hast, it is a flinty one?

Another to the River Ankor

53 Cleere *Ankor*, on whose Silver-sanded shore
   My Soule-shrin'd Saint, my faire IDEA lies,
   O blessed Brooke, whose milke-white Swans adore
   Thy Cristall streame refined by her Eyes,
   Where sweet Myrrh-breathing *Zephire* in the Spring
   Gently distills his Nectar-dropping showres,
   Where Nightingales in *Arden* sit and sing,
   Amongst the daintie Dew-impearled flowres;
   Say thus, faire Brooke, when thou shalt see thy Queene,
   'Loe, heere thy Shepheard spent his wandring yeeres;
   And in these Shades, deare Nymph, he oft hath beene,
   And heere to Thee he sacrific'd his Teares.'
     Faire *Arden*, thou my *Tempe* art alone,
     And thou, sweet *Ankor*, art my *Helicon*.

54 Yet reade at last the storie of my Woe,
   The drerie abstracts of my endlesse Cares,
   With my Life's Sorrow interlined so,
   Smoak'd with my Sighes, and blotted with my Teares;
   The sad Memorialls of my Miseries,
   Pen'd in the griefe of mine afflicted Ghost,

My Live's complaint in dolefull Elegies,
With so pure Love as Time could never boast;
Receive the Incense which I offer here,
By my strong Faith ascending to thy Fame,
My Zeale, my Hope, my Vowes, my Prayse, my Pray'r,
My Soule's Oblations to thy sacred Name:
    Which Name my Muse to highest Heav'ns shall rayse,
    By chaste Desire, true Love, and vertuous Prayse.

55 My faire, if thou wilt register my Love,
A World of Volumes shall thereof arise:
Preserve my Teares, and thou thy Selfe shalt prove
A second Floud, downe rayning from mine Eyes:
Note but my Sighes, and thine Eyes shall behold
The Sun-beames smothered with immortall Smoke;
And if by Thee my Prayers may be enrol'd
They Heaven and Earth to pitty shall provoke;
Looke Thou into my brest, and Thou shalt see
Chaste holy Vowes for my Soule's sacrifice,
That Soule (sweet Maid) which so hath honor'd Thee,
Erecting Trophies to thy Sacred Eyes;
    Those Eyes to my Heart shining ever bright,
    When Darknesse hath obscur'd each other Light.

An allusion to the Eaglets
56 When like an Eaglet I first found my Love,
For that the vertue I thereof would know,
Upon the Nest I set it forth, to prove
If it were of that Kingly kind, or no:
But it no sooner saw my Sunne appeare,
But on her Rayes with open Eyes it stood,
To shew that I had hatch'd it for the Ayre,
And rightly came from that brave mounting Brood:
And when the Plumes were summ'd with sweet desire,
To prove the Pynions, it ascends the Skyes:
Doe what I could, it needsly would aspire

110

To my Soule's Sunne, those two Celestiall Eyes:
  Thus from my Brest, where it was bred alone,
  It after thee is like an Eaglet flowne.

57 You best discern'd of my Mind's inward Eyes,
And yet your Graces outwardly Divine,
Whose deare remembrance in my Bosome lyes,
Too rich a Relique for so poore a Shrine:
You, in whom Nature chose her selfe to view,
When she her owne perfection would admire,
Bestowing all her Excellence on you,
At whose pure Eyes, Love lights his hallow'd Fire:
Ev'n as a Man that in some Trance hath seene
More then his wond'ring utt'rance can unfold,
That rapt in Spirit, in better Worlds hath beene,
So must your prayse distractedly be told;
  Most of all short, when I should shew you most,
  In your perfections so much am I lost.

58 In former times, such as had store of Coyne,
In Warres at home, or when for Conquests bound,
For feare that some their Treasure should purloyne,
Gave it to keepe to Spirits within the Ground;
And to attend it, them as strongly ty'd,
Till they return'd. Home when they never came,
Such as by Art to get the same have try'd,
From the strong Spirit by no meanes force the same;
Neerer Men come, That further flyes away,
Striving to hold it strongly in the Deepe.
Ev'n as this Spirit, so you alone doe play
With those rich Beauties Heav'n gives you to keepe:
  Pittie so left to th'coldnesse of your Blood,
  Not to availe you, nor doe others good.

To Proverbe
59 As love and I, late harbour'd in one Inne,
With Proverbs thus each other intertaine:

'In Love there is no lack,' thus I begin;
'Faire words make Fooles,' replyeth he againe;
'Who spares to speake doth spare to speed' (quoth I);
'As well (sayth he) *too forward, as too slow.'*
'Fortune assists the boldest,' I reply;
'A hastie Man (quoth he) *ne'r wanted Woe.'*
'Labour is light, where Love (quoth I) *doth pay.'*
(Saith he) *'Light Burthen's heavy, if farre borne.'*
(Quoth I) *'The Maine lost, cast the By away.'*
'You have spunne a faire Thred', he replyes in scorne.
   And having thus awhile each other thwarted,
   Fooles as we met, so Fooles againe we parted.

60   Define my Weale, and tell the joyes of Heaven;
Expresse my Woes, and shew the paines of Hell;
Declare what Fate unlucky Starres have given,
And aske a World upon my Life to dwell.
Make knowne the Faith that Fortune could not move;
Compare my Worth with others' base Desert;
Let Vertue be the Touch-stone of my Love,
So may the Heavens read wonders in my Heart.
Behold the Clouds which have eclips'd my Sunne,
And view the Crosses which my course doe let;
Tell Me, if ever since the World begunne,
So Faire a rising had so Foule a set:
   And see if Time (if he would strive to prove)
   Can shew a Second to so pure a Love.

61   Since ther's no helpe, Come let us kisse and part,
Nay, I have done: You get no more of Me,
And I am glad, yea glad with all my heart,
That thus so cleanly I my Selfe can free;
Shake hands for ever, Cancell all our Vowes,
And when We meet at any time againe,
Be it not seene in either of our Browes,
That We one jot of former Love reteyne:
Now at the last gaspe of Love's latest Breath,

When his Pulse fayling, Passion speechlesse lies,
When Faith is kneeling by his bed of Death,
And Innocence is closing up his eyes,
    Now if thou would'st, when all have given him over,
    From Death to Life thou might'st him yet recover.

62   When first I Ended, then I first Began,
    Then more I Traveld, further from my Rest;
    Where most I Lost, there most of all I Wan,
    Pined with Hunger, rising from a Feast.
    Me thinkes I Flie, yet want I legges to Goe;
    Wise in Conceit, in Act a very sot;
    Ravish'd with Joy amid'st a hell of Woe;
    What most I Seeme, that surest am I Not.
    I build my Hopes a world above the Skie,
    Yet with the Mole I creepe into the Earth;
    In plenty I am starv'd with Penurie,
    And yet I Surfet in the greatest Dearth:
        I have, I want; Despaire, and yet Desire,
        Burn'd in a Sea of yce, and drown'd amidst a fire.

63   Truce, gentle Love, a Parly now I crave;
    Me thinkes 'tis long since first these Warres begun;
    Nor thou, nor I, the better yet can have:
    Bad is the Match, where neither partie wonne.
    I offer free Conditions of faire Peace,
    My Heart for Hostage that it shall remaine;
    Discharge our Forces, here let Malice cease,
    So for my Pledge thou give me Pledge againe.
    Or if no thing but Death will serve thy turne,
    Still thirsting for subversion of my state,
    Doe what thou canst, raze, massacre, and burne,
    Let the World see the utmost of thy hate:
        I send defiance, since if overthrowne,
        Thou vanquishing, the Conquest is mine owne.

FINIS

Edmund Spenser

Amoretti

Sonnet 1

Happy ye leaves when as those lilly hands,
    which hold my life in their dead-doing might
    shall handle you and hold in love's soft bands,
    lyke captives trembling at the victor's sight.
And happy lines, on which with starry light
    those lamping eyes will deigne sometimes to look
    and reade the sorrowes of my dying spright,
    written with teares in hart's close bleeding book.
And happy rymes, bath'd in the sacred brooke
    of *Helicon* whence she derived is,
    when ye behold that Angel's blessed looke,
    my soule's long-lacked foode, my heaven's blis.
Leaves, lines, and rymes, seeke her to please alone,
    whom if ye please, I care for other none.

Sonnet 2

Unquiet thought, whom at the first I bred,
    of th'inward bale of my love-pined hart,
    and sithens have with sighes and sorrowes fed,
    till greater then my wombe thou woxen art;
Breake forth at length out of the inner part
    in which thou lurkest lyke to viper's brood,
    and seeke some succour both to ease my smart
    and also to sustayne thy selfe with food.
But if in presence of that fayrest proud

thou chance to come, fall lowly at her feet,
and with meeke humblesse and afflicted mood,
pardon for thee, and grace for me intreat.
Which if she graunt, then live and my love cherish;
if not, die soone, and I with thee will perish.

Sonnet 3

The soverayne beauty which I doo admyre,
witnesse the world how worthy to be prayzed;
the light wherof hath kindled heavenly fyre
in my fraile spirit by her from basenesse raysed:
That being now with her huge brightnesse dazed,
base thing I can no more endure to view,
but looking still on her I stand amazed
at wondrous sight of so celestiall hew.
So when my toung would speak her praises dew,
it stopped is with thought's astonishment;
and when my pen would write her titles true,
it ravisht is with fancie's wonderment:
Yet in my hart I then both speake and write
the wonder that my wit cannot endite.

Sonnet 4

New yeare forth looking out of Janus' gate,
doth seeme to promise hope of new delight;
and bidding th'old Adieu, his passed date
bids all old thoughts to die in dumpish spright:
And calling forth out of sad Winter's night
fresh love, that long hath slept in cheerlesse bower,
wils him awake, and soone about him dight
his wanton wings and darts of deadly power.
For lusty spring, now in his timely howre,
is ready to come forth him to receive,
and warnes the Earth with divers-colord flowre
to decke hir selfe, and her faire mantle weave.
Then you, faire flowre, in whom fresh youth doth raine,
prepare your selfe new love to entertaine.

Sonnet 5

Rudely thou wrongest my deare hart's desire,
    in finding fault with her too portly pride:
    the thing which I doo most in her admire
    is of the world unworthy most envide.
For in those lofty lookes is close implide
    scorn of base things, and sdeigne of foule dishonor,
    thretning rash eies which gaze on her so wide,
    that loosely they ne dare to looke upon her.
Such pride is praise, such portliness is honor,
    that boldned innocence beares in hir eies;
    and her faire countenance like a goodly banner
    spreds in defiaunce of all enemies.
Was never in this world ought worthy tride,
    without some spark of such self-pleasing pride.

Sonnet 6

Be nought dismayed that her unmoved mind
    doth still persist in her rebellious pride:
    such love not lyke to lusts of baser kynd,
    the harder wonne, the firmer will abide.
The durefull Oake, whose sap is not yet dride,
    is long ere it conceive the kindling fyre;
    but when it once doth burne, it doth divide
    great heat, and makes his flames to heaven aspire.
So hard it is to kindle new desire
    in gentle brest that shall endure for ever:
    deepe is the wound that dints the parts entire
    with chast affects, that naught but death can sever.
Then thinke not long in taking litle paine,
    to knit the knot, that ever shall remaine.

Sonnet 7

Fayre eyes, the myrrour of my mazed hart,
    what wondrous vertue is contaynd in you
    the which both lyfe and death forth from you dart
    into the object of your mighty view?

116

For when ye mildly looke with lovely hew,
   then is my soule with life and love inspired:
   but when ye lowre, or looke on me askew,
   then doe I die, as one with lightning fyred.
But since that lyfe is more than death desyred,
   looke ever lovely, as becomes you best,
   that your bright beams of my weak eies admyred,
   may kindle living fire within my brest.
Such life should be the honor of your light,
   such death the sad ensample of your might.

Sonnet 8

More then most faire, full of the living fire,
   kindled above unto the maker neere:
   no eies but joyes, in which al powers conspire
   that to the world naught else be counted deare:
Thrugh your bright beams doth not the blinded guest
   shoot out his darts to base affections' wound?
   but Angels come to lead fraile mindes to rest
   in chast desires on heavenly beauty bound.
You frame my thoughts and fashion me within;
   you stop my toung, and teach my hart to speake;
   you calme the storme that passion did begin,
   strong thrugh your cause, but by your vertue weak.
Dark is the world, where your light shined never;
   well is he borne, that may behold you ever.

Sonnet 9

Long-while I sought to what I might compare
   those powrefull eies, which lighten my dark spright,
   yet find I nought on earth to which I dare
   resemble th'ymage of their goodly light.
Not to the Sun: for they doo shine by night;
   nor to the Moone: for they are changed never;
   nor to the Starres: for they have purer sight;
   nor to the fire: for they consume not ever;
Nor to the lightning: for they still persever;

nor to the Diamond: for they are more tender;
    nor unto Christall: for nought may them sever;
    nor unto glasse: such basenesse mought offend her;
Then to the Maker selfe they likest be,
    whose light doth lighten all that here we see.

Sonnet 10

Unrighteous Lord of love, what law is this,
    that me thou makest thus tormented be,
    the whiles she lordeth in licentious blisse
    of her freewill, scorning both thee and me?
See how the Tyrannesse doth joy to see
    the huge massacres which her eyes do make,
    and humbled harts brings captives unto thee,
    that thou of them mayst mightie vengeance take.
But her proud hart doe thou a little shake
    and that high look, with which she doth comptroll
    all this world's pride, bow to a baser make,
    and al her faults in thy black booke enroll;
That I may laugh at her in equal sort,
    as she doth laugh at me and makes my pain her sport.

Sonnet 11

Dayly when I do seeke and sew for peace,
    and hostages doe offer for my truth,
    she, cruell warriour, doth her selfe addresse
    to battell, and the weary war renew'th:
Ne wilbe moov'd with reason or with rewth
    to graunt small respit to my restlesse toile,
    but greedily her fell intent poursewth,
    of my poore life to make unpittied spoile.
Yet my poore life, all sorrowes to assoyle,
    I would her yield, her wrath to pacify:
    but then she seekes with torment and turmoyle
    to force me live and will not let me dy.
All paine hath end and every war hath peace,
    but mine no price nor prayer may surcease.

Sonnet 12

One day I sought with her hart-thrilling eies
 to make a truce and termes to entertaine,
 all fearelesse then of so false enimies,
 which sought me to entrap in treason's traine.
So as I then disarmed did remaine,
 a wicked ambush which lay hidden long
 in the close covert of her guilefull eyen,
 thence breaking forth, did thick about me throng.
Too feeble I t'abide the brunt so strong,
 was forst to yeeld my selfe into their hands:
 who me captiving streight with rigorous wrong
 have ever since me kept in cruell bands.
So Ladie now to you I doo complaine
 against your eies that justice I may gaine.

Sonnet 13

In that proud port, which her so goodly graceth,
 whiles her faire face she reares up to the skie,
 and to the ground her eie lids low embaseth,
 most goodly temperature ye may descry,
Myld humblesse mixt with awfull maiesty:
 for looking on the earth whence she was borne,
 her minde remembreth her mortalitie,
 what so is fayrest shall to earth returne:
But that same lofty countenance seemes to scorne
 base thing, and thinke how she to heaven may clime,
 treading downe earth as lothsome and forlorne,
 that hinders heavenly thoughts with drossy slime.
Yet lowly still vouchsafe to looke on me:
 such lowlinesse shall make you lofty be.

Sonnet 14

Retourne agayne, my forces late dismayd,
 unto the siege by you abandon'd quite:
 great shame it is to leave like one afrayd
 so fayre a peece for one repulse so light.

Gaynst such strong castles needeth greater might
    then those small forts which ye were wont belay;
    such haughty mynds enur'd to hardy fight
    disdayne to yield unto the first assay.
Bring therefore all the forces that ye may,
    and lay incessant battery to her heart,
    playnts, prayers, vowes, ruth, sorrow, and dismay;
    those engins can the proudest love convert.
And if those fayle, fall downe and dy before her;
    so dying live, and living do adore her.

Sonnet 15

Ye tradefull Merchants that with weary toyle
    do seeke most pretious things to make your gain,
    and both the Indias of their treasures spoile,
    what needeth you to seeke so farre in vaine?
For loe, my love doth in her selfe containe
    all this world's riches that may farre be found:
    if Saphyres, loe her eies be Saphyres plaine;
    if Rubies, loe hir lips be Rubies sound:
If Pearles, hir teeth be pearles both pure and round;
    if Yvorie, her forhead yvory weene;
    if Gold, her locks are finest gold on ground;
    if silver, her faire hands are silver sheene:
But that which fairest is, but few behold,
    her mind adornd with vertues manifold.

Sonnet 16

One day as I unwarily did gaze
    on those fayre eyes, my love's immortall light,
    the whiles my stonisht hart stood in amaze,
    through sweet illusion of her looke's delight;
I mote perceive how in her glauncing sight
    legions of loves with little wings did fly,
    darting their deadly arrowes fyry bright
    at every rash beholder passing by.
One of those archers closely I did spy,

ayming his arrow at my very hart;
    when suddenly with twincle of her eye,
    the Damzell broke his misintended dart.
Had she not so doon, sure I had bene slayne,
    yet as it was, I hardly scap't with paine.

Sonnet 17

The glorious pourtraict of that Angel's face,
    made to amaze weake men's confused skil,
    and this world's worthlesse glory to embase,
    what pen, what pencill can expresse her fill?
For though he colours could devise at will,
    and eke his learned hand at pleasure guide,
    least trembling it his workmanship should spill,
    yet many wondrous things there are beside.
The sweet eye-glaunces, that like arrowes glide,
    the charming smiles, that rob sence from the hart;
    the lovely pleasance and the lofty pride,
    cannot expressed be by any art.
A greater craftesman's hand thereto doth neede,
    that can expresse the life of things indeed.

Sonnet 18

The rolling wheele that runneth often round,
    the hardest steele in tract of time doth teare;
    and drizling drops that often doe redound,
    the firmest flint doth in continuance weare.
Yet cannot I with many a dropping teare
    and long intreaty soften her hard hart,
    that she will once vouchsafe my plaint to heare,
    or looke with pitty on my payneful smart.
But when I pleade, she bids me play my part,
    and when I weep, she sayes teares are but water:
    and when I sigh, she sayes I know the art,
    and when I waile, she turnes hir selfe to laughter.
So doe I weepe, and wayle, and pleade in vaine,
    whiles she as steele and flint doth still remayne.

Sonnet 19

The merry Cuckow, messenger of Spring,
    his trompet shrill hath thrise already sounded,
    that warnes al lovers wayt upon their king,
    who now is comming forth with girland crouned:
With noyse whereof the quyre of Byrds resounded
    their anthemes sweet devized of love's prayse,
    that all the woods theyr ecchoes back rebounded,
    as if they knew the meaning of their layes.
But mongst them all which did Love's honor rayse,
    no word was heard of her that most it ought,
    but she his precept proudly disobayes,
    and doth his ydle message set at nought.
Therefore O love, unlesse she turne to thee
    ere Cuckow end, let her a rebell be.

Sonnet 20

In vaine I seeke and sew to her for grace,
    and doe myne humbled hart before her poure;
    the whiles her foot she in my necke doth place,
    and tread my life downe in the lowly floure.
And yet the Lyon that is Lord of power,
    and reigneth over every beast in field,
    in his most pride disdeigneth to devoure
    the silly lambe that to his might doth yield.
But she more cruell and more salvage-wylde
    then either Lyon or the Lyonesse
    shames not to be with guiltlesse bloud defylde,
    but taketh glory in her cruelnesse.
Fayrer then fayrest, let none ever say,
    that ye were blooded in a yeelded pray.

Sonnet 21

Was it the worke of nature or of Art
    which tempred so the feature of her face,
    that pride and meeknesse, mixt by equall part,
    doe both appeare t'adorne her beautie's grace?

For with mild pleasance, which doth pride displace,
    she to her love doth lookers' eyes allure;
    and with sterne countenance back again doth chace
    their looser lookes that stir up lustes impure.
With such strange termes her eyes she doth inure,
    that with one looke she doth my life dismay,
    and with another doth it streight recure;
    her smile me drawes, her frowne me drives away.
Thus doth she traine and teach me with her lookes,
    such art of eyes I never read in bookes.

Sonnet 22

This holy season fit to fast and pray,
    men to devotion ought to be inclynd:
    therefore, I lykewise on so holy day,
    for my sweet Saynt some service fit will find.
Her temple fayre is built within my mind,
    in which her glorious ymage placed is,
    on which my thoughts doo day and night attend
    lyke sacred priests that never thinke amisse.
There I to her, as th'author of my blisse,
    will builde an altar to appease her yre;
    and on the same my hart will sacrifise,
    burning in flames of pure and chast desyre:
The which vouchsafe, O goddesse, to accept,
    amongst thy deerest relicks to be kept.

Sonnet 23

Penelope for her *Ulisses'* sake,
    deviz'd a Web her wooers to deceave;
    in which the worke that she all day did make
    the same at night she did againe unreave.
Such subtile craft my Damzell doth conceave,
    th'importune suit of my desire to shonne:
    for all that I in many dayes doo weave,
    in one short houre I find by her undonne.
So when I thinke to end that I begonne,

I must begin and never bring to end;
    for with one looke she spils that long I sponne,
    and with one word my whole year's work doth rend.
Such labour like the Spyder's web I fynd,
    whose fruitlesse worke is broken with least wynd.

Sonnet 24

When I behold that beautie's wonderment,
    and rare perfection of each goodly part,
    of nature's skill the onely complement,
    I honor and admire the maker's art.
But when I feele the bitter balefull smart
    which her fayre eyes unwares doe worke in mee,
    that death out of theyr shiny beames doe dart,
    I thinke that I a new *Pandora* see;
Whom all the Gods in councell did agree
    into this sinfull world from heaven to send,
    that she to wicked men a scourge should bee,
    for all their faults with which they did offend.
But since ye are my scourge I will intreat,
    that for my faults ye will me gently beat.

Sonnet 25

How long shall this lyke-dying lyfe endure,
    and know no end of her owne mysery,
    but wast and weare away in termes unsure,
    twixt feare and hope depending doubtfully?
Yet better were attonce to let me die,
    and shew the last ensample of your pride,
    then to torment me thus with cruelty,
    to prove your powre, which I too wel have tride.
But yet if in your hardned brest ye hide
    a close intent at last to shew me grace,
    than all the woes and wrecks which I abide,
    as meanes of blisse I gladly wil embrace;
And wish that more and greater they might be,
    that greater meede at last may turne to mee.

Edmund Spenser

Sonnet 26

Sweet is the Rose, but growes upon a brere;
    sweet is the Junipere, but sharpe his bough;
    sweet is the Eglantine, but pricketh nere;
    sweet is the firbloome, but his braunches rough.
Sweet is the Cypresse, but his rynd is tough;
    sweet is the nut, but bitter is his pill;
    sweet is the broome-flowre, but yet sowre enough;
    and sweet is Moly, but his root is ill.
So every sweet with soure is tempred still,
    that maketh it be coveted the more:
    for easie things that may be got at will,
    most sorts of men doe set but little store.
Why then should I accoumpt of little paine,
    that endlesse pleasure shall unto me gaine?

Sonnet 27

Faire proud, now tell me why should faire be proud,
    sith all world's glorie is but drosse uncleane,
    and in the shade of death it selfe shall shroud,
    how ever now thereof ye little weene.
That goodly Idoll now so gay beseene,
    shall doffe her fleshe's borowd fayre attyre,
    and be forgot as it had never beene,
    that many now much worship and admire.
Ne any then shall after it inquire,
    ne any mention shall thereof remaine,
    but what this verse, that never shall expyre,
    shall to you purchas with her thankles paine.
Faire be no lenger proud of that shall perish,
    but that which shal you make immortall, cherish.

Sonnet 28

The laurell leafe, which you this day doe weare,
    gives me great hope of your relenting mynd;
    for since it is the badg which I doe beare,
    ye bearing it doe seeme to me inclind:

The powre thereof, which ofte in me I find,
    let it lykewise your gentle brest inspire
    with sweet infusion, and put you in mind
    of that proud mayd, whom now those leaves attyre:
Proud *Daphne* scorning Phæbus' lovely fyre,
    on the Thessalian shore from him did flee;
    for which the gods in theyr revengefull yre
    did her transforme into a laurell tree.
Then fly no more, fayre love, from Phebus' chace,
    but in your brest his leafe and love embrace.

Sonnet 29

See how the stubborne damzell doth deprave
    my simple meaning with disdaynfull scorne,
    and by the bay which I unto her gave,
    accoumpts my selfe her captive quite forlorne.
The bay (quoth she) is of the victours borne,
    yielded them by the vanquisht as theyr meeds,
    and they therewith doe poetes' heads adorne,
    to sing the glory of their famous deedes.
But sith she will the conquest challeng needs,
    let her accept me as her faithfull thrall,
    that her great triumph which my skill exceeds,
    I may in trump of fame blaze over all.
Then would I decke her head with glorious bayes,
    and fill the world with her victorious prayse.

Sonnet 30

My love is lyke to yse, and I to fyre:
    how comes it then that this her cold so great
    is not dissolv'd through my so hot desyre,
    but harder growes the more I her intreat?
Or how comes it that my exceeding heat
    is not delayed by her hart frosen cold,
    but that I burne much more in boyling sweat,
    and feele my flames augmented manifold?
What more miraculous thing may be told

that fire, which all thing melts, should harden yse:
    and yse which is congeald with sencelesse cold,
    should kindle fyre by wonderfull devyse?
Such is the powre of love in gentle mind
    that it can alter all the course of kynd.

Sonnet 31

Ah why hath nature to so hard a hart
    given so goodly giftes of beautie's grace,
    whose pryde depraves each other better part,
    and all those pretious ornaments deface;
Sith to all other beastes of bloody race
    a dreadfull countenaunce she given hath,
    that with theyr terrour al the rest may chace,
    and warne to shun the daunger of theyr wrath?
But my proud one doth worke the greater scath
    through sweet allurement of her lovely hew,
    that she the better may in bloody bath
    of such poore thralls her cruell hands embrew.
But did she know how ill these two accord,
    such cruelty she would have soone abhord.

Sonnet 32

The paynefull smith with force of fervent heat
    the hardest yron soone doth mollify,
    that with his heavy sledge he can it beat,
    and fashion to what he it list apply.
Yet cannot all these flames in which I fry
    her hart more harde then yron soft awhit,
    ne all the playnts and prayers with which I
    doe beat on th'andvyle of her stubberne wit:
But still the more she fervent sees my fit,
    the more she frieseth in her wilfull pryde,
    and harder growes the harder she is smit,
    with all the playnts which to her be applyde.
What then remaines but I to ashes burne,
    and she to stones at length all frosen turne?

Sonnet 33

Great wrong I doe, I can it not deny,
    to that most sacred Empresse, my dear dred,
    not finishing her Queene of faery,
    that mote enlarge her living prayses dead:
But Lodwick, this of grace to me aread:
    doe ye not thinck th'accomplishment of it
    sufficient worke for one man's simple head,
    all were it as the rest but rudely writ?
How then should I without another wit
    thinck ever to endure so taedious toyle,
    sins that this one is tost with troublous fit
    of a proud love, that doth my spirite spoyle?
Ceasse then, till she vouchsafe to grawnt me rest,
    or lend you me another living brest.

Sonnet 34

Lyke as a ship that through the Ocean wyde,
    by conduct of some star doth make her way,
    whenas a storme hath dimd her trusty guyde,
    out of her course doth wander far astray:
So I, whose star, that wont with her bright ray
    me to direct, with cloudes is overcast,
    doe wander now in darknesse and dismay,
    through hidden perils round about me plast.
Yet hope I well that when this storme is past
    my *Helice*, the lodestar of my lyfe,
    will shine again, and lookc on me at last,
    with lovely light to cleare my cloudy grief.
Till then I wander carefull comfortlesse,
    in secret sorow and sad pensivenesse.

Sonnet 35

My hungry eyes, through greedy covetize
    still to behold the object of their paine,
    with no contentment can themselves suffize,
    but having pine and having not, complaine.

For lacking it, they cannot lyfe sustayne,
   and having it, they gaze on it the more;
   in their amazement lyke *Narcissus* vaine
   whose eyes him starv'd: so plenty makes me poore.
Yet are mine eyes so filled with the store
   of that faire sight, that nothing else they brooke,
   but lothe the things which they did like before,
   and can no more endure on them to looke.
All this world's glory seemeth vayne to me,
   and all their showes but shadowes saving she.

Sonnet 36

Tell me when shall these wearie woes have end,
   or shall their ruthlesse torment never cease;
   but al my dayes in pining languor spend,
   without hope of aswagement or release?
Is there no meanes for me to purchace peace,
   or make agreement with her thrilling eyes,
   but that their cruelty doth still increace,
   and dayly more augment my miseryes?
But when ye have shewed all extremityes,
   then thinke how litle glory ye have gayned
   by slaying him, whose lyfe though ye despyse,
   mote have your life in honour long maintayned.
But by his death which some perhaps will mone,
   ye shall condemned be of many a one.

Sonnet 37

What guyle is this, that those her golden tresses,
   she doth attyre under a net of gold,
   and with sly skill so cunningly them dresses,
   that which is gold or heare may scarse be told?
Is it that men's frayle eyes, which gaze too bold,
   she may entangle in that golden snare;
   and being caught, may craftily enfold
   theyr weaker harts, which are not wel aware?
Take heed therefore, myne eyes, how ye doe stare

henceforth too rashly on that guilefull net,
    in which if ever ye entrapped are,
    out of her bands ye by no meanes shall get.
Fondnesse it were for any being free
    to covet fetters, though they golden bee.

Sonnet 38

Arion, when through tempest's cruel wracke,
    he forth was thrown into the greedy seas,
    through the sweet musick which his harp did make
    allur'd a Dolphin him from death to ease.
But my rude musick, which was wont to please
    some dainty eares, cannot with any skill
    the dreadfull tempest of her wrath appease,
    nor move the Dolphin from her stubborne will;
But in her pride she dooth persever still,
    all carelesse how my life for her decayse:
    yet with one word she can it save or spill:
    to spill were pitty, but to save were prayse.
Chose rather to be praysd for dooing good
    then to be blam'd for spilling guiltlesse blood.

Sonnet 39

Sweet smile, the daughter of the Queene of love,
    expressing all thy mother's powrefull art,
    with which she wonts to temper angry *Jove,*
    when all the gods he threats with thundring dart:
Sweet is thy vertue as thy selfe sweet art,
    for when on me thou shinedst late in sadnesse,
    a melting pleasance ran through every part,
    and me revived with hart-robbing gladnesse.
Whylest rapt with Joy resembling heavenly madnes,
    my soule was ravisht quite as in a traunce;
    and feeling thence no more her sorowe's sadnesse,
    fed on the fulnesse of that chearefull glaunce.
More sweet than Nectar or Ambrosiall meat
    seemd every bit, which thenceforth I did eat.

130

Sonnet 40

Mark when she smiles with amiable cheare,
    and tell me whereto can ye lyken it,
    when on each eyelid sweetly doe appeare
    an hundred Graces as in shade to sit.
Lykest it seemeth in my simple wit
    unto the fayre sunshine in somer's day,
    that when a dreadfull storme away is flit,
    thrugh the broad world doth spred his goodly ray:
At sight whereof each bird that sits on spray,
    and every beast that to his den was fled,
    comes forth afresh out of their late dismay,
    and to the light lift up theyr drouping hed.
So my storme-beaten hart likewise is cheared
    with that sunshine when cloudy looks are cleared.

Sonnet 41

Is it her nature or is it her will,
    to be so cruell to an humbled foe?
    if nature, then she may it mend with skill;
    if will, then she at will may will forgoe.
But if her nature and her wil be so,
    that she will plague the man that loves her most,
    and take delight t'encrease a wretche's woe,
    then all her nature's goodly guifts are lost:
And that same glorious beautie's ydle boast
    is but a bayt such wretches to beguile,
    as, being long in her love's tempest tost,
    she meanes at last to make her piteous spoyle.
O fayrest fayre let never it be named,
    that so fayre beauty was so fowly shamed.

Sonnet 42

The love which me so cruelly tormenteth
    so pleasing is in my extreamest paine,
    that all the more my sorrow it augmenteth,
    the more I love and doe embrace my bane.

Ne doe I wish (for wishing were but vaine)
    to be acquit fro my continuall smart,
    but joy her thrall for ever to remayne,
    and yield for pledge my poore captyved hart:
The which that it from her may never start,
    let her, yf please her, bynd with adamant chayne;
    and from all wandring loves which mote pervart
    his safe assurance, strongly it restrayne.
Onely let her abstaine from cruelty,
    and doe me not before my time to dy.

Sonnet 43

Shall I then silent be or shall I speake?
    and if I speake, her wrath renew I shall:
    and if I silent be, my hart will breake,
    or choked be with overflowing gall.
What tyranny is this both my hart to thrall,
    and eke my toung with proud restraint to tie,
    that nether I may speake nor thinke at all,
    but like a stupid stock in silence die!
Yet I my hart with silence secretly
    will teach to speak, and my just cause to plead;
    and eke mine eies with meeke humility,
    love-learned letters to her eyes to read:
Which her deep wit, that true hart's thought can spel,
    wil soone conceive, and learne to construe well.

Sonnet 44

When those renoumed noble Peres of Greece,
    thrugh stubborn pride amongst themselves did jar,
    forgetfull of the famous golden fleece,
    then *Orpheus* with his harp theyr strife did bar.
But this continuall cruell civill warre,
    the which my selfe against my selfe doe make,
    whilest my weak powres of passions warreid arre,
    no skill can stint nor reason can aslake.
But when in hand my tunelesse harp I take,

then doe I more augment my foe's despight;
    and griefe renew, and passions doe awake,
    to battaile fresh against my self to fight:
Mongst whome the more I seeke to settle peace,
    the more I fynd their malice to increace.

Sonnet 45

Leave, lady, in your glasse of christall clene
    your goodly selfe for evermore to vew,
    and in my selfe, my inward selfe I meane,
    most lively-lyke behold your semblant trew.
Within my hart, though hardly it can shew
    thing so divine to vew of earthly eye,
    the fayre Idea of your celestiall hew
    and every part remaines immortally:
And were it not that through your cruelty
    with sorrow dimmed and deformd it were,
    the goodly ymage of your visnomy
    clearer then christall would therein appere.
But if your selfe in me ye playne will see,
    remove the cause by which your fayre beames darkned be.

Sonnet 46

When my abode's prefixed time is spent,
    my cruell fayre streight bids me wend my way:
    but then from heaven most hideous stormes are sent
    as willing me against her will to stay.
Whom then shall I or heaven or her obay?
    the heavens know best what is the best for me:
    but as she will, whose will my life doth sway,
    my lower heaven, so it perforce must bee.
But ye high hevens, that all this sorrowe see,
    sith all your tempests cannot hold me backe,
    aswage your stormes, or else both you and she
    will both together me too sorely wrack.
Enough it is for one man to sustaine
    the stormes, which she alone on me doth raine.

Sonnet 47

Trust not the treason of those smyling lookes,
    untill ye have theyr guylefull traynes well tryde;
    for they are lyke but unto golden hookes,
    that from the foolish fish theyr bayts doe hyde:
So she with flattring smyles weake harts doth guyde
    unto her love, and tempte to theyr decay,
    whome being caught, she kills with cruell pryde,
    and feeds at pleasure on the wretched pray:
Yet even whylst her bloody hands them slay,
    her eyes looke lovely and upon them smyle,
    that they take pleasure in her cruell play,
    and dying doe them selves of payne beguyle.
O mighty charm which makes men love theyr bane,
    and thinck they dy with pleasure, live with payne.

Sonnet 48

Innocent paper whom too cruell hand
    did make the matter to avenge her yre,
    and ere she could thy cause wel understand,
    did sacrifize unto the greedy fyre:
Well worthy thou to have found better hyre
    then so bad end for hereticks ordayned:
    yet heresy nor treason didst conspire,
    but plead thy maister's cause unjustly payned:
Whom she, all carelesse of his griefe, constrayned
    to utter forth th' anguish of his hart,
    and would not heare, when he to her complayned
    the piteous passion of his dying smart.
Yet live for ever, though against her will,
    and speake her good, though she requite it ill.

Sonnet 49

Fayre cruell, why are ye so fierce and cruell?
    is it because your eyes have powre to kill?
    then know, that mercy is the mightie's jewell,
    and greater glory thinke to save, then spill.

But if it be your pleasure and proud will
    to shew the powre of your imperious eyes,
    then not on him that never thought you ill,
    but bend your force against your enemyes.
Let them feele th'utmost of your crueltyes,
    and kill with looks, as Cockatrices doo:
    but him that at your footstoole humbled lies,
    with mercifull regard, give mercy too.
Such mercy shal you make admyred to be,
    so shall you live by giving life to me.

Sonnet 50

Long languishing in double malady
    of my hart's wound and of my bodie's greife,
    there came to me a leach that would apply
    fit medicines for my bodie's best reliefe.
'Vayne man' (quod I) 'that hast but little priefe,
    in deep discovery of the mynd's disease,
    is not the hart of all the body chiefe,
    and rules the members as it selfe doth please?
Then with some cordialls seeke first to appease
    the inward languour of my wounded hart,
    and then my body shall have shortly ease:
    but such sweet cordialls passe Physition's art.
Then, my lyfe's Leach, doe you your skill reveale,
    and with one salve both hart and body heale.'

Sonnet 51

Doe I not see that fayrest ymages
    of hardest Marble are of purpose made,
    for that they should endure through many ages,
    ne let theyr famous moniments to fade?
Why then doe I, untrainde in lover's trade,
    her hardnes blame which I should more commend,
    sith never ought was excellent assayde,
    which was not hard t'atchive and bring to end?
Ne ought so hard, but he that would attend,

mote soften it and to his will allure:
so doe I hope her stubborne hart to bend,
and that it then more stedfast will endure.
Onely my paines wil be the more to get her,
but having her, my joy wil be the greater.

Sonnet 52

So oft as homeward I from her depart,
I goe lyke one that, having lost the field,
is prisoner led away with heavy hart,
despoyld of warlike armes and knowen shield.
So doe I now my selfe a prisoner yeeld
to sorrow and to solitary paine,
from presence of my dearest deare exylde,
longwhile alone in languor to remaine.
There let no thought of joy or pleasure vaine
dare to approch, that may my solace breed:
but sudden dumps and drery sad disdayne
of all world's gladnesse more my torment feed.
So I her absens will my prenaunce make,
that of her presens I my meed may take.

Sonnet 53

The Panther knowing that his spotted hyde
doth please all beasts but that his looks them fray,
within a bush his dreadfull head doth hide,
to let them gaze whylest he on them may pray.
Right so my cruell fayre with me doth play:
for with the goodly semblant of her hew,
she doth allure me to mine owne decay,
and then no mercy will unto me shew.
Great shame it is, thing so divine in view
made for to be the world's most ornament,
to make the bayte her gazers to embrew:
good shames to be to ill an instrument.
But mercy doth with beautie best agree,
as in theyr maker ye them best may see.

Sonnet 54

Of this world's Theatre in which we stay,
   my love lyke the Spectator ydly sits
   beholding me that all the pageants play,
   disguysing diversly my troubled wits.
Sometimes I joy when glad occasion fits,
   and mask in myrth lyke to a Comedy:
   soone after when my joy to sorrow flits,
   I waile and make my woes a Tragedy.
Yet she beholding me with constant eye,
   delights not in my merth nor rues my smart:
   but when I laugh she mocks, and when I cry
   she laughes, and hardens evermore her hart.
What then can move her? if nor merth nor mone,
   she is no woman, but a sencelesse stone.

Sonnet 55

So oft as I her beauty doe behold,
   and therewith doe her cruelty compare,
   I marvaile of what substance was the mould
   the which her made attonce so cruell-faire.
Not earth; for her high thoghts more heavenly are:
   not water; for her love doth burne like fyre:
   not ayre; for she is not so light or rare:
   not fyre; for she doth friese with faint desire.
Then needs another Element inquire
   whereof she mote be made; that is the skye:
   for to the heaven her haughty lookes aspire,
   and eke her mind is pure immortall hye.
Then sith to heaven ye lykened are the best,
   be lyke in mercy as in all the rest.

Sonnet 56

Fayre ye be sure, but cruell and unkind,
   as is a Tygre that with greedinesse
   hunts after bloud, when he by chance doth find
   a feeble beast, doth felly him oppresse.

137

Fayre be ye sure, but proud and pittilesse,
    as is a storme, that all things doth prostrate,
    finding a tree alone all comfortlesse,
    beats on it strongly it to ruinate.
Fayre be ye sure, but hard and obstinate,
    as is a rocke amidst the raging floods,
    gaynst which a ship, of succour desolate,
    doth suffer wreck both of her selfe and goods.
That ship, that tree, and that same beast am I,
    whom ye doe wreck, doe ruine, and destroy.

Sonnet 57

Sweet warriour, when shall I have peace with you?
    high time it is, this warre now ended were,
    which I no lenger can endure to sue,
    ne your incessant battry more to beare:
So weake my powres, so sore my wounds appeare,
    that wonder is how I should live a jot,
    seeing my hart through-launched every where
    with thousand arrowes, which your eies have shot.
Yet shoot ye sharpely still, and spare me not,
    but glory thinke to make these cruel stoures.
    ye cruell one, what glory can be got
    in slaying him that would live gladly yours?
Make peace therefore, and graunt me timely grace,
    that al my wounds wil heale in little space.

Sonnet 58
By her that is most assured to her selfe.

Weake is th'assurance that weake flesh reposeth
    in her owne powre, and scorneth other's ayde:
    that soonest fals when as she most supposeth
    her selfe assurd, and is of nought affrayd.
All flesh is frayle, and all her strength unstayd,
    like a vaine bubble blowen up with ayre:
    devouring tyme and changeful chance have prayd
    her glorie's pride that none may it repayre.

Ne none so rich or wise, so strong or fayre,
    but fayleth, trusting on his owne assurance:
    and he that standeth on the hyghest stayre
    fals lowest, for on earth nought hath enduraunce.
Why then doe ye, proud fayre, misdeeme so farre,
    that to your selfe ye most assured arre?

Sonnet 59

Thrise happie she, that is so well assured
    unto her selfe and setled so in hart;
    that nether will for better be allured,
    ne feard with worse to any chaunce to start;
But like a steddy ship doth strongly part
    the raging waves and keepes her course aright;
    ne ought for tempest doth from it depart,
    ne ought for fayrer weather's false delight.
Such selfe assurance need not feare the spight
    of grudging foes, ne favour seek of friends,
    but in the stay of her owne stedfast might,
    nether to one her selfe nor other bends.
Most happy she that most assured doth rest,
    but he most happy who such one loves best.

Sonnet 60

They that in course of heavenly spheares are skild,
    to every planet point his sundry yeare,
    in which her circle's voyage is fulfild,
    as Mars in three score yeares doth run his spheare.
So since the winged God his planet cleare
    began in me to move, one yeare is spent:
    the which doth longer unto me appeare
    then al those fourty which my life outwent.
Then by that count, which lovers' books invent,
    the spheare of Cupid fourty yeares containes,
    which I have wasted in long languishment,

that seemd the longer for my greater paines.
But let my love's fayre Planet short her wayes
    this yeare ensuing, or else short my dayes.

Sonnet 61

The glorious image of the maker's beautie,
    my soverayne saynt, the Idoll of my thought,
    dare not henceforth above the bounds of dewtie,
    t'accuse of pride, or rashly blame for ought.
For being as she is divinely wrought,
    and of the brood of Angels' hevenly borne,
    and with the crew of blessed Saynts upbrought,
    each of which did her with theyr guifts adorne;
The bud of joy, the blossome of the morne,
    the beame of light, whom mortal eyes admyre:
    what reason is it then but she should scorne
    base things that to her love too bold aspire?
Such heavenly formes ought rather worshipt be
    then dare be lov'd by men of meane degree.

Sonnet 62

The weary yeare his race now having run,
    the new begins his compass course anew:
    with shew of morning mylde he hath begun,
    betokening peace and plenty to ensew.
So let us, which this chaunge of weather vew,
    chaunge eeke our mynds and former lives amend;
    the old yeare's sinnes forepast let us eschew,
    and fly the faults with which we did offend.
Then shall the new yeare's joy forth freshly send
    into the glooming world his gladsome ray;
    and all these stormes which now his beauty blend,
    shall turne to caulmes and tymely cleare away.
So likewise love cheare you your heavy spright,
    and chaunge old yeare's annoy to new delight.

140

Sonnet 63

After long stormes and tempests' sad assay,
 which hardly I endured heretofore,
 in dread of death and daungerous dismay,
 with which my silly barke was tossed sore;
I doe at length descry the happy shore,
 in which I hope ere long for to arryve:
 fayre soyle it seemes from far and fraught with store
 of all that deare and daynty is alyve.
Most happy he that can at last atchyve
 the joyous safety of so sweet a rest,
 whose least delight sufficeth to deprive
 remembrance of all paines which him opprest.
All paines are nothing in respect of this,
 all sorrowes short that gaine eternall blisse.

Sonnet 64

Comming to kisse her lyps, (such grace I found)
 me seemd I smelt a gardin of sweet flowres,
 that dainty odours from them threw around
 for damzels fit to decke their lovers' bowres.
Her lips did smell lyke unto Gillyflowers,
 her ruddy cheekes lyke unto Roses red;
 her snowy browes lyke budded Bellamoures,
 her lovely eyes lyke Pincks but newly spred;
Her goodly bosome lyke a Strawberry bed,
 her neck lyke to a bounch of Cullambynes;
 her brest lyke lillyes, ere theyr leaves be shed,
 her nipples lyke yong blossom'd Jessemynes:
Such fragrant flowres doe give most odorous smell,
 but her sweet odour did them all excell.

Sonnet 65

The doubt which ye misdeeme, fayre love, is vaine,
 that fondly feare to loose your liberty,
 when loosing one, two liberties ye gayne,
 and make him bond that bondage earst dyd fly.

Sweet be the bands, the which true love doth tye,
    without constraynt or dread of any ill:
    the gentle birde feeles no captivity
    within her cage, but singes and feeds her fill.
There pride dare not approch, nor discord spill
    the league twixt them, that loyal love hath bound;
    but simple truth and mutuall good will
    seekes with sweet peace to salve each other's wound:
There fayth doth fearlesse dwell in brasen towre,
    and spotlesse pleasure builds her sacred bowre.

Sonnet 66

To all those happy blessings which ye have
    with plenteous hand by heaven upon you thrown,
    this one disparagement they to you gave,
    that ye your love lent to so meane a one.
Yee whose high worth's surpassing paragon,
    could not on earth have found one fit for mate,
    ne but in heaven matchable to none,
    why did ye stoup unto so lowly state?
But ye thereby much greater glory gate,
    then had ye sorted with a prince's pere;
    for now your light doth more it selfe dilate,
    and in my darknesse greater doth appeare.
Yet since your light hath once enlumind me,
    with my reflex yours shall encreased be.

Sonnet 67

Lyke as a huntsman after weary chace,
    seeing the game from him escapt away,
    sits downe to rest him in some shady place,
    with panting hounds beguiled of their pray:
So after long pursuit and vaine assay,
    when I all weary had the chace forsooke,
    the gentle deare returnd the selfe-same way,
    thinking to quench her thirst at the next brooke.
There she beholding me with mylder looke,

sought not to fly, but fearelesse still did bide;
    till I in hand her yet halfe trembling tooke,
    and with her owne goodwill hir fyrmely tyde.
Strange thing me seemd to see a beast so wyld,
    so goodly wonne with her owne will beguyld.

Sonnet 68

Most glorious Lord of lyfe that on this day
    didst make thy triumph over death and sin,
    and having harrowd hell didst bring away
    captivity thence captive us to win:
This joyous day, deare Lord, with joy begin,
    and grant that we for whom thou diddest dye,
    being with thy deare blood clene washt from sin,
    may live for ever in felicity:
And that thy love we weighing worthily,
    may likewise love thee for the same againe;
    and for thy sake that all lyke deare didst buy,
    with love may one another entertayne.
So let us love, deare love, lyke as we ought:
    love is the lesson which the Lord us taught.

Sonnet 69

The famous warriors of the anticke world
    used Trophees to erect in stately wize,
    in which they would the records have enrold
    of theyr great deeds and valarous emprize.
What trophee then shall I most fit devize,
    in which I may record the memory
    of my love's conquest, peerelesse beautie's prise,
    adorn'd with honour, love, and chastity?
Even this verse vowd to eternity
    shall be thereof immortall moniment;
    and tell her prayse to all posterity,
    that may admire such world's rare wonderment:
The happy purchase of my glorious spoile,
    gotten at last with labour and long toyle.

Sonnet 70

Fresh spring, the herald of love's mighty king,
 in whose cote-armour richly are displayd
 all sorts of flowers the which on earth do spring
 in goodly colours gloriously arrayd:
Goe to my love, where she is carelesse layd,
 yet in her winter's bowre not well awake:
 tell her the joyous time wil not be staid
 unlesse she doe him by the forelock take.
Bid her therefore her selfe soone ready make,
 to wayt on love amongst his lovely crew,
 where every one that misseth then her make,
 shall be by him amearst with penance dew.
Make hast therefore, sweet love, whilest it is prime,
 for none can call againe the passed time.

Sonnet 71

I joy to see how in your drawen work,
 your selfe unto the Bee ye doe compare;
 and me unto the Spyder that doth lurke
 in close awayt to catch her unaware.
Right so your selfe were caught in cunning snare
 of a deare foe, and thralled to his love;
 in whose streight bands ye now captived are
 so firmely, that ye never may remove.
But as your worke is woven all above
 with woodbynd flowers and fragrant Eglantine,
 so sweet your prison you in time shall prove,
 with many deare delights bedecked fyne.
And all thensforth eternall peace shall see,
 betweene the Spyder and the gentle Bee.

Sonnet 72

Oft when my spirit doth spred her bolder winges,
 in mind to mount up to the purest sky,
 it down is weighd with thoght of earthly things
 and clogd with burden of mortality;

Where when that soverayne beauty it doth spy,
    resembling heaven's glory in her light,
    drawne with sweet pleasure's bayt, it back doth fly,
    and unto heaven forgets her former flight.
There my fraile fancy fed with full delight,
    doth bath in blisse and mantleth most at ease;
    ne thinks of other heaven, but how it might
    her hart's desire with most contentment please.
Hart need not wish none other happinesse,
    but here on earth to have such heven's blisse.

Sonnet 73

Being my selfe captyved here in care,
    my hart, whom none with servile bands can tye
    but the fayre tresses of your golden hayre,
    breaking his prison forth to you doth fly.
Lyke as a byrd that in one's hand doth spy
    desired food, to it doth make his flight,
    even so my hart, that wont on your fayre eye
    to feed his fill, flyes backe unto your sight.
Doe you him take, and in your bosome bright
    gently encage, that he may be your thrall:
    perhaps he there may learne with rare delight
    to sing your name and prayses over all,
That it hereafter may you not repent,
    him lodging in your bosome to have lent.

Sonnet 74

Most happy letters fram'd by skilfull trade,
    with which that happy name was first desynd,
    the which three times thrise happy hath me made,
    with guifts of body, fortune and of mind.
The first my being to me gave by kind,
    from mother's womb deriv'd by dew descent:
    the second is my sovereigne Queene most kind,
    that honour and large richesse to me lent.
The third my love, my live's last ornament,

by whom my spirit out of dust was raysed,
    to speake her prayse and glory excellent,
    of all alive most worthy to be praysed.
Ye three Elizabeths for ever live,
    that three such graces did unto me give.

Sonnet 75

One day I wrote her name upon the strand,
    but came the waves and washed it away:
    agayne I wrote it with a second hand,
    but came the tyde, and made my paynes his pray.
'Vayne man', sayd she, 'that doest in vaine assay
    a mortall thing so to immortalize,
    for I my selve shall lyke to this decay,
    and eek my name bee wyped out lykewize.'
'Not so', (quod I) 'let baser things devize
    to dy in dust, but you shall live by fame:
    my verse your vertues rare shall eternize,
    and in the hevens wryte your glorious name:
Where, whenas death shall all the world subdew,
    our love shall live, and later life renew.

Sonnet 76

Fayre bosome fraught with vertue's richest tresure,
    the neast of love, the lodging of delight,
    the bowre of blisse, the paradice of pleasure,
    the sacred harbour of that hevenly spright;
How was I ravisht with your lovely sight,
    and my frayle thoughts too rashly led astray,
    whiles diving deepe through amorous insight,
    on the sweet spoyle of beautie they did pray:
And twixt her paps like early fruit in May,
    whose harvest seemd to hasten now apace,
    they loosely did theyr wanton winges display,
    and here to rest themselves did boldly place.
Sweet thoughts I envy your so happy rest,
    which oft I wisht, yet never was so blest.

146

Sonnet 77

Was it a dreame, or did I see it playne,
    a goodly table of pure yvory,
    all spred with juncats, fit to entertayne
    the greatest Prince with pompous roialty?
Mongst which there in a silver dish did ly
    twoo golden apples of unvalewd price,
    far passing those which *Hercules* came by,
    or those which *Atalanta* did entice:
Exceeding sweet, yet voyd of sinfull vice,
    That many sought yet none could ever taste;
    sweet fruit of pleasure brought from paradice
    by Love himselfe and in his garden plaste.
Her brest that table was so richly spredd,
    my thoughts the guests, which would thereon have fedd.

Sonnet 78

Lackyng my love I go from place to place,
    lyke a young fawne that late hath lost the hynd;
    and seeke each where, where last I sawe her face,
    whose ymage yet I carry fresh in mynd.
I seeke the fields with her late footing synd,
    I seeke her bowre with her late presence deckt,
    yet nor in field nor bowre I her can fynd;
    yet field and bowre are full of her aspect.
But when myne eyes I thereunto direct,
    they ydly back returne to me agayne,
    and when I hope to see theyr trew object,
    I fynd my selfe but fed with fancies vayne.
Ceasse then, myne eyes, to seeke her selfe to see,
    and let my thoughts behold her selfe in mee.

Sonnet 79

Men call you fayre, and you doe credit it,
    for that your selfe ye dayly such doe see:
    but the trew fayre, that is the gentle wit
    and vertuous mind, is much more praysd of me.

For all the rest, how ever fayre it be,
    shall turne to nought and loose that glorious hew:
    but onely that is permanent and free
    from frayle corruption, that doth flesh ensew.
That is true beautie: that doth argue you
    to be divine and borne of heavenly seed,
    deriv'd from that fayre Spirit, from whom al true
    and perfect beauty did at first proceed.
He onely fayre, and what he fayre hath made:
    all other fayre lyke flowres untymely fade.

Sonnet 80

After so long a race as I have run
    through Faery land, which those six books compile,
    give leave to rest me being halfe fordonne,
    and gather to my selfe new breath awhile.
Then as a steed refreshed after toyle,
    out of my prison I will breake anew,
    and stoutly will that second worke assoyle,
    with strong endevour and attention dew.
Till then, give leave to me in pleasant mew
    to sport my muse and sing my love's sweet praise,
    the contemplation of whose heavenly hew
    my spirit to an higher pitch will rayse.
But let her prayses yet be low and meane,
    fit for the handmayd of the Faery Queene.

Sonnet 81

Fayre is my love, when her fayre golden heares
    with the loose wynd ye waving chance to marke:
    fayre when the rose in her red cheekes appeares,
    or in her eyes the fyre of love does sparke.
Fayre when her brest lyke a rich laden barke,
    with pretious merchandize she forth doth lay:
    fayre when that cloud of pryde, which oft doth dark
    her goodly light, with smiles she drives away.
But fayrest she, when so she doth display

the gate with pearles and rubyes richly dight,
   throgh which her words so wise do make their way
   to beare the message of her gentle spright.
The rest be works of nature's wonderment,
   but this the worke of hart's astonishment.

Sonnet 82

Joy of my life, full oft for loving you
   I blesse my lot, that was so lucky placed:
   but then the more your owne mishap I rew,
   that are so much by so meane love embased.
For had the equall hevens so much you graced
   in this as in the rest, ye mote invent
   som hevenly wit, whose verse could have enchased
   your glorious name in golden moniment.
But since ye deigned so goodly to relent
   to me your thrall, in whom is little worth,
   that little that I am shall all be spent
   in setting your immortall prayses forth:
Whose lofty argument, uplifting me,
   shall lift you up unto an high degree.

Sonnet 83

My hungry eyes, through greedy covetize
   still to behold the object of theyr payne,
   with no contentment can themselves suffize,
   but having pine, and having not, complayne.
For lacking it, they cannot lyfe sustayne,
   and seeing it, they gaze on it the more:
   in theyr amazement lyke *Narcissus* vayne
   whose eyes him starv'd: so plenty makes me pore.
Yet are myne eyes so filled with the store
   of that fayre sight, that nothing else they brooke,
   but loath the things which they did like before,
   and can no more endure on them to looke.
All this world's glory seemeth vayne to me,
   and all theyr shewes but shadowes, saving she.

Sonnet 84

Let not one sparke of filthy lustfull fyre
    breake out, that may her sacred peace molest,
    ne one light glance of sensuall desyre
    Attempt to work her gentle minde's unrest.
But pure affections bred in spotlesse brest,
    and modest thoughts breathd from wel-tempred sprites,
    goe visit her in her chast bowre of rest,
    accompanyde with angelick delightes.
There fill your selfe with those most joyous sights,
    the which my selfe could never yet attayne:
    but speake no word to her of these sad plights,
    which her too constant stiffenesse doth constrayn.
Onely behold her rare perfection,
    and blesse your fortune's fayre election.

Sonnet 85

The world that cannot deeme of worthy things,
    when I doe praise her, say I doe but flatter:
    so does the Cuckow, when the Mavis sings,
    begin his witlesse note apace to clatter.
But they that skill not of so heavenly matter,
    all that they know not, envy or admyre,
    rather then envy let them wonder at her,
    but not to deeme of her desert aspyre.
Deepe in the closet of my parts entyre,
    her worth is written with a golden quill:
    that me with heavenly fury doth inspire,
    and my glad mouth with her sweet prayses fill.
Which when as fame in her shrill trump shal thunder,
    let the world chose to envy or to wonder.

Sonnet 86

Venemous toung tipt with vile adder's sting,
    of that selfe kynd with which the Furies fell
    theyr snaky heads doe combe, from which a spring
    of poysoned words and spitefull speeches well:

Let all the plagues and horrid paines of hell
    upon thee fall for thine accursed hyre,
    that with false forged lyes, which thou didst tel,
    in my true love did stirre up coles of yre:
The sparkes whereof let kindle thine own fyre,
    and catching hold on thine owne wicked hed
    consume thee quite, that didst with guile conspire
    in my sweet peace such breaches to have bred.
Shame by thy meed, and mischiefe thy reward,
    dew to thy selfe that it for me prepard.

Sonnet 87

Since I did leave the presence of my love,
    many long weary dayes I have outworne,
    and many nights, that slowly seemd to move
    theyr sad protract from evening untill morne.
For when as day the heaven doth adorne,
    I wish that night the noyous day would end:
    and when as night hath us of light forlorne,
    I wish that day would shortly reascend.
Thus I the time with expectation spend,
    and faine my griefe with chaunges to beguile,
    that further seemes his terme still to extend,
    and maketh every minute seeme a myle.
So sorrow still doth seeme too long to last,
    but joyous houres doo fly away too fast.

Sonnet 88

Since I have lackt the comfort of that light,
    the which was wont to lead my thoughts astray,
    I wander as in darknesse of the night,
    affrayd of every danger's least dismay.
Ne ought I see, though in the clearest day,
    when others gaze upon theyr shadowes vayne,
    but th'onely image of that heavenly ray,
    whereof some glance doth in mine eie remayne:
Of which beholding th' Idæa playne,

through contemplation of my purest part,
with light thereof I doe my selfe sustayne,
and thereon feed my love-affamisht hart.
But with such brightnesse whylest I fill my mind,
I starve my body and mine eyes doe blynd.

Sonnet 89
Lyke as the Culver on the bared bough
sits mourning for the absence of her mate,
and in her songs sends many a wishfull vow
for his returne that seemes to linger late;
So I alone now left disconsolate
mourne to my selfe the absence of my love;
and wandring here and there all desolate,
seek with my playnts to match that mournful dove:
Ne joy of ought that under heaven doth hove
can comfort me, but her owne joyous sight,
whose sweet aspect both God and man can move
in her unspotted pleasauns to delight.
Dark is my day, whyles her fayre light I mis,
and dead my life that wants such lively blis.

Henry Constable

Diana. The praises of his Mistress in certaine sweete Sonnets by H. C.

To his absent Diana

Sever'd from sweete Content, my live's sole light,
   banisht by over-weening wit from my desire,
   this poore acceptance onely I require,
   that though my fault have forc'd me from thy sight,
Yet that thou wouldst (my sorrowes to requite)
   review these Sonnets, pictures of thy praise,
   wherein each woe thy wondrous worth doth raise,
   though first thy worth bereft me of delight.
See them forsaken: for I them forsooke,
   forsaken first of thee, next of my sence;
   and when thou deignst on their blacke teares to looke,
   shed not one teare my teares to recompence:
      But joy in this (though Fates gainst mee repine)
      my verse still lives, to witnes thee divine.

1   Resolv'd to love, unworthie to obtaine,
    I doo no favor crave: but humble wise
    to thee my sighes in verse I sacrifice,
    only some pitie, and no helpe to gaine.

Heare then, and as my heart shall aye remaine
   a patient object to thy lightning eies,
   a patient eare bring thou to thundring cries:
   feare not the cracke, when I the blow sustaine:
So, as thyne eye bred mine ambitious thought,
   so shall thine eare make proud my voyce for joy:
   lo (Deare) what wonders great by thee are wrought,
   when I but little favours doo enjoy.
      The voyce is made the eare for to rejoyce,
      and thyne eare giveth pleasure to my voyce.

2 It maie be, Love my death doth not pretend,
   although he shootes at mee, but thinkes it fit
   thus to bewitch thee for my benefit,
   causing thy will to my wish condiscend:
For witches, which some murther doo intend,
   doo make a picture, and doo shoote at it;
   and in that part where they the picture hit,
   the partie's selfe doth languish to his end.
So Love, too weake by force thy hart to taint,
   within my hart thy heavenly shape doth paint;
   suffring therein his arrowes to abide,
   onelie to th' end he might by witches' art
      Within my hart pierce through thy picture's side,
      and through thy picture's side might wound thy hart.

3 Blame not my hart for flieng up too hie,
   sith thou art cause that it this flight begunne;
   for earthlie vapors drawne up by the Sunne
   Comets begin, and night-sunnes in the skie.
Mine humble art, so with thy heavenlie eie
   drawne up aloft, all low desires doth shunne:
   raise then me up, as thou my hart hast done,
   so during night, in heaven remaine maie I.
I saie againe, blame not my high desire,
   sith of us both the cause thereof depends.
   In thee doth shine, in mee doth burne a fire;

fire drawes up other, and it selfe ascends:
    Thine eie a fier, and so drawes up my love:
    My love a fier, and so ascends above.

4   The Sonne his journey ending in the West,
    taking his lodging up in Thetis' bed,
    though from our eyes his beames be banished,
    yet with his light th' Antipodes be blest.
Now when the Sunne time brings my Sunne to rest,
    (which mee too oft of rest hath hindered)
    and whiter skinne with white sheete covered,
    and softer cheeke doth on softe pillow rest:
Then I (O Sunne of Sunnes and Light of Lights)
    wish me with those Antipodes to bee,
    which see and feele thy beames and heate by nights.
Well, though the night both cold and darksome is,
      yet halfe the daye's delight the night graunts mee:
      I feele my Sunne's heate, though his light I misse.

5   Flie lowe deare Love, thy Sunne dost thou not see?
    Take heed, doo not so neere his rayes aspire,
    least (for thy pride, inflam'd with wreakfull ire)
    it burne thy wings, as it hath burned mee.
Thou (haply) saist, thy wings immortall bee,
    and so cannot consumed be with fire:
    the one is Hope, the other is Desire,
    and that the heavens bestow'd them both on thee.
A Muse's words made thee with Hope to flye;
    and Angel's face Desier hath begot;
    thy selfe engendred by a Goddesse' eye:
    yet for all this, immortall thou art not.
      Of heavenly eye though thou begotten art,
      Yet art thou borne but of a mortall hart.

6   Uncivill sickness, hast thou no regard,
    but dost presume my dearest to molest,
    and without leave dar'st enter in that brest

wheretoo sweete Love approach yet never dar'd?
Spare thow her health, which my life hath not spar'd;
   too bitter such revenge of my unrest:
   although with wrongs my thought she hath opprest,
   my wrongs seeke not revenge, they crave rewarde.
Cease Sicknesse, cease in her then to remaine,
   and come and welcome, harbour thou in mee,
   whom Love long since hath taught to suffer paine.
So she which hath so oft my paines increast,
    (O god, that I might so rewarded bee)
    by my more paine, might have her paine releast.

7   A frend of mine, pitieng my helplesse love,
   hoping (by killing hope) my love to slaie;
   'Let not' (quoth hee) 'thy hope thy hart betraie;
   impossible it is hir hart to move.'
But sith resolved love cannot remove,
   as long as thy divine perfections staie,
   thy Godhead then he sought to take awaie.
Deare, seeke revenge, and him a liar prove.
Gods onelie doo impossibilities:
   'Impossible' (saith he) 'thy grace to gaine'.
   show then the power of thy devinities,
   by graunting me thy favor to obtaine.
    So shall thy foe give to himselfe the lie:
    a Goddesse thou shalt prove, and happie I.

8   If true love might true love's reward obtaine,
   dumbe wonder onely might speake of my joy:
   but too much woorth hath made thee too much coy,
   and told me long agoe, I sigh'd in vaine.
Not then vaine hope of undeserved gaine
   hath made me paint in verses mine annoy;
   but for thy pleasure, that thou mightst enjoy
   thy beautie's sight, in glasses of my paine.
See then thy selfe (though mee thou wilt not heare)
   by looking on my verse; for paine in verse,

    love doth in paine, beautie in love appeare.
    So, if thou woulds't my verses' meaning see,
        Expound them thus, when I my love rehearse:
        'None loves like him, that is, None faire like mee.'

9   Thine eye the glasse where I behold my hart,
      mine eye the window, through the which thine eye
      may see my hart, and there thy selfe espye
      in bloudie colours how thou painted art.
    Thine eye the pyle is of a murdring dart,
      mine eye the sight thou tak'st thy levell by
      to hit my hart, and never shootes awry;
      mine eye thus helpes thine eye to worke my smart.
    Thine eye a fier is both in heate and light,
      mine eye of teares a river doth become:
      Oh that the water of mine eye had might
      to quench the flames that from thine eyes doo come,
        Or that the fier kindled by thine eye
        the flowing streames of mine eyes could make drie.

10   Ladie in beautie and in favor rare,
      of favor (not of due) I favor crave:
      Nature to thee Beautie and Favor gave;
      faire then thou art, and Favor thou maist spare.
    When on poore me bestow'd your favors are,
      lesse Favor in your face you shall not have:
      If favor then a wounded soule may save,
      of murther's guilte (deare Ladie) then beware.
    My losse of life a million fold were lesse
      than the least losse should unto you befall:
      yet graunt this gift, which gift when I possesse,
      both I have life, and you no losse at all.
        For by your Favour onelie I doo live,
        and Favour you may well both keepe and give.

11   Mine eye with all the deadlie sinnes is fraught,
      1. First *proud*, sith it presum'd to looke so hie:
      a watchman being made, stood gazing by,

    2. and *idle,* tooke no heede till I was caught:
3. And *envious,* beares envie that my thought
    should in his absence be to her so nie:
    to kill my hart, mine eie let in her eie,
       4. and so consent gave to a *murther* wrought:
5. And *covetous,* it never would remoove
    from her faire haire, gold so doth please his sight:
      6. *Unchast*, a baud betweene my hart and love:
      7. a *glutton* eie, with teares drunke everie night.
      These sinnes procured have a Goddesse'ire:
      Wherefore my hart is damnd in Love's sweete fire.

12 My *Reason* absent did mine eyes require
    to watch and ward, and such foes to descrie
    as they should neere my hart approching spie:
    but traitor eies my hart's death did conspire;
(Corrupted with *Hope's* giftes) let in *Desire*
    to burne my hart; and sought no remedie,
    though store of water were in either eie,
    which well imploid, might well have quencht the fire.
Reason returned, *Love* and *Fortune* made
    judges, to judge mine eies to punishment:
Fortune, sith they by sight my hart betraid,
    from wished sight adjudgd them banishment:
      Love, sith by fire murdred my hart was found,
      adjudged them in teares for to be drownd.

13 Falslie doth envie of your praises blame
    my tongue, my pen, my hart of flatterie:
    because I said there was no sunne but thee,
    it calld my tongue the partiall trumpe of fame;
And saith my pen hath flattered thy name,
    because my pen did to my tongue agree;
    and that my hart must needs a flattrer bee,
    which taught both tongue and pen to say the same.

No, no, I flatter not, when I thee call
   the sunne, sith that the sunne was never such:
   but when the sunne thee I compar'd withall,
   doubtles the sunne I flattered too much.
      Witnes mine eies I saie the truth in this:
      they have seene thee and know that so it is.

14   Wonder it is, and pitie ist, that shee,
   in whom all beautie's treasure we may finde
   that may inrich the bodie or the minde,
   towards the poore should use no charitie.
My Love is gone a begging unto thee,
   and if that Beautie had not been more kinde
   than Pitie, long ere this he had been pinde;
   but Beautie is content his food to bee.
Oh pitie have, when such poore Orphans beg;
   Love (naked boy) hath nothing on his backe:
   and though he wanteth neither arme nor leg,
   yet maym'd he is, sith he his sight doth lacke.
      And yet (though blinde) he beautie can behold:
      And yet (though nak'd) he feeles more heat than cold.

15   Much sorrow in it selfe my love doth move,
   more my dispaire, to love a hopelesse blisse:
   my follie most, to love whom sure to misse:
   oh helpe me but this last griefe to remove.
All paines if you commaund it, joy shall prove,
   and wisdome to seeke joy: then say but this:
   'Because my pleasure in thy torment is,
   I doo commaund thee without hope to love.'
So, when this thought my sorrow shall augment,
   that my owne follie did procure my paine,
   then shall I say, to give my selfe content,
   obedience onely made me love in vaine.
      It was your will, and not my want of wit:
      I have the paine, beare you the blame of it.

16   Pitie refusing my poore Love to feed,
        a beggar starv'd for want of helpe he lies,
        and at your mouth (the doore of Beautie) cries
        that thence some almes of sweete grants may proceed.
    But as he waiteth for some almes-deed,
        a cherrie-tree before the door he spies;
        'Oh deare,' (quoth he) 'two cherries may suffice,
        two onely may save life in this my need.'
    But beggars, can they naught but cherries eate?
        Pardon my Love, he is a Goddesse' sonne,
        and never feedeth but on daintie meate,
        els need he not to pine as he hath done:
            For onely the sweete frute of this sweete tree
            can give food to my Love, and life to me.

17   My Ladie's presence makes the Roses red,
        because to see her lips, they blush for shame:
        the Lillie's leaves (for envie) pale became,
        and her white hands in them this envie bred.
    The Marigold the leaves abroad doth spred,
        because the sunne's; and her power is the same:
        the Violet of purple colour came,
        di'd in the bloud she made my hart to shed.
    In briefe, all flowers from her theire vertue take;
        from her sweete breath theire sweet smells doo proceed;
        the living heate which her eie beames doth make,
        warmeth the ground, and quickeneth the seed:
            The raine wherewith she watereth these flowers
            falls from mine eyes, which she dissolves in showers.

18   The Fouler hides (as closelie as he may)
        the net, where caught the sillie bird should bee,
        least he the threatning prison should but see,
        and so for feare be forc'd to flie away.
    My Ladie so, the while she doth assay
        in curled knots fast to entangle mee,
        puts on her vayle, to th' end I should not flee

the golden net, wherein I am a pray.
Alas (most sweete) what need is of a net,
    to catch a bird that is alreadie tame,
    sith with your hand alone you maie it get,
    for it desires to flie into the same?
        What neede such art my thoughts then to intrap,
        When (of themselves) they flie into your lap?

19   When your perfections to my thoughts appeare,
    they say among themselves, 'O happie wee,
    which ever shall so rare an object see':
    but happie hart, if thoughts lesse happie were;
For their delights have cost my hart full deare,
    in whom of love a thousand causes bee,
    and each cause breedes a thousand loves in mee,
    and each love more than thousand harts can beare.
How can my hart so manie loves then hold,
    which yet (by heapes) encrease from day to day?
    but like a ship that's over-charg'd with golde,
    must either sinke, or hurle the golde away.
        But hurle out love thou canst not, feeble hart:
        In thine owne blood thou therefore drowned arte.

20   Sweete hand, the sweet but cruell bowe thou art,
    from whence at mee five yvorie arrowes flie:
    so with five wounds at once I wounded lie,
    bearing in breast the print of everie dart.
Saint Frances had the like, yet felt no smart,
    where I in living torments never die:
    his wounds were in his hands and feete, where I
    all these five helplesse wounds feele in my hart.
Now (as Saint Frances) if a Saint am I,
    the bowe that shot these shafts a relique is:
    I meane the hand, which is the reason whie
    so manie for devotion thee would kisse:
        And some thy glove kisse, as a thing divine,
        this arrowes' quiver, and this relique's shrine.

Last sonnet

Faire Sunne, if you would have me praise your light,
    when night approacheth, wherefore doe you flie?
    Time is so short, Beauties so manie bee,
    as I have need to see them day and night,
That by continuall view my verses might
    tell all the beames of your divinitie;
    which praise to you, and joy should be to mee,
    you living by my verse, I by your sight.
I by youre sight, but not you by my vearse:
    neede mortall skill immortall praise rehearse?
    no, no, though eies were blinde, and verse were dumb,
    Your beautie should be seene, and your fame knowne.
      For by the winde which from my sighes doo come,
      Your praises round about the world be blowne.

Barnabe Barnes

From Parthenophil and Parthenophe Sonnettes, Madrigals, Elegies and Odes

36   And thus continuing with outrageous fier,
      My Sunne proceeding forward to my sorrow
      Tooke up his court, but willing to retier
      Within the Lyon's denne, his rage did borrow:
    But whiles within that mansion he remayned,
      How cruell was Parthenophe to me,

And when of my great sorrowes I complained,
She Lyon-like wish't they might tenfold be.
Then did I rage and in unkindly passions
I rent mine heare, and rac'd my tender skinne,
And raving in such frantique fashions
That with such crueltie she did beginne
To feede the fier which I was burned in.
Can women brooke to deale so sore with men?
She manne's woe learn'd it in the Lyon's denne.

37 But pitie which sometimes doth Lyons move,
Remov'd my sunne from moodie Lyon's cave,
And into Virgoe's boure did next remove
His fierie wheeles: but then she answere gave
That she was all vow'd to virginitie,
Yet said bove all men she would most affect me.
Fye, Delian goddesse, in thy companie
She learn'd with honest colour to neglect me;
And underneath chast vayles of single life
She shrowdes her craftie clawes, and Lyon's hart,
Which with my sences now do mingle strife
Twixt loves, and vertues, which provoke my smart:
Yet from these passions can I never part,
But still I make my suites importunate
To thee, which makes my case infortunate.

54 When I was yong, indewd'd with nature's graces,
I stoule blind love's strong bow and golden arrowes,
To shoote at redbrestes, goldfinches and sparrowes.
At shrew'd gyrles, and at boyes in other places
I shot when I was vexed with disgraces:
I perc't no skinne, but melted up their marrowes.
How many boyes and gyrles wish't mine embraces?
How many prayz'd my favour 'bove all faces?
But once (Parthenophe) by thy sweet side sitting,
Love had espyed me in a place most fitting,
Betray'd by thine eyes' beames, which makes blind see:

163

He shot at me, and said 'For thine eyes' light,
 This daring boy that durst usurpe my right,
 Take him, a wounded slave to love, and thee.'

60 Whilst some the Troiane warres in verse recount,
  And all the Grecian Conquerours in fight,
 Some valiant Romaine warres 'bove starres do mount,
  With all their warlike leaders, men of might:
 Whilst some of Bryttish Arthure's valure sing,
  And register the prayse of Charlemayne;
 And some of doughtie Godfrey tydinges bring,
  And some of Germaine broyles, and warres of Spayne:
 In none of those myselfe I wounded finde,
  Neither with horseman, nor with man on foote:
 But from a cleare bright eye, one captaine blinde
  (Whose puisance to resist did nothing boote)
 With men in golden armes, and dartes of golde,
  Wounded my hart, and all which did beholde.

63 Jove for Europae's love tooke shape of Bull,
  And for Calisto playde Dianae's parte,
  And in a golden shower he filled full
  The lappe of Danae with coelestiall arte.
 Would I were chang'd but to my mistresse' gloves,
  That those white lovely fingers I might hide;
  That I might kisse those hands, which mine hart loves,
  Or else that cheane of pearle, her necke's vaine pride,
 Made proude with her necke's vaines; that I might folde
  About that lovely necke, and her pappes tickle,
  Or her to compasse like a belt of golde;
 Or that sweet wine, which downe her throate doth trickle,
  To kisse her lippes, and lye next at her hart,
  Runne through her vaynes, and passe by pleasure's part.

65 Oh that I had no hart, as I have none,
  (For thou mine harte's full spirite hast possessed)
  Then should myne argument be not of mone,

Then under love's yoke should I not be pressed:
Oh that without myne eyes I had been borne,
   Then had I not my mistresse' bewtie vewed,
   Then had I never been so farre forlorne,
   Then had I never wep't, then never rewed:
Oh that I never had been borne at all,
   Or beeing, had been borne of shephearde's broode;
   Then should I not in such mischances fall,
Quyet my water and content my foode:
   But now disquieted, and still tormented,
   With adverse fate, perforce must rest contented

66 Ah sweet content, where is thy mylde abode?
   Is it with shepheardes and light-harted swaynes,
   Which sing upon the downes and pype abroade,
   Tending their flockes and cattell on the playnes?
Ah sweet content, where doest thou safely rest?
   In heaven, with Angels which the prayses sing
   Of him that made and rules at his behest
   The mindes, and harts of every living thing?
Ah sweet content, where doth thine harbour hold?
   Is it in Churches, with Religious men,
   Which please the goddes with prayers manifold,
   And in their studies meditate it then?
Whether thou doest in heaven, or earth appeare,
   Be where thou wilt, thou will not harbour here

34 My sweet Parthenophe, within thy face
   My passion's Calender may plaine be red:
   The golden number told upon thine hed;
   The sunne dayes (which in carde I holy place
And which divinely blesse me with their grace)
   Thy chearefull smiles which can recall the dedde:
   My working dayes, thy frownes from favours fledde,
   Which set a-worke the furies in my brest,
These dayes are six to one more then the rest:
   My leape yeare is (oh when is that leape yeare?)

When all my cares I overleape, and feast
With her fruition whom I hould most deare.
And if some Calenders the truth tell mee,
Once in fewe yeares that happie leape shall bee.

Giles Fletcher, the Elder

From Licia

Sonnet 1

Sadde all alone, not long I musing satte,
But that my thoughtes compell'd me to aspire:
A Laurell garland in my hande I gatte,
So the Muses I approch'd the nyer.
My sute was this, a Poet to become,
To drinke with them, and from the heavens be fedde.
Phaebus denyed, and sware there was no roome,
Such to be Poets as fonde fancie ledde.
With that I mourn'd, and sat me downe to weepe:
Venus she smil'd, and smyling to me saide,
'Come drinke with me, and sitt thee still and sleepe.'
This voyce I heard, and Venus I obayde.
      That poyson (sweete), hath done me all this wrong,
      For nowe of love must needes be all my song.

Sonnet 17

As are the sandes (faire Licia) on the shore,
Or colourd floures, garlands of the spring,
Or as the frosts not seene, nor felt before,
Or as the fruites that Autume foorth doth bring;
As twinckling starres, the tinsell of the night,
Or as the fish that gallope in the seas,

As aires, each part that still escapes our sight,
So are my sighes, controllers of my ease.
Yet these are such, as needes must have an end,
For things finite, none els hath nature done:
Onlie the sighes, which from my heart I send,
Will never cease, but where they first begunne.
    Accept them (sweete) as incense due to thee:
    For you immortall made them so to be.

Sonnet 26
I live (sweete love) whereas the gentle winde
Murmures with sport, in midst of thickest bowes,
Where loving Wood-bine doth the Harbour binde,
And chirping birdes doe eccho foorth my vowes;
Where strongest elme can scarce support the vine,
And sweetest flowres enameld have the ground,
Where Muses dwell: and yet hereat repine
That on the earth so rare a place was found.
But windes delight: I wish to be content.
I praise the Wood-bine, but I take no joye:
I moane the birdes that musicke thus have spent:
As for the rest, they breede but mine annoye.
    Live thou (fayre Licia) in this place alone:
    Then shall I joye, though all of these were gone.

Sonnet 27
The Chrystal streames, wherein my love did swimme,
Melted in teares, as partners of my woe;
Her shine was such as did the fountaine dimme,
The pearlike fountaine, whiter than the snowe.
Then lyke perfume, resolved with the heate,
The fountaine smoak'd, as if it thought to burne:
A woonder strange, to see the colde so great,
And yet the fountaine into smoake to turne.
I searcht the cause, and found it to be this:

She toucht the water, and it burnt with love.
Now by her meanes, it purchast hath that blisse
Which all diseases quicklie can remoove.
    Then if by you, these streames thus blessed be:
    (Sweet) graunt me love, and be not woorse to me.

Sonnet 28

In tyme the strong and statelie turrets fall,
In tyme the Rose, and silver Lillies die,
In tyme the Monarchs captives are and thrall,
In tyme the sea, and rivers are made drie:
The hardest flint in tyme doth melt asunder,
Still-living fame in tyme doth fade away,
The mountaines proud, we see in tyme come under,
And earth for age, we see in tyme decay:
The sunne in tyme forgets for to retire
From out the east, where he was woont to rise:
The basest thoughtes, we see in time aspire,
And greedie minds in tyme do wealth dispise.
    Thus all (sweet faire) in tyme must have an end,
    Except thy beautie, vertues, and thy friend.

Sonnet 31

When as her lute is tuned to her voyce,
The aire growes proude, for honour of that sound;
And rockes doe leape, to shewe howe they rejoyce,
That in the earth such Musicke should be found.
When as her haire, more worth, more pale, then golde,
Like silver threed, lies waffting in the ayre,
Diana-like she lookes, but yet more bolde:
Cruell in chase, more chaste, and yet more fayre.
When as she smyles, the cloudes for envie breakes;
She Jove in pride encounters with a checke:
The Sunne doeth shine for joye when as she speakes:

Thus heaven, and earth doe homage at her becke.
    Yet all these graces blottes, not graces are,
    Yf you my love, of love doe take no care.

Sonnet 41

If (aged Charon), when my life shall end,
I passe thy ferrye, and my wafftage pay,
Thy oares shall fayle thy boate, and maste shall rend,
And through the deepe shall be a drye-foote-way.
For why? My heart with sighs doth breath such flame,
That ayre and water both incensed be:
The boundless Ocean from whose mouth they came,
For from my heate not heaven it selfe is free.
Then since to me thy losse can be no gaine,
Avoyd thy harme and flye what I foretell.
Make thou my love with me for to be slaine,
That I with her, and both with thee may dwel.
    Thy fact thus (Charon) both of us shall blesse:
    Thou save thy boat, and I my love possesse.

Sonnet 42

For if alone thou thinke to waft my love,
Her cold is such as can the sea commaund:
And frosen Ice shall let thy boate to move,
Nor can thy forces rowe it from the land.
But if thou friendly both at once shalt take,
Thy selfe mayst rest. For why? My sighes will blowe.
Our colde and heate so sweete a thawe shall make,
As that thy boate without thy helpe shall rowe.
Then will I sitte and glut me on those eyes,
Wherewith my life, my eyes could never fill.
Thus from thy boate that comfort shall arise,
The want whereof my life and hope did kill.
    Together plac'd so thou her skorne shalt crosse,
    Where if we part, thy boate must suffer losse.

Thomas Lodge
From Phillis: Honoured with Pastorall Sonnets, Elegies and amorous delights

4   Long hath my sufferance labored to inforce
One pearle of pittie from hir prettie eyes,
Whilest I with restlesse rivers of remorse,
Hath bathde the bankes where my faire Phillis lies.
    The moning lines which weeping I have written,
And writing red unto my ruthfull sheepe,
And reading sent with teares that never fitten,
To my love's Queene, that hath my heart in keepe,
    Have made my Lambkins lay them downe and sigh:
But Phillis sittes, and reades, and cals them trifles:
Oh heavens why clime not happie lines so high,
To rent that ruthlesse heart, that all hearts rifles?
    None wrightes with truer faith, or greater love,
    Yet out, alas, I have no power to move.

22   Faire art thou Phillis, I, so faire (sweet mayd)
As nor the sunne, nor I have seene more faire,
For in thy cheekes sweet roses are embayde,
And golde more pure then gold doth guilde thy haire.
    Sweet Bees have hiv'd their hony on thy tongue,
And Hebe spic't hir Necter with thy breath:
About thy necke do all the graces thronge,
And lay such baites as might entangle death.
    In such a breast what heart would not be thrall?

170

From such sweet armes who would not wish embraces?
At thy faire handes who wonders not at all,
Wounder itselfe through ignorance embases?
    Yet naithelesse tho wonderous giftes you call these,
    My faith is farre more wonderfull then all these.

34   I would in rich and golden coloured raine,
With tempting showers in pleasant sort discend,
Into faire Phillis' lappe (my lovely friend)
When sleepe hir sence with slomber doth restraine.
    I would be chaunged to a milk-white Bull,
When midst the gladsome fieldes she should appeare,
By pleasant finenes to surprise my deere,
Whilest from their stalkes, she pleasant flowers did pull:
    I were content to wearie out my paine,
To bee Narsissus so she were a spring
To drowne in hir those woes my heart do wring:
And more I wish transformed to remaine;
    That whilest I thus in pleasure's lappe did lye,
    I might refresh desire, which else would die.

35   I hope and feare, I pray and hould my peace,
Now freeze my thoughtes and straight they frie againe;
I now admire and straight my wounders cease,
I loose my bondes and yet my selfe restraine:
    This likes me most that leaves me discontent,
My courage serves and yet my heart doth faile;
My will doth clime whereas my hopes are spent,
I laugh at love, yet when he comes I quaile.
    The more I strive, the duller bide I still,
I would be thrald, and yet I freedome love;
I would redresse, yet hourly feede myne ill,
I would repine, and dare not once reprove;
    And for my love I am bereft of power,
    And strengthlesse strive my weaknes to devoure.

(Anonymous)

From Zepheria

8 Illuminating Lamps, ye Orbs christallite,
Transparant mirrolds, globes devining beautie,
How have I joyd to wanton in your light?
(Though was I slayne by your artillerie.)
 Ye blithsome starres, (like Leda's lovely twins,
When cleare they twinckle in the firmament,
Promise esperance to the Sea-men's wandrings)
So have your shine made ripe mine heart's content:
 Or as the light which Sestyan Hero show'd
Arme-finnd Leander to direct in waves,
When through the raging Hellespont he row'd,
Steering to Love's port: so by thine eyes' cleere rayes
  Blest were my wayes: but since no light was found,
  Thy poore Leander in the deepe is drownd.

17 How shall I deck my love in love's habiliment,
And her embellish in a right depaint?
Sith now is left nor Rose, nor Hyacint,
Each one their beauties with their hue acquaint.
 The golden seeling of thy browe's rich frame
Designes the proud pomp of thy face's architure:
Chrystall transparant casements to the same
Are thine eyes' sunne, which doe the world depure,
 Whose silverie canopie gold wier fringes:
Thy brow the bowling place for Cupid's eye:
Love's true-love knots, and lilly-lozenges
Thy cheekes depaynten in an immortall dye.
  If well thou limn'd art now by face immagerie,
  Judge how by life I then should pencill thee.

20   How often hath my pen, mine heart's solicitour,
Instructed thee in breviat of my case?
While fancie-pleading eyes (thy beautie's visitour)
Have patternd to my quill an angel's face.
     How have my Sonnets (faithfull counsellers)
Thee without ceasing mov'd for day of hearing?
While they my plaintive cause (my faith's revealers)
Thy long delay, my patience, in thine eare ring.
     How have I stood at barre of thine owne conscience,
When in requesting court my suite I brought?
How have thy long adjournments slow'd the sentence,
Which I through much expence of teares besought?
       Through many difficulties have I run:
       Ah sooner wert thou lost (I wis) then wonne.

21   And is it by immutable decree
(Immutable, yet cruell ordenance)
Ordayn'd (still forst I cry, 'Oh strange impietie')
On true-love to impose such tyrant penance,
     That we unto each other shall surrender
The seal'd indentures of our love compacted,
And that thereof we make such loyall tender,
As best shall seeme to them that so enacted?
     Then list while I advertize once againe:
Though we yeeld up our charters so ensealed,
Yet see that thou safe-guard my counterpanc,
And I in heart shall keepe thy bond uncanceled:
       And so hereafter (if at least you please)
       Weele plead this redeliverie was by duresse.

37   When last mine eyes dislodged from thy beautie,
Though serv'd with proces of a parents' writ,
A Supersedeas countermanding dutie
Even then I saw upon thy smiles to sit.
     Those smiles which me invited to a partie,
Disperpling clowdes of faint respecting feare
Agaynst the summons which was serv'd on me,

A larger priviledge of dispence did beare.
   Thine eyes' edict, the statute of repeale,
Doth other duties wholly abrogate,
Save such as thee endeere in heartie zeale:
Then be it farre from me that I should derogate
   From nature's law enregistred in thee:
   So might my love encur a premunire.

38   From the revenew of thine eyes' exchequer,
My faith his subsidie did neare detract:
Though in thy favour's booke I rest thy debter,
Yet 'mongst accomptants who their faith have crackt,
   My name thou findest not irrotulat.
I list not stand indebted to infame;
Fowle them befall who pay in counterfaite;
Be they recogniz'd in black booke of shame.
   But if the rent which wont was of assise
Thou shalt enhance, through pride and coy disdayne,
Exacting double tribute to thine eyes,
And yet encrochest on my heart's demayne,
   Needs must I wish, though gaynst my foyaltie,
   That thou unsceptred be of nature's royaltie.

B. Griffin

From Fidessa, more chaste then kinde

3 Venus, and yong Adonis sitting by her,
   Under a Myrtle Shade began to woe him:
She told the yong-ling how god Mars did trie her,
   And as he fell to her, so fell she to him.

'Even thus' (quoth she) 'the wanton god embrac'd me,'
    (And then she clasp'd Adonis in her armes)
'Even thus' (quoth she) 'the warlike god unlac'd me,'
    As if the boy should use like loving charmes.
But he a wayward boy refusde her offer,
    And ran away, the beautious queene neglecting;
Shewing both folly to abuse her proffer,
    And all his sex of cowardise detecting.
Oh that I had my mistris at that bay,
To kisse and clippe me till I ranne away!

13   Compare me to the child that plaies with fire,
    Or to the flye that dyeth in the flame:
Or to the foolish boy that did aspire,
    To touch the glorie of high heaven's frame.
Compare me to Leander struggling in the waves,
    Not able to attaine his safetie's shore:
Or to the sicke that doe expect their graves,
    Or to the captive crying ever more.
Compare me to the weeping wounded Hart,
    Moning with teares the period of his life;
Or to the Bore that will not feele his smart,
    When he is stricken with the butcher's knife.
No man to these can fitly me compare:
These live to dye: I dye to live in care.

15   Care-charmer sleepe, sweet ease in restles miserie,
    The captive's libertie, and his freedome's song:
Balme of the brused heart, man's chiefe felicitie,
    Brother of quiet death, when life is too too long.
A Comedie it is, and now an Historie:
    What is not sleepe unto the feeble minde?
It easeth him that toyles, and him that's sorrie;
    It makes the deaffe to heare, to see the blinde.
Ungentle sleepe, thou helpest all but me,
    For when I sleepe my soule is vexed most:
It is Fidessa that doth master thee;

If she approach (alas) thy power is lost.
But here she is: see how he runnes amaine,
I feare at night he will not come againe.

16   For I have loved long, I crave rewarde;
     Rewarde me not unkindlie: thinke on kindnes:
Kindnes becommeth those of high regarde:
     Regard with clemencie a poore man's blindnes.
Blindnes provokes to pittie when it crieth:
     It crieth 'Give'. Deere Lady shew some pittie;
Pittie, or let him die that daylie dieth:
     Dieth he not oft, who often sings this dittie?
This dittie pleaseth me although it choke me;
     Me thinkes dame Eccho weepeth at my moning,
Moning the woes, that to complaine provoke me.
     Provoke me now no more, but heare my groning:
Groning both night and day doth teare my hart;
My hart doth know the cause, and triumphs in his smart.

31   Tongue, never cease to sing Fidessae's praise;
     Heart (how ever she deserve) conceave the best;
Eyes, stand amaz'd to see her beautie's raies;
     Lippes, steale one kisse and be for ever blest.
Hands, touch that hand wherein your life is closed;
     Brest, locke up fast in thee thy live's sole treasure;
Armes, still imbrace and never be disclosed;
     Feete, runne to her without or pace or measure:
Tongue, hart, eyes, lipps, hands, brest, armes, feete,
     Consent to doe true homage to your Queene;
Lovelie, faire, gentle, wise, vertuous, sober, sweete,
     Whose like shall never be; hath never beene.
Oh that I were all tongue her praise to show:
Then surelie my poore hart were freed from woe.

39   My Ladies haire is threads of beaten gold,
     Her front the purest Christall eye hath seene;
Her eyes the brightest starres the heavens hold,

Her cheekes red Roses, such as seld have been;
Her pretie lips of red vermilion dye,
Her hand of yvorie the purest white;
Her blush Aurora or the morning skye,
Her breast displaies two silver fountaines bright;
The Spheares her voyce, her grace the Graces three,
Her bodie is the Saint that I adore;
Her smiles and favours sweet as honey bee,
Her feete faire Thetis praiseth evermore.
But ah the worst and last is yet behind,
For of a Gryphon she doth beare the mind.

William Smith
From Chloris or the Complaint of the passionate despised shepheard

5 You Fawnes and Silvans, when my Chloris brings
Hir flocks to water on your pleasant plaines,
Sollicite hir to pitie Corin's stings,
The smart whereof for hir he still sustaines,
For she is ruthlesse of my wofull song.
My oaten reede she not delights to heare.
O Chloris, Chloris, Corine thou dost wrong,
Who loves thee better than his owne hart deere.
The flames of Aetna are not halfe so hot,
As is the fire which thy disdaine hath bred.
Ah cruell fates, why do you then besot
Poore Corin's soule with love when love is fled?
    Either cause cruell Chloris to relent,
    Or let me die upon the wound she sent.

18   My Love, I cannot thy rare beauties place
      Under those formes which many writers use.
      Some like to stones compare their mistres' face;
      Some in the name of flowers do love abuse;
      Some makes their love a goldsmith's shop to be,
      Where orient pearles and pretious stones abounde.
      In my conceite these farre do disagree,
      The perfect praise of beautie foorth to sounde.
      O Chloris thou dost imitate thy selfe;
      Self's imitating passeth pretious stones,
      Or all the Easterne Indian golden pelfe:
      Thy red and white with purest faire attones:
          Matchlesse for beautie nature hath thee framed,
          Onely unkinde, and cruell thou art named.

20   Yee wastefull woods beare witnes of my woe,
      Wherein my plaints did oftentimes abound:
      Ye carelesse birds my sorrowes well do knoe,
      They in your songs were wont to make a sound.
      Thou pleasant spring canst record like wise beare
      Of my designes and sad disparagment,
      When thy transparent billowes mingled weare
      With those downfals which from mine eies were sent.
      The eccho of my still-lamenting cries
      From hollow vaults in treble voice resoundeth,
      And then into the emptie aire it flies,
      And backe againe from whence it came reboundeth.
        That Nimphe unto my clamors doth deplie,
        Being likewise scorned in love as well as I.

26   Though you be faire and beautiful withall,
      And I am blacke for which you me despise,
      Know that your beauty subject is to fall
      Though you esteeme it at so high a prise.
      And time may come when that whereof you boast,
      (which is your youth's chief wealth and ornament)
      Shall withered be by winter's raging froast,

When beautie's pride and flowring yeeres are spent.
Then wilt thou morne when none shall thee respect:
Then wilt thou think how thou hast scornd my tears:
Then pitilesse ech one will thee neglect,
When hoary gray shall die thy yellow hears.
    Then wilt thou thinke upon poore Corin's case,
    Who lov'd thee deere yet liv'd in thy disgrace.

Sir John Davies

Gullinge Sonnets

[*Dedication.*]

To his good freinde Sir Anthony Cooke

Here my Camelion Muse her selfe doth chaunge
To divers shapes of gross absurdities,
And like an Antick mocks with fashion straunge
The fond admirers of lewde gulleries.
Your judgement sees with pitty and with scorne
The bastard Sonnetts of these Rymers bace,
Which in this whiskinge age are daily borne
To theire owne shames, and Poetrie's disgrace.
Yet some praise those, and some perhappes will praise
Even these of myne: and therefore thes I send
To you that pass in Courte your glorious dayes,
That if some rich, rash gull these Rimes commend,
Thus you may sett his formall witt to schoole,
Use your owne grace, and begg him for a foole.
                         J.D.

Gullinge Sonnets

1   The Lover under burthen of his Mistress' love,
    Which lyke to *Aetna* did his harte oppresse,

Did give such piteous grones that he did move
The heav'nes at length to pitty his distresse.
But for the fates in theire highe Courte above
Forbad to make the grevous burthen lesse,
The gracious powers did all conspire to prove
Yf miracle this mischeife mighte redresse.
Therefore regardinge that the loade was such
As noe man mighte with one man's mighte sustayne,
And that mylde patience imported much
To him that shold indure an endles payne,
By their decree he soone transformed was
Into a patiente burden-bearinge Asse.

2   As when the brighte Cerulian firmament
    Hathe not his glory with black cloudes defas'te,
    Soe were my thoughts voyde of all discontent
    And with noe myste of passions overcast;
    They all were pure and cleare, till at the last
    An ydle, carles thoughte forthe wandringe wente,
    And of that poysonous beauty tooke a taste
    Which doe the harts of lovers so torment.
    Then as it chauncethe in a flock of sheepe
    When some contagious yll breedes first in one,
    Daylie it spreedes, and secretly doth creepe
    Till all the silly troupe be overgone;
    So by close neighbourhood within my brest,
    One scurvy thoughte infecteth all the rest.

3   What Eagle can behould her sunbrighte eye,
    Her sunbrighte eye that lights the world with love,
    The world of Love wherein I live and dye,
    I live and dye and divers chaunges prove,
    I chaunges prove, yet still the same am I,
    The same am I and never will remove,
    Never remove untill my soule dothe flye,
    My soule dothe fly and I surcease to move,
    I cease to move which now am mov'd by you,

Am mov'd by you that move all mortall hartes,
All mortall hartes whose eyes your eyes doth veiwe,
Your eyes doth veiwe whence Cupid shoots his darts,
Whence Cupid shootes his dartes and woundeth those
That honor you, and never weare his foes.

4   The hardnes of her harte and truth of myne
When the all seeinge eyes of heaven did see,
They streight concluded that by powre devine
To other formes our hartes should turned be.
Then hers as hard as flynte, a Flynte became,
And myne as true as steele, to steele was turned,
And then betwene our hartes sprange forthe the flame
Of kindest love which unextinguish'd burned.
And longe the sacred lampe of mutuall love
Incessantlie did burne in glory brighte,
Untill my folly did her fury move
To recompence my service with despighte,
And to put out, with snuffers of her pride,
The lampe of love which els had never dyed.

5   Mine Eye, myne eare, my will, my witt, my harte,
Did see, did heare, did like, discerne, did love,
Her face, her speche, her fashion, judgement, arte,
Which did charme, please, delighte, confounde and move.
Then fancie, humor, love, conceipte, and thoughte
Did soe drawe, force, intyse, perswade, devise,
That she was wonne, mov'd, caryed, compast, wrought,
To thinck me kinde, true, comelie, valyant, wise.
That heaven, earth, hell, my folly and her pride
Did worke, contrive, labor, conspire and sweare
To make me scorn'd, vile, cast of, bace, defyed
With her my love, my lighte, my life, my deare;
So that my harte, my witt, will, eare, and eye
Doth greive, lament, sorrowe, dispaire and dye.

6   The sacred Muse that firste made love devine
     Hath made him naked and without attyre;
     But I will cloth him with this penn of myne
     That all the world his fashion shall admyre:
     His hatt of hope, his bande of beautye fine,
     His cloake of crafte, his doblett of desyre;
     Greife for a girdell shall aboute him twyne;
     His pointes of pride, his Iletholes of yre,
     His hose of hate, his Codpeece of conceite,
     His stockings of sterne strife, his shirte of shame;
     His garters of vaine glorie, gaye and slyte,
     His pantofels of passions I will frame;
     Pumpes of presumption shall adorne his feete,
     And Socks of sullennes excedinge sweete.

7   Into the Midle Temple of my harte
     The wanton Cupid did himselfe admitt,
     And gave for pledge your Eagle-sighted witt
     That he wold play noe rude uncivill parte.
     Longe tyme he cloak'te his nature with his arte,
     And sadd and grave and sober he did sitt;
     But at the last he gan to revell it,
     To breake good rules, and orders to perverte.
     Then love and his younge pledge were both convented
     Before sadd Reason, that old Bencher grave,
     Who this sadd sentence unto him presented
     By Dilligence, that slye and secreate knave:
     That love and witt for ever shold departe
     Out of the Midle Temple of my harte.

8   My case is this: I love Zepheria brighte.
     Of her I hold my harte by fealtye
     Which I discharge to her perpetuallye,
     Yet she thereof will never me accquite.
     For now supposinge I withold her righte,
     She hathe distreinde my harte to satisfie
     The duty which I never did denye,

And far away impounds it with despite.
I labor therefore justlie to repleave
My harte which she unjustly doth impounde,
But quick conceite which nowe is love's highe Shreife
Retornes it as esloynde, not to be founde:
Then, which the lawe affords, I onely crave
Her harte for myne in withername to have.

9   To Love, my lord, I doe knighte's service owe,
And therefore nowe he hath my witt in warde;
But while it is in his tuition soe,
Me thincks he doth intreate it passinge hard.
For thoughe he hathe it marryed longe agoe
To Vanytie, a wench of noe regarde,
And nowe to full, and perfect age doth growe,
Yet nowe of freedome it is most debarde.
But why should love, after minoritye,
When I am past the one and twentith yeare,
Perclude my witt of his sweete libertye
And make it still the yoake of wardshippe beare?
I feare he hath an other Title gott,
And holds my witt now for an Ideott.

Mark Alexander Boyd

Sonet

Fra banc to banc, fra wod to wod, I rin
   Owrhailit with my feble fantasie,
   Lyc til a leif that fallis from a trie
   Or til a reid owrblawin with the win'.
Twa gods gyds me: the ane of tham is blin',
   Ye, and a bairn brocht up in vanitie;
   The nixt a wyf ingenrit of the se,
   And lichter nor a dauphin with hir fin.

Unhappie is the man for evirmaire
    That teils the sand and sawis in the aire,
    Bot twyse unhappier is he, I lairn,
That feidis in his hairt a mad desyre,
    And follows on a woman throu the fyre,
    Led be a blind and teichit be a bairn.

Notes

SIR PHILIP SIDNEY ASTROPHEL AND STELLA (c. 1582)
MODERN EDITIONS
Astrophel and Stella ed. Mona Wilson (Nonesuch) 1931.
The Poems of Sir Philip Sidney ed. William A. Ringler Jr
(Oxford) 1962.
Sir Philip Sidney. Selected Poems ed. Katherine Duncan-Jones
(Oxford Paperback English Texts) 1973.

The sonnet cycle first appeared in print in 1591 in two incomplete
and unauthorized quartos (Q1,Q2). The complete text was printed
at the end of the 1598 Folio of the *Arcadia*, apparently under the
supervision of the Countess of Pembroke herself. I have used the
1598 Folio (F) as my text, with minor emendations from the
Quartos and from Ringler (R). All substantial variations from 1598
are indicated below. Where these agree with Ringler, as most of
them inevitably do, I have acknowledged the debt, and where I have
retained the 1598 or quarto reading in preference to Ringler, the
fact is also noted. I have followed Ringler and the Quartos in
replacing the rigid sonnet pattern used by the printers of 1598 by a
variety of forms designed to draw attention to the variations in
Sidney's rhyme schemes. I have retained the spelling of 1598, but
have modernized the punctuation where necessary. I have kept the
spelling 'Astrophel' of 1598, although Ringler's 'Astrophil' — 'star-
lover' — with its play on Sidney's christian name, is more apt.

1 2. *she (deare she)* (F). R, 'the deare She'.   10. *Invention*:
   See general introduction pp. xvii   13. *Trewand*: truant.
2 1. *dribbed*: random.   3. *mine*: tunnel dug under the walls in
   a siege — cf. 'undermine'.

3   1—8. An ironic and very concentrated description of those poets who invoke the nine Muses to help them dress up their fancies in fine words (1—2); or who become servile imitators of the Greek rhapsodic poet, Pindar, in overlaying their commonplace thoughts with the various colours of rhetoric (3—4); or who use new-fangled figures of speech (Tropes) which are so inept that even the most hackneyed themes expressed through them serve to improve them (5—6); or who embellish their poems with extravagant similes from natural history (as in Lyly's *Euphues*). By *Pindar's apes*, Sidney may be alluding to Ronsard's claim 'Le premier de France/ J'ai Pindarisé', or more likely to the claim of the hack sonneteer, Soowthern in the Ode prefacing his *Sonnets to Diana* (c. 1584) that 'never man before/ Now in England, knewe Pindar's string'.

4   2. *bate*: debate.   5. *Catoe*: Roman moralist and ascetic.   11. *prove*: test.

6   1—4. A list of the commonest clichés of the Petrarchan sonnet.   2. *wot*: know.   5—6. *Jove's strange tales*: reference to Jove's metamorphoses when wooing Europa, Leda and Danae.   6. *Brodered*: embroidered. R, 'Broadred'. F, 'Bordred'. *powdred*: dusted over.   7—8. A hackneyed theme of the pastoral romance.   8. *vaine*: vein.

7   7. *vaile*: veil.   8. *then*: than.   13. *weed*: garment.

8   1. *his native place*: Cyprus, home of Cupid's mother, Venus, captured by the Turks in 1573.   6. *clips*: embraces.

9   2. *choisest* (F). R, 'chiefest'.   12. *touch*: multiple word play on 'touch' which, in addition to its primary meaning, signified a jet-like substance able, when rubbed, to attract straws etc. by static electricity. Also 'touchstone', used for testing gold, and 'touch', tinder for lighting fires.   13. *mine* (R). F, 'mind'.

10   1. *brabling*: disputing.   11. *fence*: use of the sword.

11   6. *Velume*: vellum.   10. *lookst babies*: looked at your own reflection.   11. *pitfould*: trap.   12. *bopeepe or couching*: nursery game involving hiding and peeping out unexpectedly.

12   2. *day-nets* (R). F, 'daunces'. Nets of hair in which small birds

were caught after being attracted by mirrors – in this case, Stella's eyes.   3. *swell* (R). F, 'sweld'.

13   2. *armes*: coat-of-arms. That of Jove includes the eagle in which form he carried off the boy, Ganymede. Mars' coat-of-arms represents love's war and the triumph of Venus over him. Cupid's shield proclaims (blazes) the red and white of Stella's cheeks, but also alludes to the Devereux arms, three scarlet circles on a silver ground.   11. *'sables', 'Vert',* and *'gueuls'*, heraldic colours; black green and scarlet respectively.   14. *scantly* (F). R, 'scarcely'.

14   2. *Upon whose breast*: Prometheus, whose punishment for stealing fire from heaven was to be chained to a rock and have his liver devoured by Jove's vulture each day.   *tire*: tear.   5. *Rubarb*: purgative.   10. *staid*: unchanging.

15   2. *Parnassus*: mountain in Greece sacred to Apollo and the Muses.   8. *denisend*: naturalized in a foreign country.   9. *far-fet*: far-fetched.   10. *inward tuch*: judgment and inspiration.

16   2. *Carrets*: carat, as of gold.   8. *soule* (F). R, 'love'.   9. *young* (Qs, R), omitted F.

17   3. *pricking*: a typical Sidneyan double entendre.   *he*: i.e. Cupid.   6. *prove*: make trial of.   7. *chafe*: anger.   13. *wags*: mischievous boys.

18   1. *shent*: disgraced.   4. *hath* (R). F, 'have'.   5–6. *Nature's rent . . . birthright*: unable to perform the duties he owes to nature, including even that of begetting children.

19   2. *wracke*: wreck.   8. *Avise*: apprise.   12. *prop*: find a support for.

20   5. *Tyran*: tyrant.   6. *levell*: level place from which to take aim.   *stay*: resting-place.   9. *passenger*: passer-by.

21   1. *caustiks*: corrosives.   2. *windlas*: go round about to intercept the game in hunting.   5. *but if*: unless.   6. *coltish gyres* (R). 'youthfull running around'. F, 'yeeres'.

22   2. *faire twinnes*: Gemini, the zodiacal sign governing May/June when the sun is at its highest.   11. *the wealth*: her beauty which owed nothing to cosmetics.   12. *where*: F, 'were'.

23   2. *Bewray*: make visible.

24   1. *Rich*: for this play on Stella's married name, see also sonnets **35**, **37** & **79**.   2. *hatching*: a play on the double meaning of the word; to hatch out, i.e. breed more, and to close up, shut in; cf. sonnet **38**.   3. *Tantal*: Tantalus, whose punishment in hell was to suffer the torments of hunger and thirst whilst standing in water which never rose as high as his lips, and in sight of fruit always out of reach.   4. *blist*: blessed.

25   1. *The wisest scholler*: Plato, whose teacher, Socrates, was judged the wisest of mankind by Apollo's oracle at Delphi.   5. *But for that*: But because.   6. *wayes*: weighs.   8. *inward sunne*: the Right Reason in man which kindles an instinctive love of virtue so long as it is not obscured by the passions.   9. *ster*: stir, arouse.

26   3. *ways* (R). F, 'weighs'.   7. *brawle*: a French dance.   11. *those Bodies high raigne on the Low*: Sidney is playing with the traditional conception of the power of the stars, but it is likely that he believed in it himself. He had his horoscope cast; he was a friend of Dr Dee, the queen's astrologer; and Giordano Bruno, the noted Italian Hermeticist, dedicated two books to him. The relationship between eyes and stars is more than merely a conceit. It is a commonplace of the Renaissance neo-Platonic belief in the real affinities between different levels of the universe — eyes at the material level embodying the same 'Platonic Idea' as stars at the celestial.

27   5. *doome*: judgment, cf. **25**, 2.

28   7. *raines*: reins. *slake*: slack.   9. *I beg no subject*: I don't appropriate any subject simply as an excuse to show off my eloquence.   11. *quintessence*: inner truth and meaning.

30   A series of references to contemporary affairs which might be expected to preoccupy the mind of a young statesman such as Astrophel/Sidney in 1582. For a full analysis see Ringler, pp. 470–1.   1. *The Turkish new-moone*: the Crescent, standard of the Turks who were expected to attack Spain in 1582.   3. *Poles' right king*: the elected king of Poland, Stephen Bathory, who invaded Russia in 1580–1.   5. *three*

parts: the three French factions before Henry of Navarre gained the throne; Catholics, Huguenots and the moderate Politiques.   6. *Dutch*: Germans (Deutsch).   *full diets*: the Diet of the Holy Roman Empire at Augsburg, July—September, 1582.   8. *Orange*: William of Orange lost a number of towns to the Spaniards in 1581—2.   9. *golden bit*: Sir Henry Sidney, three times governor of Ireland, subdued Ulster in 1576—8, in part by imposing a land-tax on the great land-owners to pay for the maintenance of his troops there.   11. *weltring*: the conflict of factions in the Scottish Court. Changed in F to 'If in the *Scotch* Court be no weltring yet', perhaps as a tactful move towards James VI of Scotland, soon to become James I of England.

31   7. *thy languisht grace*: presumably a waning moon.   8. *descries*: proclaims.   14. *Do they call Vertue there ungratefulnesse?* An ambiguous line. Ringler suggests a simple inversion, 'Do the ladies there consider ungratefulness a virtue?' There is no need, however, to change Sidney's order. From the male point of view, Stella's virtue could in this case be considered a form of ungratefulness since the traditional courtly lover expects by right a reward for his constant love, a reward which Stella's virtue denies him. Astrophel is making this point but ruefully showing, at the same time, that he is fully aware of the sophistry of his plea.

32   1. *Morpheus*: son of Somnus, the god of sleep. He was responsible for bringing dreams which appear in human form to sleepers, '*them that living die*'. Such dreams were either prophetic (3), out of memory (3), or out of fantasy, (4), depending on which bodily humour was predominant.   7. *descrie*: discover by observation.   9. *of all acquaintance*: cf. 'auld acquaintance', long-standing fellowship.

34   3. *glasses*: mirrors.   7. *fond*: foolish.   8. *close*: unpublished.   9. *hard*: heard.   12. *wreake*: revenge.

35   5. *Nestor*: oldest and wisest of the Greeks at the seige of Troy, hence the prototype of the wise counsellor.   6. *blow the cole*: blow up the fire.

36   2. yelden (R). F, 'golden'. Qs, 'yeelding'.   8. *now* (F). R,

189

'new'.   14. *by Sence's priviledge*: even though they lack feeling.

37   5. *Aurora's Court*: Aurora, goddess of the dawn; hence the east, where Lord Rich had his family seat in Essex.   13. *make the patents*: entitle one to the possession of.

38   2. *hatch*: close. *unbitted*: without a bit, uncontrolled.   4. *leave the scepter*: give up the rule of.   7. *curious drought*: skilful draftsmanship.   14. *him, her host*: sleep, destroyed by Stella's image, 'that unkind guest'.

39   2. *baiting place*: inn where travellers rest and horses are fed and watered.   4. *indifferent*: impartial.   5. *prease*: attack.

41   7. *sleight*: skill coming from practice rather than natural ability alone.   12. *shoote* (R). F, 'shot'.   14. *race*: course in a tournament.

42   1. *Spheares*: Stella's eyes are like the angelic 'intelligences' which move the planetary spheres (cf. sonnet 26)   14. *Wrackes*: wrecks, defeats.

43   2. *pray*: prey.   13. *rome*: room.

44   5. R, 'yet I no pitty find'.   7. *overthwart*: adverse.   11. *those daintie dores*: her ears.

45   3. *cannot skill*: is not able.   7. *gate*: got.   11. *Then*: than. *wracke*: ruin.

46   6. *Rogue*: a vagrant without master or possessions.   11. *misse*: fail to learn.   12. *this* (R). F, 'his'.   13. *myche*: play truant.   13–14. 'Let love be pardoned for playing truant and forsaking your chaste rules to follow desire, until you yourself are able to arouse love without arousing the passion which fuels it'.

47   2. *those blacke beames*: one of the many references to the paradox of the brightness of Stella's dark eyes.   6. *sprite*: spirit.   12. *Let her go* (R). F, 'Let her do'.

49   4. *descrie*: perceive.   5. *raines*: reins.   9. *Wand*: whip. *Will*: sexual desire.   14. *Manage*: the training of a horse in its paces.

50   2. *staid*: contained.   6. *behest*: command.   8. *portrait*: portray.   11. *those* (R). F, 'these'. *poor babes*: i.e. his verses.

51 5. *silly*: unsophisticated.   7—8. *Hercules*: Atlas supported the weight of the heavens on his shoulders until Hercules relieved him for a time.   7. *in steed*: instead.   10. *cunningst* (R). F, 'cunning'.

52 2. *pretends*: makes a legal claim.   12. *demurre*: legal objection.

53 1. *cunning*: skill.   2. *stave*: shaft of a lance.   5. *descride*: caught sight of.   6. *presse*: the thick of the fight.   7. *I would no lesse*: 'You must do as well for me as you have for Mars'.   13. *beat the aire*: His opponent gallops up the tilting yard but finds no one there to oppose him, since Astrophel, gazing at the window, has not stirred.

54 2. *set colours*: Stella's colours, as a declaration of his love.   4. *a full point*: a full stop.   9. *And thinke so still*: 'And let them continue to think so, as long as Stella knows my mind'.   13. *pies*: magpies.

55 2. *choisest flowers*: the 'flowers' or adornments of rhetoric.   4. *in your sweet grace* (F). R, 'in your sweet skill'.   8. *their blacke banner*: how, by the inspiration of the Muses and the embellishments of rhetoric, the words might be made most tragic and moving: cf. Marlowe, *Tamburlaine* I. v, 1.

56 2. *without booke*: by heart.   4. *misse*: begin to ignore.   11. *flegmatike*: Phlegm, the cold and dull humour.

57 1. *fights*, F. Qs, 'sighes'.

58 This sonnet refers to the traditional debate as to whether the orator owes his power of persuasion primarily to his fine language and strength of argument or to his mode of utterance and the impression of his personality. In this case, the latter wins.   6. *tropes*: figures of speech.   12. *maugre*: in spite of.

59 9. *clips*: see sonnet 8.   14. *clog*: hindrance.

61 3. *assayll* (R). F, 'assaid'. Qs, 'assailde'.   8. *Thence* (R). F, 'Then'.   12—13. *Doctor*: teacher, associated especially with the medieval Schoolmen, among whom Thomas Aquinas was called the Angelic doctor. Scholasticism was out of fashion by Sidney's day; hence 'Angel's sophistrie'.   14. *without I leave to love*: unless I leave off loving.

63 2. *So children*: 'let children continue to study you with eyes full of awe so long as . . .' 9. *Io Pean*: paeon of triumph or joy, especially a marriage song. 12. *weigh* (R). Qs, 'waye'. F, 'nay'. 14. *affirme*: make a positive.

First song 5. *state*: dignity and decorum. 10. *deckes and stayneth*: adorns and puts to shame by outshining. 13. *all* (R). F, 'of'. 24. *rueth*: grieves. 28. *the flatterer*: 'flattery can't improve on the truth'. 32. *not miracles*: 'wonders are not miracles but natural'.

64 12. *wishe* (R). F, 'with'.

65 3. *my good turnes*: my good services. 14. *the arrow head*: Sidney's own arms were a blue arrow-head on a gold background.

66 6. *Fortune wheeles . . . slow* (R). F, 'Fortunes'. Q, 'Fortunes windes . . . blowe'.

67 4. *take time*: cf. 'carpe diem'.

68 6. *Amphion's lyre*: Amphion, son of Jupiter and inventor of music, whose lyre had the power to move stones, and build the walls of Thebes. 8. *kindled* (R). F, 'blinded'.

69 11. *I, I, O I*: cf. sonnet 63. In a sonnet vowing chastity, the verse ironically echoes the 'Io' of the traditional marriage song. 14. *covenants*: legal agreements to do or refrain from doing certain acts.

70 5. *annoy*: misery. The traditional Petrarchan sonnet is a lament over the denial of love.

72 3. *descrie*: distinguish. 6. *Dian's wings*: Diana, the patron goddess of chastity. 8. *Vertue's gold*: as opposed to Cupid's golden-headed arrow which kindled passion.

Second song 17. *danger*: the traditional medieval 'daunger', the terrifying power of the mistress' anger.

73 3. *misse*: ignore. 4. *so soft a rod*: typical *double entendre*. 11. *Those scarlet judges*: her lips.

74 1. *Aganippe*: a fountain on Mount Helicon, sacred to the Muses. *Tempe*: a vale in Thessaly much celebrated by poets: more specifically, the place where Daphne, in flight from Apollo, was turned into a laurel, which became henceforth the symbol of poetic achievement, the poet's 'bays'.

Astrophel is dissociating himself from all high-flown pretensions to poetic inspiration, but also denying that he is copying Petrarch, whose verses to his 'Laura' were the source of the sonnet tradition.   6. *wot*: know.

75 Ringler suggests that this is a sonnet written with tongue-in-cheek, since Edward IV was mainly known in the period for his notorious love affair with Shore's wife and the murder of his brother Clarence, drowned in a butt of malmsey.   4. *impe*: engraft feathers to improve the flight of a falcon.   5–6. *His Sire's revenge*: Edward usurped the throne in 1461, avenging his father, the Duke of York, killed in battle by the Lancastrians.   8. *The Ballance weigh'd*: he ruled with justice the kingdom he had gained by the sword.   9–11. He invaded France (the Floure delice) and was bought off by Louis XI.   *bloudy Lyon*: the Red Lion of Scotland, though in this case the 'old alliance' between France and Scotland against England was not in operation.   14. *To lose his crowne*: Edward was driven into temporary exile by Warwick the Kingmaker because he married Lady Elizabeth Gray while Warwick was, under his orders, negotiating a French marriage for the King.

77 2. *lecture*: reading.   8. *sublime the quintessence*: alchemical terms: 'refine and produce the purest essence'.   11. *consterd*: expressed.

78 11. *as stirre still*: which keep on treading, even though on thorns.   12. *ay*: ever.   14. *wants hornes*: is not cuckolded. Astrophel turns his general statement about jealousy into a specific reference to Lord Rich.

79 3. *consort*: group of musical instruments in harmony.   4. *coupling Doves*: Venus' chariot was drawn by doves.   5. *retrait*: retreat.   9. *meane*: means.   12. *ostage*: hostage.

80 3. *stall*: seat of office and dignity.   8. *graine*: a fast dye.   12. *resty*: indolent, lazy. Feeling such hyperbolic praise must be flattery, his mouth refuses to utter further praise unless another kiss convinces it that even such hyperboles fall short of the truth.

81 6. *only Nature's art*: the art of nature herself.   8. *shade out*:

literally, to represent the shadows on an object in painting it; hence to suggest some part of.

82   3. *His*: Narcissus who was drowned through falling in love with his own reflection in the water.   4. *Hers*: Venus at the judgment of Paris.   6. *th' Esperian taste*: the golden apples of the Hesperides.

83   1. *Philip*: Traditional name for a sparrow: cf. John Skelton's *Philip Sparrowe*.   3. *your cut to keepe*: to know your place.   6. *peepe*: chirp.

Third song   4. *Amphyon's lyre*: see sonnet **68**.   7–10. Reference to stories in Pliny's *Natural History* of an Arcadian rescued from brigands by a snake which he had fed when he was a child (III, xxii) and of an eagle which flew into the funeral pyre of a maiden of Sestos who had reared it (III, vi) (Loeb).   11. *trow*: believe.   12. *O birds, O beasts* (R). F, 'O beasts, O birds,'. Ringler reverses the order to restore the elaborate pattern of Chiasmus around which the poem is organized: Verse 1: trees, stones. stones, trees. Verse 2: Lyzard, Eagle; birds, beasts. Verse 3: birds, beasts, stones, trees; trees, stones, beasts, birds. *Also*, Verse 1, hearing; Verse 2, sight: Verse 3, eyes, ears.

85   6. *pointing*: appointing.   13. *indentures*: contracts.

Fourth song   9. *Danger*: cf. Second song, 17. *hence*: Danger is on guard elsewhere but not here.   15. *flowers*: embroidered on the bed-spread, but also like 'flowers', i.e. figures of rhetoric wooing 'in their best language'.   33. *stay*: postponement.   38. *curtaines*: drawn around the four-poster-bed.   40. *endite*: a *double entendre* related to the Elizabethan euphemism, 'to have ink in one's pen'.   50. *but*: unless. The tone changes in the last verse from tragic to half humorous. Stella will not grant but neither will she damn.

86   14. *one's* (R). F, 'once'. A pun is probably intended.

Fifth song   This rather laboured poem differs from the other songs in its hostile attitude to Stella; and Ringler and earlier critics have argued convincingly that it was not designed for a place in *A. and S.* but belongs to the sequence of Philisides/Mira poems in the *Old Arcadia*. I omit it, therefore.

Sixth song   3. *whether*: which of the two: cf. line 53.   4. *former*: foremost.   5. *bate*: debate.   14. *wage*: plead at the bar.   31. *affected*: inclined towards.   40. *The judgement* (R). F, 'Eye-judgement'.   42. *exceptions*: legal objections.   43. *The common sence*: the faculty by which the soul receives impressions from the senses and transmits them to the reason.   47. *on this*, (R). F, 'on this side'.

Seventh song   3. *closde* (F). R, 'cloyed'. I retain 'closde', shut in, in opposition to the 'things past bounds of wit' in line 6.   8. *wodden*: wooden.

Eighth song   40. *to acquaintance*: to the level of human understanding.   71. *such wise*: in such a way.   74. *in these effects*: 'Do not try to test my love by arousing it in this way' — i.e. by his hands 'in their speech'.   94. *try*: undergo.   102. *so* (R). F, 'to'.

Ninth song   30. *sterved*: starved.   40. *But*: unless.   49. *blaying*: bleating.

87   8. *saddest* (F). R, 'sadded'.

88   3. *heere marcheth she*: another mistress who offers immediate rewards.   8. *cates*: delicacies.

90   6. *Lawrell tree*: cf. sonnet **74**. He doesn't seek fame as a poet.   9. *Ne*: nor. *could I* (R). F, 'I could'.   11. *Without*: unless.

91   4. *Vaile*: veil.   8. *seeing jets blacke*: her dark eyes (Ringler's emendation). F, 'seeing gets blacke'. Qs, 'seeming jett blacke'.   11. *wood globes*: wooden globes showing the disposition of the constellations; hence, painted, artificial reproductions.

92   1. *Indian ware*: rare and precious materials as from the Indies.   3. *cutted*: abrupt, brief (cf. George Puttenham, 'Brachiologia or the cutted comma', *Arte of English Poesie*.) The Spartans were notoriously men of action rather than of words.   5. *totall*: curt.   9. *did*: omitted F.

Tenth song   6. *thy* (R). F, 'the'.   7. *O if I my selfe* (R). F, 'Or if I me selfe'.   12. *aymes at*: can hope to achieve.   33. *licorous*: sensual, lecherous.   41. *depart*: yield, share. R, 'imparte'.   43. *surcease*: stop.

93 5. *may* (F). R, 'might'.   8. *misse*: fall into error.   11. *quite*: acquit.

94 6. *tries*: undergoes.   8. *harbengers*: Officers who rode ahead of the court when it was travelling, to secure accommodation in advance.   9—10. 'if grief, normally so given to lamenting, refuses to inspire my lament on the grounds that I deserve my punishment,'.

95 2. *best*: (Q1). R, 'least'. F, 'left'. All three are tenable, but 'best', besides balancing 'worst', agrees with 'as you with my breast I oft have nurst'.   9. *maine*: strong.

96 2. *kind*: nature.   4. *sunne's* (R). F, 'sun'.   8. *expresse*: as well as the normal meaning, the literal sense, 'press out'.   9. *mazefull*: bewildering.   10. *stur*: go abroad.   12. *fur*: by far.

97 1—4. *Dian . . mortall wight*: Diana, the huntress goddess of the moon, accompanied by her nymphs, the stars, which shoot their rays at and influence human beings.   4. *standing*: position from which to shoot. *wight*: person. *Phoebus*, who drove the chariot of the sun.   8. *dight*: array herself.

98 4. *lee shores*: sheltered shores.   7. *gald* (R). F, 'gold'. Q1, 'held'.   *and shortly raind*: made sore with rubbing of saddle or harness, and with the reins pulled back hard.   11. *marks* (R). F, 'makes'.   12. When dawn comes.   13. *winke*: shut.

99 3. *marke-wanting*: lacking a target.   9. *charme*: tune their voices.   14. light in the world of the senses, in contrast to the 'inward night' 'of the mind'.

100 1. *O teares, no teares*: Kyd may have taken a hint for his famous line in *The Spanish Tragedy* from this, 'O eyes! no eyes but fountain fraught with tears.'   9. *conserv'd*: preserved in sugar. *sugred* (R). F, 'surged'.

101 3. *such fine conclusions tries*: tries out such experiments.   6. *paleness*: spotlessness.   7—8. *And joy . . . in thee*. There is a compressed syllogism in these lines: joy is inseparable from Stella's eyes: Stella weeps with her eyes: therefore Stella unites joy with weeping.   8. *Love moves thy paine*: as in **31**.   14. Ringler suggests an inversion: 'Thy pain moves love who runs up and down . . .' Such a distortion of normal syntax is not characteristic of Sidney. Possibly 'moves' could convey the sense of 'plead', 'utter': 'Love proclaims thy pain.' 10. *sturre*: 'as your fevered glances dart in different directions'. 'runs' (R). F, 'comes'. 11. *prest*: prompt. 12. *with care*: full of fear.

102 3. *kindly*: natural. *badge of shame*: i.e. blushes. 5. *vade*: fade. 6. *engraind*: dyed with a fast dye. 9. *Gallein's adoptive sonnes*: doctors, followers of the Greek physician, Galen, who stick to the old and out of date methods of diagnosis. 11. *feeling proofe*: the evidence of my feelings.

103 4. *those faire planets*: her eyes. 9. *those Aeols' youth*: breezes. Aeolus was the god of the winds.

104 8. *rigour's* (F). Q1, 'rigorous'. R, 'rigrows'. 10. *stars*: they see a reference to Stella. 11. *empty glasse*: linked both with 'thirsty' and with Stella's windows. 12. *your morall notes*: cf. the medieval *Ovid Moralised*: finding meanings under the surface.

Eleventh song 2. *playneth*: mourns, sings a lover's complaint. 12. *Leave*: leave off. 23. *theye* (R). F, 'thy'. 27. *minds*: states of mind. 40. *there* (R). F, 'thee'. *Argus*: a beast with a hundred eyes set by the jealous Juno to watch Io. 43. *unjustest* (R). F, 'unjust'.

105 3. *Dead glasse*: his eyes which missed seeing Stella because of the darkness of the night, the speed of the coach and the fact that the page dropped the torch. 6. *dazling race*: dazzled beam. 11. *whome* (R). F, 'whence'.

106 3. *Bare me in hand*: amused yourself by deceiving me. 10. *charme*: cf. sonnet 99 line 9.

107 7. *Lieftenancy*: delegated authority.

From Certaine Sonnets

These two sonnets are the last two pieces in the collection of assorted sonnets and songs, *Certaine Sonnets written by Sir Philip Sidney: Never before Printed*, which follow the *Arcadia* and precede *The defence of Poesie* and *Astrophel and Stella* in the 1598 Folio.

Nineteenth-century editions often included them as the conclusion of *Astrophel and Stella*, but it is generally accepted now that they were composed earlier, perhaps as early as 1577.

1 4. *web*: woven fabric.   *never wrought*: never complete.

2 Sidney uses the Shakespearean sonnet form occasionally in *Certaine Sonnets*, but abandons it totally for variations on the Petrarchan form in *Astrophel and Stella*.

SAMUEL DANIEL TO DELIA (Text of 1594)
MODERN EDITIONS
The Complete Works in Verse and Prose of Samuel Daniel (5 volumes) ed. Grosart, 1885: reprinted 1963, vol. i.
Poems and a Defence of Ryme, ed. A. C. Sprague, London (1930, 1950, 1972).

Daniel, like Constable, is one of the earlier among the Elizabethan sonneteers. Twenty-seven sonnets of Delia were printed together with Sidney's *Astrophel and Stella* in the pirated edition of 1591, which may have driven Daniel to print his own edition of fifty sonnets in 1592, *Delia. Contayning certayne Sonnets: with the complaint of Rosamond*. The book was not surprisingly dedicated to Sidney's sister, the Countess of Pembroke, who later became his patron. *Delia* was reprinted thereafter, with constant revisions and additions, again in 1592, in 1594, 1595, 1598, 1601, 1602, 1611, and in *The Whole Workes of Samuel Daniel* (1623), by which time it had reached a total of 60 sonnets, many of the original ones being omitted. I have chosen the text of 1594, *Delia and Rosamond Augmented,* since this, while published at the height of the sonnet vogue, indicates in its revisions the direction in which Daniel was developing.

The identity of Delia cannot be established with any certainty. The Countess of Pembroke has been suggested, but sonnet 53 indicates that Delia lived near Daniel's own home at Beckington near the Wiltshire Avon. In his successive revisions of the sonnets, Daniel eliminated many of the autobiographical hints in the earlier versions, and Delia is reduced to the role of the generic Petrarchan mistress. The name Delia is, in any case, one of the names of Diana, the chaste goddess of the moon. For an examination of the whole question of identity, see Joan Rees, *Samuel Daniel. A Critical and Biographical Study* (Liverpool University 1964), ch. ii.

1   For a similar use of the image from accountancy, cf. Sidney, *A & S,* **18** and Drayton, *Idea* **3.**   12. *crosse*: draw a line under and finish the sum.

2   2. *Minerva*: born out of Jupiter's forehead.

3   10. *outcast Eaglets*: cast out of the nest because, unlike true eaglets, unable to gaze directly at the sun.

4   1. *Posts*: messengers.   5. *lymned*: painted.   6. *For that*: because.   10. *cleer-ey'd Rector*: Apollo.   14. *steemes*: esteems.

5   The sonnet uses the story of Actaeon who, for spying on Diana while she was bathing, was pursued by her hounds.

8   4. *even*: equal.   8. *treate*: entreat.   10. *processe*: the formal proceedings in a legal action.

9   2. *Paint on floods* . . .: 'paint on water which holds no lasting impression; plough the sea-shore where no crops can grow; cry to the empty air.'

10   6. *Laughter-loving goddess*: Venus.   7. *Intenerat*: make tender.   11. *Trophey*: memorial of victory.   13. *Once*: at once.

11   3. *convart*: convert.

13   Refers to Pygmalion who fell in love with the statue of a woman which he had carved. The gods favoured him by bringing it to life. 1. *hap*: fortune.   6. *Table*: blank sheet on which a picture is to be painted.   8. *proper*: play on double meaning of the word, 'own' and 'excellent'.   13. *joy'd*: had joy of.

14   1. *snary*: ensnaring. Changed from 'amber' in 1592 text. 11. *salve*: ointment.   13. *least*: lest. *travailes*: labours.

15   8. *Vultur-gnawne*: like that of Prometheus, continually torn by Jupiter's vulture.

16   2. *Imbracing clowdes*: reference to Ixion who thought he was embracing Juno when he was only embracing a cloud in her likeness.   9. *Hydra*: a monster slain by Hercules which grew two new heads for every one which he cut off.

18 11. *innated*: born and established within.

19 2. *Citherea's sonne*: Venus's son, Cupid. *those Arkes*: the arcs of her eyebrows to make him a bow. (cf. Sidney, *A and S*, 17). 7. *Aurora*: goddess of the dawn. 8. *Thetis*: 'silver-footed Thetis' of the *Iliad*. 9. *her resign'd*: by her resigned. 10. *the Spheares*: cf. 'the music of the spheres'. 12. *Hyrcan Tygers*: Hyrcania, an Asian country noted for its wild beasts: cf. *Macbeth*, III, iv, 100.

20 7. *Sith*: since.

21 5. *prospective*: scene.

25 12. *rain'd*: reined, with possibly a pun on 'Raigne' of line 1.

27 1. *trace*: track.

29 6. Reference to Icarus whose wings, fastened on by wax, melted as he approached the sun, so that he fell into the sea and was drowned.

30 3. *venter*: venture. 10. *Meane-observer*: who keeps the middle way.

31 1—5. The reference is to the giants who rebelled against Jupiter and attempted to scale the heavens by heaping mount Pelion upon mount Ossa. Jupiter struck them down with his thunderbolts and piled the mountain on top of them. From their rage came volcanoes, 'all this fire'. 13. *spill*: perish.

32 2. *Gazing*: gazing at. 12. *Narcissus*: who fell in love with his own image in a stream, and pining away, was transformed into a flower.

33 1. *wreck*: avenge.

34 1. *steeme*: cf. 4. 14.

35 7. *done*: spelt 'dunne' in 1592 edition, probably involving a pun.

36 2. *carefull*: full of care.

39 2. *Bewray*: reveal.

40 4. *ear'd*: ploughed. 12. *instarre*: set among the stars, make immortal. *Raile*: garment, kerchief or decoration on a gown. The image would seem to refer back to 'the fairest vaile' – her body, and to mean 'Though time destroys her beauty, it makes immortal through poetry those qualities which created that beauty', (the needle which sewed the veil and the garment which decorated it — i.e. that grace, that virtue).   13. *t' in-woman*: to make her a woman.

41   2. *Leander*: drowned while swimming the Hellespont to reach Hero.   11. 1592 has the more aggressive version, 'Ile not revenge olde wrongs, my wrath shall cease'.

42   The metaphor refers to Helen, and the burning of Troy as described in the *Iliad*.

43   6. *the night's pale Queene*: Cynthia, the moon which governs the tides. 1592 has 'Cynthia' for 'Delia' in the first line.   7. *impost*: tribute.   12. *joy*: have joy of.   13. *I doubt to finde*: I don't think that I should find.

45   3. *but till*: only until.   12. *Kalends*: the first day of the month — in this case, the beginning of the last period of our lives.

47   This sonnet 'At the author's going into Italie', which first appeared in 1594, forms a marked contrast in tone to the happier sonnet 'made at the author's being in Italie' (no 48) published in 1592 and presumably written earlier. Joan Rees (op. cit. p. 20—1) suggests that both sonnets are autobiographical, referring, in the case of 48, to a visit to Italy which Daniel made in 1590—1, and in 47, to a second visit about which no detail is known. While accepting that 48 is autobiographical, I would suggest that in the 1594 text Daniel was attempting a dramatic development of the sonnet situation. Having written his sonnet from Italy (48), he prefaces it by a conventional sonnet about the pains of parting, very much in the mode of the late sonnets of *Astrophel and Stella*.

48   2. *cost*: coast.   3. *My joyfull North*: because Delia is in England.   4. *levell*: mark aimed at.

49   4. *With darke forgetting*: forgetting in sleep.   13. *imbracing clowdes*: cf. sonnet 16 line 2.

50   1. *Palladines*: heroes.   2. *aged . . . untimely*: perhaps a slighting reference to the archaisms of *The Faerie Queene*, as line 3 may refer to its allegory. *imaginarie*: out of imagination.   6. *Autentique*: authentic, possessing authority.

51   1. *the Roman*: Brutus.

52   1. *joyes or else dislikes*: pleases or displeases.   7. *deskant . . .*

  ground: variations played around the basic tune.
53 *Avon*: the Wiltshire Avon which runs near Beckington, where
  Daniel may have been born, and to which he retired in his
  later years. 11. *'poore in fame and poore in waters'*: an
  example of Daniel's increasing literalness. 1592 has 'rich in
  fame, though poore in waters'.
54 5. *unrespecting*: heedless.
55 1. *impost*: cf. 43, 7.

MICHAEL DRAYTON IDEA IN SIXTIE THREE SONNETS
(1619 text)
MODERN EDITIONS
The Works of Michael Drayton. ed, J. W. Hebel. 4 volumes. Vol.
v, Notes and Variant Readings, ed. Kathleen Tillotson and
Bernard Newdigate (Oxford, 1931—41). Vol. ii reprints
Drayton's collected works published 1619 and includes *Idea*. In
the same series Bernard H. Newdigate, *Michael Drayton and His
Circle*. Oxford, 1941.
Michael Drayton. *Poems,* 1619 (Scolar Press Facsimile, 1969).
Poems of Michael Drayton. ed. John Buxton (London 1963) 3
vols, includes a selection from *Idea* in vol. i.

Drayton's sonnet sequence first appeared in 1594 under the title of
Ideas Mirrour. Amours in quatorzains (Hebel, vol. i). It comprises
fifty-one sonnets. The subsequent editions in 1599, 1600, 1602,
1605 and 1619 embody a process of revision in which thirty-two of
the more conceited or plaintive sonnets of the original version were
omitted, and forty-four new sonnets were added. Like Daniel,
Drayton was an inveterate reviser and persevered with the sequence
long after the sonnet fashion had passed. He was also extremely
sensitive to criticism and to changes in poetical fashion (see his
prefatory sonnet *To the Reader of these sonnets*, and also sonnet
31), and his later sonnets contain qualities of irony and concentra-
tion of meaning which have affinities with the drama and the poetry
of the Metaphysicals (e.g. sonnets **6, 8, 15, 21, 61**) rather than with
the Elizabethan love sonnet. I have used the edition of 1619,
however, although it is a less typical sonnet sequence than that of

1594, because it reveals Drayton in his prime and is an immeasurably more impressive collection. The notes indicate the edition in which each sonnet first appeared, but I have not commented on Drayton's revisions of earlier sonnets which he retained.

The name *Idea* suggests the Platonic Idea of a woman; but the sonnets are also a specific tribute to Anne Goodere, younger daughter of Sir Henry Goodere, friend of Sidney, and Drayton's early patron. Drayton knew her all his life from the time that he was a page in her father's household, and his affection survived her marriage to Henry Rainsford in 1595 and continued after her husband's death in 1622. It is not necessary to assume, however, as Bernard Newdigate does (op. cit.) that the sonnets resulted from a passionate attachment on Drayton's part. He wrote an elegie 'upon the death of his incomparable friend' when Sir Henry Rainsford died, and he was clearly a valued friend of the family. Like so many other sonnet sequences of the period, *Idea* is the sort of compliment which could be paid by a poet to a friend and patron.

To the Reader of these sonnets: first printed 1599. 9. *the true image of my Mind*: a conventional pose, since the description, 'Ever in motion, still desiring change', embodies the stock symptoms of the generic lover whose mind, like that of Orsino in *Twelfth Night*, is a 'changeable opal'. For the type of the lover, see Puttenham, *Arte of English Poesie*, Bk I, ch. xxii.

1 (1619). 8. *As how the Pole*: according to the direction of the north pole. 11. *spent*: worn down.

2 (1599). 5. *the view*: inspection by a jury. 6. *quit*: acquit the dead heart of slaying itself. 7. *prov'd by you*: i.e. to be done by you.

3 (1594). 1. *cast*: calculate. 6. *crosse*: draw a line under and complete the sum; cf. *Delia,* Sonnet 1. 7. *Substracting*: subtracting his pains from his joys. 8. *arrerage*: deficit.

4 (1600).

5 (1599). A sequence of word-play on 'I' and 'Aye'. 5. *sleightly*: cunningly.

6 (1619).

7   (1599). 1. *Humor*: whim: see sonnet 19.   10. *Ruffin*: bully.

8   (1619). 13. *thou* (Hebel). Omitted 1619.

9   (1600). 2. Invention: see *Astrophel and Stella*, Sonnet 1 and note.   9. *Bedlam*: as in a mad-house.   10. *twaine*: divided.   11. *nine yeeres*: suggesting that Drayton's affection for Anne Goodere may have begun around 1591.

10   (1599). 2. *Penny-father*: skin-flint.   5. *chest*: coffer.

11   (1599). 10. *but*: only.

12   (1599). 1. *That learned Father*: Saint Augustine.   3. *Offices*: functions.   4. *Anima*: the vital principle.   7. *Mens*: 'the same in kind', i.e. Mind.   10. *Sensus*: consciousness.

13   (1594). 3. *once*: one day.   6. *of force*: necessarily.   13—14. 'so that everything which has a shadow may find in it a reminder of my love story, since my poem is like the shadow of my love produced by the brightness of Idea, my sun'.

14   (1600). Prometheus stole fire from heaven and with it, animated the clay from which he made men and women. For his punishment, see *Delia*, 15.

15   (1619). 1. *sted*: avail.

16   (1594). The Phoenix, the mythical bird of which only one at a time exists. It dies in a fire of spices and is born anew from its own ashes.   3. *is knowne*: its qualities are best reproduced and made known by yours.

17   (1594). 5. *Tralucent*: clear.

18   (1594). Drayton bases his conceit on the traditional 'Nine Worthies', the nine famous heroes of antiquity, *These with the Gods are ever resident.*

19   (1599). 7. *meane*: middle way.   10. *coyle*: perplexity.

20   (1599). 9—12. Drayton plays on the traditional temptations to suicide with which the devil attacks the man who is in despair. (cf. *The Faerie Queene*, I. ix.)

21   (1619).

22   (1600). 1—2. 'Discretion makes allowances for fools and children, so bear with Cupid, the child and me, the fool.   5. *Gawdes*: trinkets, toys.   14. 'some who appear wise are in

fact more foolish than they are'.

23 (1599).

24 (1600). cf. *Astrophel and Stella,* **54**.

25 (1599). 4. *Piren's*: Pyrenees. 5. *to Scotland*: Drayton may have visited Scotland at this period, and possibly had his mind on James VI, shortly to succeed Elizabeth. 6. *Orcades*: the Orkneys. 9. *the Bards*: for Drayton's knowledge of the Irish bards, see his *Ode, To himselfe, and the Harpe*, (Hebel, Vol II, Odes). 11. *the stiffe-neck'd Rebels*: Many of the Irish chieftains had fled to the continent or Spain during the Irish wars of 1595—9. 12. *Galliglasse*: galloglass, Irish soldier.

26 (1594). A complex play of words around the paradox that despair alone makes hope necessary, so that to stop despairing is to stop hoping. Thus love, freed from despair is also removed from hope and is thus, so to speak, imprisoned in nothingness.

27 (1619). 13. *partiall*: biased. *Or . . . or*: Either . . . or.

28 (1600). 5. *then*: than. 7—8. 'What I invest would yield them nothing, even at the most favourable rates, but gives me back triple interest.

29 (1599).

30 (1599). *Vesta,* the Roman goddess of fire. 4. *Being stedfastly opposed*: Being turned always to face the sun. 11. *Desire,* (Hebel). 1619, 'Desires'.

31 (1599). 1. *crooked Mimicke*: for an account of the contemporary criticism of the sonnet and its probable effects on Drayton's revisions, see Hebel, vol. v, pp. 137—8, Introduction and Notes to *Idea*. 4. *Antike*: in grotesque parody. 7. *pack-Horse*: routine, hackneyed. 8. *Dudgen*: mean, ordinary. 9. *imprest*: turned out in print, massproduced. 10. *satiate*: satiated. 14. *Scarabies*: beetles.

32 (1594). See Drayton's *Poly-Olbion* for a full catalogue of English rivers and their special qualities. 4. *Avon's Fame*: Kathleen Tillotson suggests that this may be a compliment to Daniel: cf. *Delia, 53.* 13—14. *Arden's sweet Ankor*: a reference to the Goodere home at Polesworth on the banks of the Ancor in Warwickshire.

33   (1594). *Imagination*: the image-making faculty which allows the heart to retain an image of Idea when the eyes cannot see her.   7. *These*: the eyes. *the other's*: the heart's.

34   (1599). 1. *admire*: wonder at. 'Don't marvel, Love, that in spite of the more than human things I attempt under your domination, the only reward I get is refusal. The only thing to marvel at is that I find nothing to marvel at in this'.

35   (1594). 7. *by Kind*: by Nature.   8. *One*: the dumb-borne Muse able to speak through the virtue of Idea's name. *the other*: the cripple hand able to write by the virtue of her touch.   12. *lyne*: lain.

36   (1619). 1. *purblind*: blind.   3. *Wracke*: destruction.   5. *Styx*: one of the rivers of the underworld by which the gods, including Jupiter the thunderer, swore their most binding oaths.   6. *thy faire Mother*: Venus. *unavoided*: inescapable.   7. *Hecat's Names*: because of her power in earth, heaven and hell she was known as the triform goddess and called Diana on earth, Luna in heaven and Hecat in hell. *Proserpine*: carried off to the underworld by Pluto.   9. *Psyche*: Cupid's Psyche.

37   (1602).

38   (1594). 10. *Despiteth*: shows contempt for.   11. *contemning*: despising.   13. *put back*: repulsed.

39   (1594). cf. *Astrophel and Stella,* 6 and **74**.   2. *Exordium*: the introductory part of a composition.   5. *Elizium*: the Paradise to which the heroes were transported after death.   6. *Phlegeton*: the burning river of the underworld.   8. *Like they* . . . 'Let those like them who want to: I don't.'   9. *Erinnis*: one of the Eumenides, the Furies.   10. *Ate*: Goddess of Discord.   11. *charming*: having magical powers. Hecate was also the chief goddess of magic arts.   12. *in Apollo's cell*: in connection with poetry.   13. *I passe not*: I don't care for. *Minerva . . Astrea*: goddesses of wisdom and justice respectively.

40   (1594). 10. *gleed*: ember.   13. *Sisiphus*: punished in Hades by being forever forced to push uphill a huge rock which always rolled down again.   14. *Ixion*: tied to a fiery wheel

by Jupiter for trying to seduce Juno.

41 (1594). 3. *prove*: experience.

42 (1594). 1. *Method*: the basic order and arrangement of a discourse according to the rules of logic and rhetoric.   2. *Vaine*: vein.   4. *Humor*: my own particular line of fancy.   6. *As Poets doe*: refers to the common renaissance conception of poetry as 'imitation' or feigning. See Sidney's *Defence of Poesie* where it is so defined.   7. *And in bare words . . .*: 'though using plain words, still give a false colouring to my pain'.   9. *I passe not*: cf. sonnet **39** line 13.

43 (1605). 8. *bent*: limit.

44 (1599). 6. *Medea-like*: by her magic she made Aeson young again.

45 (1599).

46 (1605). 2. *evidently*: plainly.   3. *Schoole-men*: learned man.   7. *happily*: haply, by chance.

47 (1605). 5—6. Drayton worked as a writer of plays for Henslowe, the theatre owner and entrepreneur between 1599—1602.   6. *in the Circuit of the Lawrell*: in pursuit of poetic fame.   10. *the proud Round*: the circular auditorium: cf. 'this wooden O' (Prol., *Henry V*).

48 (1619). 3. *Fascia*: fillet around the head.   6. *preferre*: offer yourself for employment.   8. *Practise thy Quiver*: shoot your arrows to scare away the birds.   11. *blind*: cf. Sidney's reference in the *Defence* to the blind crowder singing the old songs of Percy and Douglas.   13—14. For the reference to Venus and Mars, cf. *Astrophel and Stella*, **17**.

49 (1599). 2. *move*: stir the reader.   5. *Packe-Horse*: drudge.   13. *refines*: purifies.

50 (1605). 7. *Coarse*: corpse.

51 (1605). 5. *Lastly*: lately. The references are to the execution of Essex (1601); the surrender and pardon of Tyrone in Ireland, the death of Elizabeth, the arrival of James, whom Drayton welcomed with a *Paean Triumphall* (1603); the Treaty of Hampton Court with Spain (1604) which allowed James to keep his garrison towns in the Low Countries provided they gave no help to the Dutch rebels against Spain.

52   (1619). 6. *Rebate*: diminish.   7. *scorse*: exchange.

53   (1594). cf. sonnet **32**.   10. *thy Shepheard*: in 1593, Drayton had published his first collection of pastoral eclogues, *Idea, The Shepheards Garland*, using himself the pseudonym of Rowland, the shepherd poet.   13. *Tempe*: vale in Thessally sacred to Apollo.   14. *Helicon*: home of the Muses.

54   (1594).

55   (1594). 3. *prove*: experience.

56   (1594). 6. For the ability of eagles to gaze unblinded at the sun, see *Delia* **3**.   9. *summ'd*: fully grown.   10. *Pynions*: flight feathers of the wing.   11. *needsly*: of necessity.

57   (1605). 1. *best discern'd of*: best perceived by.

58   (1605). 9. *That*: i.e. the guardian spirit.

59   (1600). 1. *harbour'd*: lodged.   11. *the By*: the secondary matter.

60   (1594). 10. *let*: obstruct.

61   (1619).

62   (1594). 3. *Wan*: won.   4. *Pined*: starved.   6. *Conceit*: thought.

63   (1599). cf. *Amoretti*, **14**.

EDMUND SPENSER AMORETTI (1595)

MODERN EDITIONS

The Poetical Works of Edmund Spenser ed. de Selincourt (Oxford 1910). Vol. i: Spenser's Minor Poems.

Daphnaida and other Poems ed. W. L. Renwick (London 1929).

The Works of Edmund Spenser (Variorum). Vol. ii: *The Minor Poems.*

The Amoretti and Epithalamion was entered in the Stationers' Register in November 1594 and published in 1595 by William Ponsonby when Spenser was in Ireland. The precise date of composition is not known; but Ponsonby's description 'written not long since', together with the reference to *The Faerie Queene* in sonnet **33**, would suggest a date some time later than 1590 when the first three books of *The Faerie Queene* appeared. 1593–4 seems the most probable period. Unlike other sonnet cycles, Spenser's does not have a woman's pseudonym for its title: 'Amoretti' is a term normally applied to cheerful Italian love songs dealing with the exploits of Cupid. Because of the association of the sequence with Spenser's Marriage Song, *The Epithalamion*, however, it has been generally assumed that both were addressed to Spenser's second wife, Elizabeth Boyle, whom he married in 1594 and to whom he refers in sonnet **74**.

The Amoretti and Epithalamion was republished in the Folios of 1609, 1611 and all subsequent ones. The Folio texts are virtually identical with the text of 1595, and I have used the latter, therefore, with very minor emendations and some modernization of the punctuation.

1   2. *dead-doing*: death-dealing.   6. *lamping*: lighting as with a lamp.   8. *close bleeding*: secret inward bleeding.   10–11. *Helicon . . . Angels*: Spenser has identified the hill of the Muses with the Christian heaven.

2   2. *bale*: misery. *love-pined*: love-starved.   3. *sithens*: since.   6. *viper's brood*: which were thought to be born by gnawing their way out of their mother's belly. (See Pliny, *Natural History* X, lxxxii).   11. *humblesse*: humility.

4   1. *Janus' gate*: god of entrances, doors, beginnings; (*Janua*: a door). In this case, the opening of the year, hence January. He was normally depicted with two faces, one 'forth looking', the other backwards, 'bidding th' old Adieu.'   4. *dumpish spright*: dejected spirits.   7. *dight*: make ready.   13. *raine*: reign.

5   2. *portly*: stately, magnificent.   4. *envide*: envied.   6. *sdeigne*: disdain.   10. *boldned*: confident.

6   5. *durefull*: long-lasting.   7. *divide*: dispense.   11. *dints*: impresses.   12. *affects*: passions.   13. *thinke not long*: don't think it a long time.

7   1. *the myrrour*: this is either a very difficult or an imprecise image. The eyes could be the mirror in which the heart sees its own bewilderment, or a mirror in the sense of a magic crystal which causes the disturbance; or even a burning glass which

concentrates the suns rays upon an object. The last interpretation is supported by line 3 as well as by the reference to living fire in line 12 and in sonnet **8**. The eyes would thus be like a lens transmitting the living fire from the mistress to the heart of the lover.   14. *ensample*: example.

8   One of Spenser's rare attempts at the Shakespearean sonnet form.   2. *unto the maker neere*: near to God himself.   5. *the blinded guest*: Cupid.   6—8. *to base affections' wound* . . .: to wound by arousing lustful passions, 'But the angelic nature of your glances converts them to chaste adoration'.   12. *strong . . . weak*: 'passions strong since caused by your beauty but weak because of your virtue.'

9   7. *for they have purer sight*: they appear brighter.   11. *sever*: cleave, separate.

10   3. *licentious*: unrestrained by law.   10. *comptroll*: control.   11. *bow to a baser make*: either 'bow that high look to a baser mate' or — since so many of the lines end with verbs — 'make that high look bow to someone baser'.

11   5. *rewth*: compassion.   7. *fell*: cruel.   9. *assoyle*: purge, get rid of.   14. *surcease*: bring to an end.

12   7. *eyen*: eyes.

13   1. *port*: bearing.   3. *embaseth*: lowers.   4. *temperature*: combination of opposite humours and qualities.   5. *awfull*: creating awe.

14   4. *peece*: fortress.   6. *wont belay*: accustom to beseige.   7. *enur'd*: inured, used to.   12. *engins*: instruments of war.

15   1. *tradefull*: busy.   3. *both the Indias*: East and West Indies.   10. *weene*: think.   11. *on ground*: in the world.   12. *sheene*: shining.

16   4. *illusion*: deceptive because ultimately causing pain.   5—8. *glauncing sight . . . arrowes*: this very common conceit of Cupid shooting his arrows through the mistress' glances is based on the traditional physiological theory of the animal spirits. These were thought to consist of fine particles which, generated in the heart, flowed out in streams through the eyes, and entering through the eyes of the other person,

penetrated to the heart where they set up the disturbance
which is love. Many sonnet conceits are variations on this. cf.
Astrophel and Stella, **17, 20, 42, 48**, etc.

17 1. *skil*: reason.   4. *fill*: fullness.   11. *pleasance*: courtesy,
desire to give pleasure.

18 3. *redound*: flow.   9. *play my part*: a stage metaphor; 'carry
on with my act'.

19 A spring sonnet following the new year of sonnet 4.   4.
girland: garland.   5. *resounded*: uttered loudly.   10. *of
her*: from her. *ought*: play on the double meaning, 'owed' and
'owned'. She ought to honour love and deserved to be
honoured by love.   14. *rebell*: 'let her be proclaimed a
rebel'.

20 14. *blooded*: stained with blood.

21 2. *tempred*: blended.   9. *inure*: exercise.   11. *recure*:
restore.   14. *in bookes*: i.e. an art based on nature not on
learning.

22 1. *This holy season*: Lent leading up to Good Friday, 'so holy
day'.

23 1—6. *th' importune suit*: to keep her importunate wooers at
bay during Ulysses' long absence, Penelope swore not to
remarry until her tapestry was finished, but she unravelled
each night what she had woven during the day.   4. *unreave*:
unwind.   11. *spils*: destroys.

24 3. *complement*: fulfilment.   8. *Pandora*: the beautiful
woman endued with all gifts from Jupiter created and sent to
earth as a punishment for Prometheus because he had
stolen fire from heaven. She brought with her a box full of
plagues and disasters which, when opened, flew out among
mankind. Spenser moralizes the myth by making them a
scourge to 'wicked men'. Of all the qualities, only Hope
remained in Pandora's box, which may account for the hope-
ful plea in the last couplet.

25 4. *depending*: hanging.   10. *close*: hidden.   14. *meede*:
reward.

26 1. *brere*: briar.   4. *firbloome*: furze-bloom (Renwick).   6.
pill: peel.   8. *Moly*: a mythical plant with a white flower

and a black root possessing magical properties; mentioned in the *Odyssey*, Bk X.

27   4. *weene*: think; cf. sonnet **15**.   5. *beseene*: appearing.

28   1. *The laurell leafe*: the bays. The wreath of laurel bestowed upon poets (hence laureate) and conquerors (see sonnet) **29**).   8. *whom now those leaves attire*: Daphne, having broken her faith with Apollo, fled from him and at her entreaty, was turned by the gods into a laurel, which henceforth was sacred to Apollo. Spenser changes the myth at line 11. The gods metamorphosed Daphne out of pity, not revenge. (cf. *Astrophel and Stella* **74**).

29   5. *The bay*: see sonnet **28**.   11. *triumph*: an extension of the metaphor of conquest: the public demonstration and procession awarded to the conqueror.   12. *trump*: trumpet. *blaze*: proclaim.

30   14. *kynd*: nature.

31   9. *scath*: damage.   12. *embrew*: stain.

32   1. *paynefull*: painstaking, labouring with care.   3. *sledge*: hammer.   4. *list*: pleases.   6. *soft awhit*: soften the smallest bit.

33   2. *that most sacred Empresse*: *The Faerie Queene* was dedicated 'to the most mighty and magnificent Empresse Elizabeth'. *dear dred*: both loved and feared.   3. *not finishing*: the first three books of *The Faerie Queene* were published in 1590, the second three in 1596. Spenser's apology implies a date of writing a considerable time later than 1590, e.g. 1594.   5. *Lodwick*: Lodovick Bryskett, friend of Spenser in Ireland.   5. *aread*: counsel.

34   5. *wont*: was accustomed.   10. *Helice*: the Great Bear near the North Pole, or Spenser may be confusing it with the Little Bear in which the Pole Star lies, (*Variorum*).   13. *carefull*: full of care.

35   This sonnet is printed again with minor variations as sonnet **83**.   2. *still*: ever. *Narcissus*: See *Delia*, **32**.   10. *brooke*: enjoy.

36   6. *thrilling*: piercing.   12. *mote*: might.

37   4. *heare*: hair (cf. False Florimel, *F.Q.* Bks III and IV).   13.

Fondness: foolishness.

38 1. *Arion*: the lyric poet of Lesbos whose myth forms the basis of this sonnet, although Spenser alters it considerably. Arion was about to be murdered by the crew for his riches and he asked, therefore, to be allowed to sing one last song before he died, which charmed the dolphins and brought them to his rescue. Spenser replaces the crew by the tempest, and turns both it and the dolphin into attributes of the lady.

39 3. *temper*: moderate, assuage.

41 9. *ydle boast*: promising much but performing nothing.

42 7. *thrall*: slave.   9. *start*: break away.   11. *pervart*: pervert.   14. *doe*: make.

43 14. *construe*: interpret.

44 1. *those renoumed noble Peeres*: the Argonauts who under the command of Jason gained the Golden Fleece. Orpheus was among them.   7. *of passions warreid are*: ravaged by warring passions.   8. *aslake*: abate, control.

45 4. *semblant*: resemblance.   6. *Idea*: the Platonic Idea, the essential being.   11. *visnomy*: physiognomy; features as they indicate inner qualities.

47 2. *traynes*: deceits.   12. *beguyle*: distract by pleasure.

49 3. *the mightie's*: the Almighty's.   10. *Cockatrice*: basilisk; a mythical serpent hatched from a cock's egg, having the power to kill with its glance.

50 3. *leach*: doctor.   5. *quod*: quoth. *priefe*: experience.   9. *cordialls*: medicines designed to cure heart trouble.

51 4. *moniments*: records of something to be commemorated.   7. *assayde*: attempted.   9. *attend*: to apply oneself long enough.

53 1. *The Panther*: a common myth derived from Pliny's *Natural History*.   2. *fray*: frighten.   11. *embrew*: stain with blood.

54 3. *pageants*: scenes on a stage.   4. *disguysing*: dressing up, covering as with a mask. cf. 'guisers'.   9. *constant*: unchanging.

55 9. *the skye*: the immaterial element, purer than fire, the highest of the terrestrial elements.

56 4. *felly*: cruelly. 11. *desolate*: destitute.

57 3. *lenger*: longer. *sue*: follow. 7. *through-launched*: shot through. 10. *stoures*: combats.

58 5. *unstayd*: unsteady. 7. *prayd*: preyed upon.

59 A complementary sonnet to the previous one, in praise of self-assurance. 4. *feard*: frightened. *to any chaunce to start*: to change to any unconsidered course. 11. *stay*: support.

60 2. *his sundry yeare*: the planetary year, in the Ptolemaic system of astronomy, was the length of time that a planet and the sun, moving on their separate courses, took to return to the position relative to each other from which they started. Ptolemy calculated the period for Mars as 79 years (see Dodge, *Variorum*). Spenser's conceit extends the principle to Cupid, 'the winged God' although he was not a planetary deity. 8. *al those fourty*: this reference has led to much speculation, both about the dates of composition of the *Amoretti*, and of Spenser's birth, which would seem to be between 1550—4. The 'fourty', however, could simply be a round figure. *outwent*: preceded it and exceeded it in number. 13. *short*: shorten.

61 3. *dare not*: addressed to himself or to the reader: 'do not dare to accuse'.

62 A new yeare's sonnet. 1. *race*: course. 2. *compast*: circular. 11. *blend*: trouble.

63 1. *assay*: trials.

64 In this sonnet Spenser is concerned exclusively with the scents not the colours of the flowers, and in ignoring the latter produces occasionally ludicrous images. 5. *Gillyflowers*: wall-flowers. 7. *Bellamoures*: no longer identifiable. 8. *newly spred*: newly opened. 12. *Jessemynes*: jasmine.

65 1. *misdeeme*: misjudge. 4. *earst*: formerly. 13. *brasen towre*: unlike Danae, whom Jupiter seduced in the form of a shower of gold, even though her father shut her in a brazen tower for protection.

66 5. *paragon*: excellence. 9. *gate*: got. 10. *sorted*: consorted.   14. *reflex*: reflection.

68   1. *on this day*: Easter day.   11. *all lyke deare*: all alike dearly.

69   4. *emprize*: undertakings.   13. *spoile*: spoils of war.

70   2. *cote-armour*: coat of arms.   9. *make*: mate.   12. *amearst*: punished.

71   1. *drawen work*: embroidery.   9. *above*: 1595 and Folio read 'about'. Emended de Selincourt and most modern editions.

72   10. *mantleth*: spreads its wings.

74   The three Elizabeths, his mother, the Queen and Elizabeth Boyle, his wife.

75   5. *assay*: attempt.

77   3. *juncats*: sweetmeats.   6. *unvalewd*: beyond valuation.   7. *Hercules*: the eleventh labour, to procure the golden apples of the Hesperides.   8. *Atalanta*: the golden apples which Hippomenes dropped in his race with her, thus enticing her to stop and pick them up, so that he won.

78   5. *synd*: signed.

79   1. *credit*: believe.   8. *ensew*: succeed, come afterwards.

80   As Renwick and others have pointed out, this sonnet proves that the first six books of *The Faerie Queene*, published in 1596, were completed by 1594.   7. *assoyle*: absolve, set free; hence, release, let forth. *that second worke*: presumably the second six books promised in the letter to Raleigh published with the 1590 edition of *The Faerie Queene*.   9. *mew*: retreat.   13. *low and meane*: a compliment to Queen Elizabeth but also, perhaps, a reference to the literary hierarchy, the sonnet being a lower 'kind' than the heroic poem.

81   6. *forth doth lay*: Elizabethan fashion allowed the breasts to be exposed.   10. *the gate*: her mouth. *dight*: furnished, arrayed.

82   4. *embased*: lowered.   5. *equall*: just.   7. *enchased*: set in gold.   14. *hart's*: a pun on Art (v. Nature).

83   This sonnet repeats 35 except for minor alterations of spelling, and line 6, 'seeing it': 35, 'having it'.

85   3. *Mavis*: thrush. 5. *skill*: understand. 7. *then*: than. 8. 'but not aspire to judge of her desert'.

86   2. *the Furies fell*: a cliché out of the popular Senecan drama. cf. Bottom's speech, 'Approach ye furies fell'. Certainly by the time of *M.S.N.D.* and possibly even as early as 1594 this phrase had become a joke. 6. *hyre*: reward.

87   4. *protract*: tedious continuance. 6. *noyous*: vexations. 7. *forlorne*: deprived.

88   9. *th' Idaea*: he glimpses the Platonic Idea by contemplating the actual image retained in memory.

89   1. *Culver*: dove. 3. *vow*: 1595 and 1609 Folio, 'vew'. Corrected in Folio 1611. 9. *hove*: remain. 12. *pleasauns*: pleasantness; but *sight, aspect,* suggest that the meaning of 'pleasance' as a pleasure garden is also there.

HENRY CONSTABLE DIANA (1592 text)
MODERN EDITIONS
The Poems of Henry Constable ed. Joan Grundy (1960) English Texts and Studies, Liverpool University Press.

Constable's *Diana, The praises of his Mistres in certaine sweete sonnets* was first published in 1592. One of its sonnets, however, 'A calculation of the nativitye of the Ladie Riche's daughter borne upon friday in the yeare 1588' suggests an earlier beginning for the sequence, and that Constable was one of the first of the Elizabethan sonneteers, writing at a time when *Astrophel and Stella* was still circulating in manuscript, before the pirated edition of 1591. Constable himself, having been converted to Catholicism, went to the Continent in 1591 and stayed there until the accession of James I, so that his edition was published in his absence. It is a small volume, consisting of twenty-three sonnets, including an introductory one 'To his absent Diana', a concluding sonnet, and that on the birth of Ladie Rich's daughter. In 1594 or thereabouts, there appeared another edition, *Diana or the excellent conceitful Sonnets of H.C. Augmented with divers Quatorzains of honorable and lerned personages*. This contains seventy-six sonnets, divided into eight decades, of which the last is incomplete; and this is the edition on which Sidney Lee and earlier editors based their texts, although there has always been uncertainty about which of the new sonnets were by Constable and which by the other 'honorable and lerned personages'. Joan Grundy's recent edition, however, goes back beyond the printed texts and relies primarily upon manuscript sources, especially the version of *Diana* included in MS.Dyce 44, commonly known as the Todd manuscript, which she argues very convincingly was probably arranged and supervised by Constable himself. This version is built around the mystical numbers 7 and 3, consisting of three parts, each part subdivided into three sections, each of which has seven sonnets. All the sonnets of 1592 appear in the Todd manuscript except the dedicatory sonnet 'To his absent Diana', which suggests that it is an authentic text and that Constable gave his approval to it by composing the dedication while he was in exile. Only twenty-seven of the sonnets in the 1594 edition are in the Todd MS and most of these had already appeared in 1592. The authorship of the rest, apart from eight identified as by Sidney, remains uncertain.

There is not room in this edition for the full canon of Constable's love sonnets and I print therefore the text of 1592, excluding the sonnet on Lady Rich's daughter which does not properly belong to the sequence. The 1592 text has not been reprinted since its original appearance, and includes enough sonnets to give an adequate idea of Constable's quality. I have emended it in the light of Miss Grundy's text only on the occasions where 1592 is obviously inaccurate, and I have included the original version in the notes. The spelling and lay-out is retained, but the punctuation is emended where the sense demanded it.

The identity of Diana herself has never been established, although Constable addressed a number of sonnets to Lady Rich, Sidney's Stella; and the printer's dedication of 1592, *To the Gentlemen Readers*, describes the poet as one 'whose eies were acquainted with Beautie's Riches'. The second part of the Todd MS *Diana,* is written to 'the generall honoure of this Ile, through the prayses of the heads thereof', and to 'celebrate the memory of particular ladies whoe the author most honoureth'. As well as three sonnets to Lady Rich, there are seven to the King and Queen of Scotland, later to succeed Elizabeth to the throne, two to Lady Arabella Stuart, also in the line of royal succession, and others to various noble ladies with whom he had dealings. It would seem that Constable's sonnets were more social and political than amatory in their motivation.

To his absent Diana: absent presumably because of Constable's exile in France. The dedication of the volume 'To the Gentlemen Readers' refers to 'these insuing Sonnets . . . by misfortune left as Orphans'.

1 14. *thyne eare* (Grundy). 1592/4, 'your eare'. *my voyce* (1592/4). Grundy, 'the voyce'.

2 1. *pretend*: intend.   4. 'causing your will to stoop to favour my wish'.   14. *thy hart* (Grundy). 1592/4, 'my hart', which is clearly a misunderstanding of the argument of the sonnet.

3 4. *Comets*: traditionally believed to be caused by hot and dry exhalations which rose from the earth to form the element of fire of which the highest layer of the terrestrial sphere was composed. This, when heated further by the friction from the rotating lunar sphere which surrounded and enclosed it, produced comets and shooting stars. *begin* (1592/4): 'are the cause of'. Grundy, 'become'.

4 4. *Thetis*: here confused with Tethys, goddess of the sea.

5 1–4. reference to Icarus.

6 13. *rewarded* (Grundy). 1592/4, 'revenged'.

7 1. *helplesse* (Grundy). 1592/4, 'hopelesse'.   2. *my love to slaie* (Grundy). 1592/4, 'my hope to slaie'.

8 2. *dumbe wonder*: i.e. my joy would be beyond expression.

9 5. *pyle*: the pointed metal head of an arrow or lance.   6. *the sight . . . levell*: the sight by which you take aim.

12 2. *descrie*: observe and cry out against.

13 4. *partiall*: biased.

14 7. *pinde*: starved.

15 1–3. 'my love in itself produces much sorrow, my despair more . . . my folly most of all'.   4. *this last griefe*: i.e. the grief produced by my folly in loving one I am sure to miss.   5. *All paines if you commaund it, joy* (Grundy). 1592/4, 'All paines if you commaund, it joy': i.e. 'All pains

will prove pleasures if you command it, and it is wisdom to seek pleasure'.

18   10. *tame* (Grundy). 1592/4, 'tane'.

19   13. *But hurle out love thou canst not* (Grundy). 1592/4, 'But hurle not love: thou canst not'.

20   5. *Saint Frances had the like*: i.e. the marks of Christ's wounds which he found on his body after his vision of the cross.

Last Sonnet.   9. *but not* (Grundy). 1592/4, 'and not'.   14. *be* (Grundy). 1592/4, 'is'.

BARNABE BARNES PARTHENOPHIL AND PARTHENOPHE.
Sonnettes, Madrigals, Elegies and Odes (1593)
  MODERN EDITIONS
  Parthenophil and Parthenophe: A Critical Edition. ed.
  Victor A. Doyno (Southern Illinois University Press, 1971).

Barnes' work, probably published in 1593, is of considerable size. It consists of three parts, the first comprising more than a hundred fourteen- and fifteen-line sonnets, interspersed with madrigals in the manner of the songs in *Astrophel and Stella*; the second, a series of love elegies; and the last, a collection of Odes, canzoni, a sonnet and a final sestine. The whole sequence is strung along the story of Parthenophil, the lover, wooing in vain and driven to distraction by the mixture of coquetry and coldness on the part of Parthenophe, until in the end he resorts to magical charms in the manner of Theocritus' Idyll and gains his desire. The consummation is described in the last sestine with considerable dramatic power and understanding, and the Petrarchan sequence ends in a very Ovidean manner.

The only part of the work relevant to this volume is the first section, which is an orthodox Petrarchan sonnet cycle. Barnes is one of the most lively, varied and 'conceited' of the minor Elizabethan sonneteers. His verse ranges from the extravagance of the 'Zodiac' sonnets (36—7) to the sweet pastoral nostalgia of his best known sonnet, 'Ah sweet content' (66), and he has a line of witty audacious sexuality which is all his own. Although some of the individual sonnets have dramatic quality, there is no overall dramatic development as in *Astrophel and Stella*, for example, and nothing is lost by separating particular sonnets from their context. No firm identity has been established for Parthenophe, and Victor Doyno has pointed out that both of the title names derive from the Greek root meaning 'virgin'. Only one original copy of the text is extant, that in the British Museum. I have retained the original spelling and format but modernized the punctuation where necessary.

36 and 37 These are two of the twelve sonnets which Barnes wrote around the signs of the Zodiac. He charts the fortunes of his 'unbridled Phaeton', his 'worlde's bright fierie sunne', by which he means his passionate and ambitious heart, as it takes its course through the zodiac of love; and he describes with great ingenuity both his own sufferings and the various moods of his mistress in terms of the predominant sign.

36 Leo, July/August.   8. *they* (Doyno). 1593, 'the'.   10. *rac'd*: tore.   14. *manne's woe*: Doyno points out the traditional play upon this and 'woman'.

37 Virgo, August/September.   7. *Delian goddesse*: Diana, the virgin Goddess.   8. *with honest colour*: in the name of Diana, she could hide her real inclinations under a pose of virginity, which set up a conflict between his love and his desire.   14. *infortunate*: unsuccessful.

60 3. *'bove starres do mount*: raise to poetic immortality.   5. *valure*: valour.   7. *Godfrey*: Godfrey of Bouillon, hero of Tasso's *Jerusalem Delivered*   11. *one captaine blinde*: Cupid.   12. *did nothing boote*: nothing availed to resist his power.

63 1—4. reference to the most frequently quoted of Jupiter's metamorphoses.   4. *coelestiall*: celestial.   8—9. a play on vain and vein.   14. For critical reactions to this very unpetrarchan wish, see Doyno's notes to the sonnet.

84 3. *The golden number*: the number of the year in terms of the nineteen year cycle which the moon takes to return to the same apparent position in relation to the sun.   4. *in carde*: in the chart.

GILES FLETCHER THE ELDER (1593) LICIA OR POEMES OF
LOVE
    MODERN EDITIONS
    The English Works of Giles Fletcher the Elder, ed. Lloyd E.
    Berry (University of Wisconsin Press, 1964).

The dedicatory epistle 'To the worthie, kinde, wise, and vertuous
Ladie, the Ladie Mollineux . . .' is dated 1593, the probable year of
publication; and internal evidence suggests that the sonnets were
written after 1591. The full description of the work on the title
page, 'In honour of the admirable and singular vertues of his Lady,
to the imitation of the best Latin Poets, and others' is an indication
of how Fletcher saw his own work. His dedication to Lady
Mollineux presents it very much as a literary exercise, beginning
with a general defence of love as a passion, and going on to justify
the writing of love poetry on the best humanist grounds: 'Peruse
but the writings of former times, and you shall see not onely others
in other countryes, as Italie, and France, men of learning and great
partes to have written Poems and Sonnets of Love; but even
amongst us, men of best nobilitie, and chiefest families, to be the
greatest Schollers and most renowned in this kind.' The writing of
verse is a proper leisure occupation for a gentleman and a scholar,
both of which Fletcher could claim to be — in his younger days he
had been Fellow of Kings and Public Orator. He makes it refresh-
ingly clear that to write love poetry one need not be in love — 'I am
so liberall to graunt thus much, a man may write of love, and not bee
in love, as well as of husbandrie, and not goe to the plough'.

    I include a selection of *Licia* in this volume because it may be
said to embody the norm of sonnet sequences. It makes no claim to
be original and avoids all that is extravagant or outlandish: it rings
the changes on the traditional sonnet *topoi* with graceful com-
petence and considerable lyric charm: above all, it is always under
control, always clear. It provides an excellent demonstration of
how a poet of limited ability and ambition may be helped by a
strong convention.

17   14. *immortall.* 1593, 'immotall'.

27   4. *pearlike*: i.e., pearl-like.   5. *resolved*: changed into vapour.

41   Charon's job was to conduct the souls of the dead in his boat
and   over Styx and Acheron to the underworld. Fletcher's conceit
42   is based, like many others in his sequence, on the poetry of Renaissance Latinists (see Berry, Explanatory Notes to *Licia*).

41   2. *wafftage*: conveyance across water.   3. *rend*: split.

42   3. *let*: obstruct.

THOMAS LODGE PHILLIS: HONOURED WITH PASTORALL SONNETS, ELEGIES AND AMOROUS DELIGHTS (1593)
    MODERN EDITIONS
    The Complete Works of Thomas Lodge, 4 volumes. Hunterian Club 1883. Vol. ii. (reprinted Johnson Reprint Coy 1966).

This sequence, published in 1593, is an example of the fashion for pastoral sonnets established by the poems in Sidney's *Old Arcadia*. Lodge's verse, however, has a colour and a sensuous use of mythology which owes something to the University Wits, Marlowe, Peele and Greene.

(ANON) ZEPHERIA (1594)

Nothing is known of the author of *Zepheria*, but the book was printed in London in 1594, and the strongly legal flavour of so many of the conceits suggests that it was written by a young Inns of Court man for an audience of fellow lawyers. The author apologizes in his Proem for his 'artless pen' and his 'home-spun Verse', but this conventional disclaimer need not be taken too seriously: of all the Elizabethan sonnet sequences, this is the most extravagantly rhetorical, the most ostentatiously 'artificial'. There is little dramatic development in the series, though if one can penetrate the tangle of legal metaphors in sonnets 21 and 37, for example, it would seem that the lovers are under parental pressure to separate and are doing their best to resist it. The general impression, however, is of a poet whose main objects were to display his rhetorical virtuosity, to show his mastery over language by inventing new words or putting old ones to new uses, and to make 'in' jokes for the entertainment of his colleagues. Yet the poet has remarkable skill in handling extended double meanings and making legal puns, and some of the sonnets have vitality and real if very idiosyncratic charm. *Zepheria,* however, was notorious in its own day, and is the only sonnet cycle to be mentioned specifically by name in Davies' *Gullinge Sonnets.* It is to be found in Sidney Lee's *Elizabethan Sonnets,* vol. ii.

8   2. *devining*: rendering divine.   5. *Leda's lovely twins*: Castor and Pollux, begotten by Jupiter in the guise of a swan.   7. *esperance*: hope.   8. *ripe*: probably a pun: Latin, *ripa*, a shore.

17   1. *habiliment*: proper attire.   2. *depaint*: painting or description.   4. *acquaint*: accustomed, appropriate.   5. *The golden seeling*: presumably her golden hair.   6. *architure*: architecture.   8. *depure*: make pure.   13. *limn'd*: painted.

20   2. *breviat*: a lawyer's brief, a summary.

21   6. *indentures*: deeds of contract, originally executed in duplicate with the edges correspondingly indented for the purpose of identification.   9. *advertize*: call attention to the matter.   11. *counterpane*: connected with counter-pawn, counter-point, i.e. counterpart. Also a pun on counter-pane in its modern sense of a bed-cover.   14. *duresse*: illegal constraint.

37   2. *process*: the formal commencement of an action at law.   3. *Supersedeas*: writ commanding the stay of legal proceedings.   5. *to a partie*: to become an accessory in an action at law.   6. *Disperpling*: dispersing.   8. *dispence*: relaxation of the law.   14. *premunire*: a legal summons.

38   2. *neare*: never.   4. *accomptants*: accountants. *crackt*: gone bankrupt.   5. *irrotulat*: entered in the roll.   6. *list*: care.   9. *of assise*: normally assessed.   13. *foyaltie*: allegiance.

B. GRIFFIN GENT FIDESSA, MORE CHASTE THEN KINDE (1596)

Fidessa, dedicated to the gentlemen of the Inns of Court, was published in 1596. It is a relatively late cycle which has absorbed the more obvious and fashionable mannerisms of its time and borrows extensively from its English predecessors. It is nevertheless a competent sequence and a good example of the run-of-the-mill sonneteering against which the originality of the greater writers should be assessed. There is no modern edition, but it is included in vol. ii of Sidney Lee's *Elizabethan Sonnets* (1904).

13   This sonnet runs through the whole gamut of 'lover' comparisons, as Donne does in *The Canonization*, but without the ironic self-consciousness and the dramatic dimension which transform them in Donne's poem.

13   3. *the foolish boy*: Phaethon, who borrowed the chariot of the sun and could not control it.

15   Borrowed directly from Daniel, *Delia*, sonnet 49.

16   The figure of rhetoric around which this sonnet is built is called (by Puttenham) Clymax or the marching figure in his *Arte of English Poesie*. It is parodied in number 3 of Davies' *Gullinge Sonnets*.

WILLIAM SMITH CHLORIS OR THE COMPLAINT OF THE PASSIONATE DESPISED SHEPHEARD (1596)

Chloris, published in 1596, is another pastoral sequence, whose debt to previous cycles in English is unusually obvious. This sequence is in vol. ii of Sidney Lee's *Elizabethan Sonnets*.

18   1—4. cf. Sidney, *Astrophel and Stella*, 3, 6, etc.

20   A sonnet heavily indebted to the pastoral eclogues of the *Old Arcadia*.

26   cf. Daniel *Delia*, 36, 37.

SIR JOHN DAVIES GULLINGE SONNETS
   MODERN EDITIONS
   The Complete Poems of Sir John Davies, ed. Grosart (1876).
   Vol. ii.
   The Poems of Sir John Davies, ed. Robert Krueger (Oxford,
   1975).

These sonnet parodies were not printed until Grosart discovered
them in manuscript form in Chetham's library, Manchester. He
published them in 1873 in *The Dr Farmer Chetham MS* Part I
(Chetham Society vol. 89), and subsequently in his edition of
Davies's poems three years later. The sonnets were probably written
round 1594 since they attack *Zepheria* by name, and they thus
anticipate the main onslaught on the sonnet from Hall and Marston
by several years. Davies was himself an Inns of Court man, and his
sonnets were written for the kind of sophisticated audience he
would find there.

Dedicatory sonnet. 3. *Antick*: jester.   4. *fond*: foolish. *lewde
   gulleries*: illiterate shams.   7. *whiskinge*: light, superficial.   13. *formall*: capable of making only the conventional judgement.   14. *beg him for*: set him down as.

1   5. *But for*: but because.   7. *gracious*: emended Krueger.
     MS, 'gracous'.
2   8. *Which doe* (MS). Krueger, 'Which does'.
3   See Griffin, *Fidessa,* sonnet **16** and note for 'Clymax or the
     Marcher'.   14. *weare*: i.e. were.
5   Sidney started the fashion in England for this kind of 'Corre-
     lative verse', mainly as an exercise in verbal skill. The most
     elaborate example is Philoclea's sonnet in Book III of the *Old
     Arcadia.*
6   8. *pointes*: laces joining the doublet and hose through
     'Iletholes'.   12. *pantofels*: slippers. There is no logical
     affinity in this extended metaphor between Love's garments
     and the qualities they represent. See, as a contrast, *Astrophel
     and Stella,* **49.**

7—9 Three sonnets parodying the legal conceits of Barnabe Barnes and the anonymous author of *Zepheria*.

8   9. *repleave*: bail out.   11. *Shriefe*: sheriff. MS, 'Sheife', emended Krueger.   12. *esloynde*: removed out of the jurisdiction of.   14. *withername*: in an action of replevin, the reprisal of other goods in lieu of those taken and esloynde, (O.E.D.). Grosart emended 'in wit her name'.

9   2. *in warde*: The crown was the legal guardian of all minors, unmarried female orphans and idiots who held their land in return for military service which they could not render. In practice, wardship was often farmed out to individuals who were entitled to the revenues of the estate, dowries, etc.   4. *intreate*: treat.

MARK ALEXANDER BOYD (1563—1601)

Boyd was a Scottish writer noted mainly for his Latin poems. This sonnet, the only one he is known to have written, was printed c. 1590.

2. *Owrhailit*: carried away.   5-6. *blin'* . . . *bairn*: blind Cupid. 7. *wyf*: Venus rising from the sea.   8. *Lichter*: lighter. *dauphin*: dolphin.   10. *teils*: tills. *sawis*: sows.

Index of first lines

E

If n
thi
d